The Dead Beside Us

A MEMOIR OF GROWING UP IN DERRY

TONY DOHERTY

FOR EDDIE O'DONNELL

MERCIER PRESS

Cork

www.mercierpress.ie

© Tony Doherty, 2017

ISBN: 978 1 78117 512 5

10 9 8 7 6 5 4 3 2 1

A CIP record for this title is available from the British Library

Printed and bound in the EU.

Contents

Acknowledgements

At home I am extremely grateful to my wife, Stephanie, for supporting me throughout the writing process and delivering several sharp critiques of the later chapters. Also my son, Rossa, for interrupting his busy social media schedule to read over several chapters and telling me that I wasn't such a goat after all.

On the wider family front, thanks to Uncles Eugene and Gerard for helping me restore sensible order to events after my father's death and to my wee brother Paul for taking the rubbish out to the bin.

Thanks to Christopher (Dooter) McKinney and Brian McCool, for helping me clarify several snippets of memory of my Brandywell days. I am really glad that I spent time with my old friend Benny McLaughlin, who was of enormous help keeping me straight about our shared Galliagh and Shantallow days in the 1970s. Thanks also to Kevin (Boiler) Boyle, his brother Bobby, and Brenda Cooley (now Kearney) for a variety of memory jogs and for teaching me to jive (Brenda, I mean). I am very grateful to Tommy Carlin for his support and input, albeit regarding much more serious matters.

On the production side of things I am indebted to Mickey Dobbins for his enthusiasm and encouragement during our many tours to and from Belfast. Also Amanda Doherty and Catherine Murphy for their help and feedback; and Dave Duggan for providing me with the overview of my memoir without reading a word! I am especially grateful to Freya McClements for her valuable and insightful assistance in too many ways to mention.

Readers, please note that Patrick Brown (now deceased) and Paddy Brown are two different people.

I would like to thank Christine Spengler for allowing me to use her brilliant photograph on the cover.

Finally, I apologise to all those whose names I have changed or simply left out of the later chapters due to good sense and sensibility.

1

HUNGER IN THE HEART

My earliest memory is of my granny's house in Creggan. It was 1966, when I was three. The singer sang 'What a Day for a Daydream' on the transistor radio in the scullery, and me granny was standing at the table, the sleeves of her pale blue jumper rolled up, kneading dough with her floury fists. I stood in the doorway of the sitting room with a mixed-fruit jam piece in my hand as the sun shone through the large window, catching dust and fine fluff in its streaming rays.

I found myself once again standing in the sitting room of me granny's house, after we buried me da on a cold, wet and windy February day in 1972. The house was choc-a-bloc. A huge fire roared in the hearth as the inviting aroma of homemade chicken soup struggled to win over the gloom and the less inviting smells of steaming hair, soggy shoes and damp clothing. We took turns heating up and drying off in front of the fire as me granny took charge in the scullery. She always made more than enough to feed everyone; her cooking pots were huge and she had enough bowls to feed an army. She'd arranged for Mr McLaughlin, the bread man, to deliver a full wooden tray of Hunter's sliced pan loaves, which lay, neatly packed in their blue and yellow wrappers, on the floor beside the front door. It was a strange gathering, though, as me granny's house was always a place for the craic, scone bread and feeling good, and now here we were not knowing what to do or say, feeling the loss of me da in the same room where he'd sung 'The Black Velvet Band' to me ma at the Christmas party only a few weeks ago.

When your da dies so suddenly, killed by a soldier's bullet, it does things to your head and body that you can't really work out. I felt a terrible hunger of a strange and different kind than I'd ever felt before. At least, I can only explain it as a hunger, but it could've been something else, as food didn't seem to take it away. I could feel it right up to my throat. Food didn't taste the same and I would still feel the strange hunger soon after eating. In the few days since me da was killed, over the wake and after the funeral, I felt this hunger. Something had changed in me as a nine-year-old, in both body and mind. The mysteries of how, why and where me da died were great unknowns to me that I couldn't yet begin to explore. I didn't even know the right questions or who to ask about it.

In hushed, mysterious tones, spoken as much with the eyes as the mouth, word went around the thawing-out gathering that Josie Brown had seen a *rath* of me da in St Mary's

Chapel.[1] Josie was me granny's friend who lived around the bend of the Cropie, across the street from No. 26 Central Drive. She always had a smiling, thoughtful face, her head shaking slightly when she spoke. It didn't shake when she was quiet. She smoked, like almost all the older people, but she often kept her fag drooping at the corner of her mouth, gangster-like, allowing the smoke to crawl its way up the side of her face and out through her soft white curls, shrouding her head in a smoky mist.

Josie was special. She saw things differently from everyone else, me granny used to tell us. They held nights in each other's houses so that Josie could read their tea leaves. She told me ma one such night, after reading her tea leaves, that she would wear two wedding rings.

Josie told whoever was gathered around the scullery table that she'd seen Patsy Doherty's *rath* when she was in the queue for Holy Communion at Mass the previous day. She stood near the main door of the chapel at the end of the long queue and saw Patsy Doherty walking towards her with his hands clasped in front of him and his eyes towards the floor. When he reached Josie, he smiled and winked an eye at her as he passed by. When she looked around, he was nowhere to be seen. She said she nearly died with the shock of it.

---

1   A *rath* is like the ghost of the dead person appearing at their own funeral or somewhere shortly after their death.

Word of Josie's meeting with me da's *rath* spread throughout me granny's packed house. It was Aunt Siobhán I heard it from, when she was telling someone else in the hall beside the sitting-room door. The news brought a strange comfort to me and I'm sure to the rest of us Doherty wains; it was as if he was still here with us and would look after us.

Me granny always served her chicken soup with a few boiled spuds, sitting like floury balls in the middle of the wide bowl. I sat with my sister Karen and brothers Patrick and Paul, lined up along the sofa with the steaming soup bowls on the low coffee table, and we bent forward as best we could to slurp the soup and dip the sliced pan bread into it. Others, including my Uncle Joe (about the same age as Karen) and Aunt Lorraine (three years younger than me), hunkered down on the floor and blew the hot steam from the soup to cool it down, dipping the bread into it and shaping their mouths to trap it before it came away, splashing its soggy weight back into the bowl. The large, metal-framed windows of the sitting room were steamed up, keeping the heavy, grey February day at bay for the time being. If me granda had been himself, he would have said, 'It's like a buckin' Turkish bath in here'; but he didn't.

***

With me da gone and in his grave, me ma's head was elsewhere. Her face was pale and angst-ridden, her voice frail and distant. She was twenty-nine. She had six wains, the youngest only seven months old. Everything around us seemed different. The emptiness was everywhere and it was as if we all had to get to know one another all over again. Like strangers. There was always someone else around the house helping out, or just being there – my Aunts Siobhán (about seven years older than me) and Mary, or me Uncle Patsy and his wife Geraldine. Maisie McKinney from up the street came in very often and took us to her house for our tea while me ma rested in bed. We spent time, including a few nights, at me granny's in Central Drive. Me and our Paul even stayed a night in Maisie's, had our tea and toast for supper, and got packed into the bed 'heads and thraws' beside Dooter and Michael. It was strange falling asleep with someone's smelly feet near your pillow, like the old days in Moore Street.

We stayed off school for a week after me da's death. I'd never missed a single day of school before. At the end of Primary Four, Mrs Radcliffe had awarded me a KitKat for the achievement of never missing a day since I started in Primary One.

The following Monday morning, Patrick, Paul and me were sent back to Long Tower Primary School. For some reason we were allowed to go in late, and as we walked from the Bishop Street gate past the Primary One, Two and Three classrooms I realised that there wasn't another boy to be seen outside. The yard was empty, cold and grey. They were all inside in the warm. We walked in silence through the chilly schoolyard and split up into our separate classrooms. Patrick was in Primary Six; I was in Primary Five; and Paul was in Primary Four. It felt odd that I was at school and when I got home afterwards me da wouldn't be there.

The three of us walked home together in silence after school. We were watching TV when there was a noise at the front door and Patrick got up to see who it was. Our Uncle Michael was in the hall and he came through the door with a cardboard box in his arms. Uncle Michael was a tall, gangly teenager who always wore jeans and his hair was dark and styled like Rod Stewart's – spiked at the front and long at the back. When he put the box down on the floor we could see a wee brown pup inside, lying on a bed of straw and newspaper. We had our own dog at last!

'It's a bitch,' he declared.

Maisie McKinney came in shortly after and had her dog, Dandy McKinney, with her. Dandy sniffed around the cardboard box and nosed and licked our new pup, wagging her stubby, sandy-coloured tail.

'She's takin' to the wee pup,' said Maisie. 'She loves pups.'

We all sat around the box on the floor while the pup slept on her straw and newspaper, and the older and wiser Dandy lay down beside it with her head between her front paws.

'Now, make sure and train the wee pup,' said Maisie. 'You don't want it cackin' all over the house; and a dog has to know that it *is* a dog or it won't know its place. Our Terry will give yis a hand. He's great wi' dogs.'

Me ma came in with Uncle Patsy and Aunt Geraldine. Geraldine was a small woman with short, dark, curly hair, horn-rimmed glasses and a slight country accent. She drove a car. She was the only woman I knew who drove a car. Uncle Patsy wasn't that much taller than her. He had black hair and his shadowy face always looked like he needed a shave. They were nearly always together; you rarely saw one without the other.

'We got a new wee pup, Ma!' said our Paul.

Me ma came over to the box, sat down on the edge of the sofa and lifted the pup onto her lap. It opened its eyes for a second as it was moved, then settled back into the warmth and slept on.

'Ach dear, look at the wee critter. What'll we call it?' she asked, smiling. Because the wee pup had a brown coat of hair we named her Brandy, after me ma's favourite drink. Brandy Doherty, one of the family.

Patsy and Geraldine were in the scullery getting something ready for us to eat.

'We got a couple of beef curries and rice from the new Chinese restaurant in Shipquay Street,' said me ma. We'd never had curry before and could smell its strange aroma coming from the scullery table, where Patsy and Geraldine were dividing it out from tinfoil cartons onto plates. It smelled really different from anything we'd ever eaten.

'I'd better get home and get a spud on for the dinner,' said Maisie, and me ma walked her and Dandy out to the hall and closed the sitting-room door behind them. By the time she came back in we were sitting around the room eating our first Chinese beef curry. We got a cup of tea as well, which tasted strange along with the curry. Everything tasted strange to me anyway since me da died, so I wasn't that put out.

'I'm not really hungry,' said me ma as she forked the curry around her plate.

'I know, Eileen, but ye have to eat to keep your strength up,' said Patsy, standing by the scullery door with his plate in his hand, looking concerned. Everyone agreed that the Chinese curry was delicious and we Dohertys all licked the curry sauce from the plates until they were clean.

'We won't have to wash the plates now, Patsy, look at the clean of mines!' Paul said, holding up his white plate for everyone to see. Patsy laughed and said, 'I know, Paul, but you'll still have to wash it in the sink.'

Patsy and Geraldine gathered up the plates and forks while we drank our tea. Everyone agreed the tea tasted very strange because of the hot curry sauce, so most of it went cold in the cups. Patsy and Michael went into the scullery to wash the dishes.

'He was tryin' to reach his cousin's flat in Joseph Place, ye know,' said me ma, drifting her eyes towards the sitting-room window. It was now dark outside.

'What, Eileen?' said Geraldine, looking at us through her horn-rims. We were all listening. Brandy was sleeping in her cardboard box.

'Paddy. I think he must've been trying to reach his cousin's flat in Joseph Place. That's where he was shot.'

'D'ye think so, Eileen?' asked Geraldine, looking around at us as we listened. This was the first time me ma had spoken about it since it happened.

'We went out after dinner and left Karen to watch the three boys. We took Colleen and Glenn up to me ma's in the pram and then went over to the shops for the march. We had great craic as we walked down Southway; people were calling to one another and all, but when the rioting started I turned round to see where he was. We got separated. Then I met me da and stayed wi' him. That's when the shooting started. He had to nearly drag me over the barricade because I couldn't get over it myself.' She smiled a soft smile as she spoke, remembering, but her eyes were dull and sad.

She stopped talking and the room fell silent. She kept looking towards the window. She was probably too pained to look us in our own eyes. The newspaper rustled inside the box on the floor and we all dived down to see Brandy waking up. She opened her brown eyes and we lifted her out and took turns at petting her. Michael brought in a saucer with milk in it and placed it down beside the cardboard box and the wee dog got up on her four paws and started lapping the milk, making slight splashing noises with her tongue. We all laughed at this.

'Give her a wee bit of space and don't pet her when she's drinkin' or eatin'; dogs don't like that,' said Michael.

Brandy finished the milk, licked it off her lips and nose, put her two front paws out in front of her, stretched and yawned with a slight squeak. It was the first noise she'd made. She then began to move unsteadily along the oilcloth floor. We followed her every move with squeals of laughter and excitement, and took turns at holding her in our warm laps.

Just as Uncle Michael said, 'We'll have to put some papers down for her …', our Patrick jumped up from the sofa with the wee brown pup in both hands, saying 'She's pishin'! She's pishin'!' and put her back down on the floor where she continued peeing, looking up at us as we looked down at her, the pee forming into a yellowy puddle around her feet on the red-patterned oilcloth. Like Pineappleade. Everyone laughed, including Patrick, who went out to the scullery to get dried off.

We had our own dog! Brandy even rhymed with Dandy, the rat-catcher!

'As I was saying about the newspaper!' said Michael, and we all laughed again. I caught sight of me ma not laughing, though, and she continued to look out the window into the darkness.

'I ordered me breakfast by phone from me bed the day he

was killed, ye know,' she said, smiling sadly towards Geraldine, who by this stage was waiting for more.

After a brief silence, Geraldine, looking a bit puzzled, said, 'But yous don't have a phone, Eileen.'

'Aye, we do! Aye, we do!' we all replied, and Patrick bounded out to the telephone table, lifted the receiver of the phone and turned the dial with his finger. The phone dinged upstairs in me ma and da's room.

'See?' me ma said, smiling to Geraldine, who nodded back to her, smiling as well. 'It only works up and down the stairs.' She went quiet again for a wee while.

'He was a wile man, that Paddy,' me ma said. She always called him Paddy, while a lot of other people called him Patsy. She also said he *was* a wile man, not *is* a wile man. It was the first time anyone had spoken of me da as *was*. She suddenly started laughing at her own recent memory of him.

'He rings me up and says in a snobby voice, "Hello, Mrs Doherty, this is the hotel manager. Do you want breakfast in bed this morning?" I put on a snobby voice as well and said back to him, "Oh, yes please! Bring me two eggs, toast and tay up on a tray – and make it snappy!" "Did you say tay, madam?" he said down the phone, and I said, "Don't be ridiculous, man! Of course I didn't say tay! Now hurry up, man!" and put the phone down with a ding,' she laughed, as she remembered. She looked both happy and sad at the same time, as she sat on the sofa telling her story. She was laughing but her eyes were tearful. We all laughed as well and were all ears for more.

She went on: 'He brought the breakfast up and then took the four bigger wains to Mass. Glenn is a great sleeper and so's Colleen, so I brought her into the bed beside me and went back to sleep.' She went silent again for a few seconds.

'It's doing a cack!' whispered our Paul, pointing at Brandy the pup, who was squatting down near the hearth over a watery, yellowy-brown cack. We all giggled as Michael lifted the wee cack with his hand through a sheet of newspaper and took it to the bin in the yard. As he came back in he said, 'Tony, get Terry McKinney the marra and get him to give yous a hand wi' the wee pup's training. She'll shite and pish all over the place unless she gits properly trained.' Michael lifted the wee pup and went into the scullery with it. The rest of us stayed in the sitting room, wondering if me ma was going to say any more. After a few moments of silence, she started again.

'Ye know, when he was shot, a man called Paddy Walsh came out to help him. He drinks in Mailey's.'

Patsy nodded in agreement and said, 'Aye, Eileen, that's right. So he does.'

'He crawled out on his belly as the soldiers continued to fire at him and Paddy. A bullet passed through his coat collar when he reached your daddy. He said an Act of Contrition in his ear as your father passed away.'

She fell silent again as she continued to stare into the blackness of the early evening.

***

I missed me da very much, but I didn't put it in words to anyone except our Paul at night in bed. Paul and me, at eight and nine, were sent upstairs earlier than Patrick and Karen, who were ten and eleven. They were bigger and were allowed to stay down longer and watch TV with me ma or Uncle Eugene, or whoever else was in.

'I really miss me da wile,' I said to Paul as we lay side by side in bed. Paul was always on the inside, with me on the outside. The words nearly choked me and I could feel them tighten my throat. I'd been dying to say them all night but hadn't.

'Same as me,' said Paul, with his head, like mine, resting back on the pillow and us both staring into the dark grey of the bedroom ceiling, which had an orange glow from the streetlights.

Before we went to bed, both of us knelt at the side of it to say our prayers. Me da had trained us to do it every night before we got in, and would kneel himself to say the Hail Mary and ask God to look after the family. Me and Paul kept doing it, saying the Hail Mary together and asking God to look after us all. I said to myself at the end before we climbed into bed 'but me ma especially'.

After a while I heard Paul crying softly beside me. He'd turned his head to the wall to do it but I could tell he was crying. It's in the breathing and the stiffness of the body. I felt that I could cry too then, and stayed lying on my back, staring at the ceiling, and let the warm tears come out the sides of my eyes and seep into the white pillowcase. When I turned to go to sleep later I felt the damp patch on my cheek, so I turned the pillow over to its dry side. Paul had cried himself to sleep.

When Karen and Patrick came up a wee bit later to go to bed, I pretended to be asleep but listened to them praying too, getting into their beds and then both of them crying silently into the night. I could tell by their breathing.

One night, as I was lying half-awake, my eyes shot open when I thought I heard me da whistling his way down the street towards our house, and I half expected to hear the front door opening as he came in. But the whistling continued on down the street, passing our house, rounding the corner at Foyle Road and fading away.

Each morning I woke up to a brand new day and, as my brain started to work its way out of sleep, everything was normal for a few seconds, but then I would realise, as I opened my eyes, that me da was dead. It was the same every morning.

2

STARMAN

There was a huge explosion around the corner on Foyle Road. We were at school when we heard it and the school shook slightly, the panes of glass rattling in their white-painted wooden frames. We heard explosions nearly every day; mostly bombs going off in the city centre, which was very close to our school, on the other side of the Derry Walls. Some would be close and others would be distant rumbles and tremors. A few times we were sent home early because of bomb-scares near the courthouse, just inside the Walls; too close for comfort. A wee boy in Primary Four by the name of Healy from Lone Moor Road, not far from our house in Hamilton Street, had his finger blown off after he lifted a detonator from the ground. The teacher said he was very lucky he wasn't killed or injured worse. I didn't know what a detonator was but was afraid to show myself up by asking. When the wee boy Healy came back to school a few weeks later he showed off his hand with his pointing finger missing along with half of the next one to it.

While the town centre was now considered a very dangerous place because of the IRA bombings, I still loved going up the town with me ma or granny or granda, or anyone else for that matter, as long as we went to Wellworths. Me granny used to go down the town from Creggan early on a Saturday for her messages to avoid the bombings. 'I'll have to get down the town for the messages before that oul bombin' starts,' she would say, as if the bombings started at a certain time, rushing out the door with her straw shopping bags over to the Creggan shops to get a Sticky Taxi. The Sticky Taxis ran from the Creggan shops to Rossville Street; people queued up and piled in when the taxi came, sharing the car. The bus service was hit and miss, as more often than not buses would be hijacked, driven across the road and set alight. No one ever hijacked the Sticky Taxis.

The Sticky Taxis got their name because people believed that they were set up by the Official IRA. In early 1970 the IRA had split into the Official IRA and the Provisional IRA. People, families, streets and neighbourhoods were divided as to which IRA they supported. Depending on what you were told, your beliefs usually led you to support one or the other, though many hedged their bets and pretended to support both. The Officials' nickname was the Stickies, and the Provisionals became the Provos. The Officials began to be called the Stickies when, in 1971, they produced a green, white and orange Easter Lily badge with a sticky back to commemorate the 1916 Easter Rising. The Provisionals made a non-sticky badge, which needed a pin to attach it to your coat or jumper. They were called the 'Pinheads' for a while but the name wasn't as popular as the 'Stickies'. By 1972 both the Stickies and the Provos were fairly well armed, displaying their guns on foot-patrols and checkpoints in the Brandywell, where we lived, and in the huge Creggan estate where me granny and granda Quigley lived.

One Saturday me ma took me to Wellworths to help her with the messages. We walked down William Street and went through the British Army (BA) checkpoint on the corner, and as we did, the soldier asked me ma to open her bag. The soldier smiled at me ma but she looked straight through him and didn't smile back. Another soldier asked me to raise my arms, which I did and me ma said, 'He's only a wain; what are you searching him for?' and I thought, *I'm not a wain, I'm nearly nine and a half!* I raised my arms anyway and the soldier patted his hands along my coat, my waist and down the outside of my legs. This was the first time I was searched in my life and I couldn't wait to get back to the street to tell everybody. When we got out the other side of the sandbagged checkpoint the soldiers called something to us and they all laughed, but we just walked on towards Wellworths to get the shopping. Some of the shops on Waterloo Street and Waterloo Place had been blown up and had barrels outside them with tape strung across to keep people out. You could see right into the backs of the shops which the bombs had gouged out. Other shops had 'Bomb Damage Sale' signs on their windows.

As luck had it, lorries used to dump bomb-damaged goods out on the Line (an old railway track that ran parallel to the river) behind the Mex army camp. Everything from clothes to food, to household goods and glasses got dumped, and we made it our business to scavenge through the rubble to get at the buried treasure in the form of trays of tinned stewed steak, Fray Bentos steak and kidney pies in their sealed tins, trays of tinned beans with sausages actually in the tin as well, rubber boots, kitchen clocks and annuals for girls and boys. One day Dooter McKinney picked up a box with four fancy glasses in it and when he took it home his ma sent him down to get another two as, apparently, they came in sixes! Dooter headed back out to the dump and sure enough found the other two.

One day, while out scavenging, we noticed a pile of long, brass army shells lying in a heap beside the bomb-damaged goods. Terry McKinney said they were flare shells fired by the BA from the Mex to light up the area at night in search of IRA gunmen. They were shaped like bullet shells only much heavier, fatter and about eighteen inches longer. We took two each home with us, shined them up with Brasso, and me ma and Maisie McKinney put big plastic reeds into them and used them as ornaments, sitting on the floor on either side of the hearth in the sitting room. When the other mammies in the street saw them or heard about them, they sent their wains out to the dump to bring them back two as well. Soon, almost every hearth in the street was adorned with the BA flare shells.

***

In Wellworths, you had to pass the sweet counter and then the cake counter on the way in. Some of the sweets came in purple, red, orange and green wrappers, some had see-through plastic wrappers, and others had none. They were all stacked there in their thousands, laid out in terraces as me ma called them, starting low at the front of the counter where the customer was and rising gradually towards the back, where the women shop assistants stood in their white coats and pretty make-up.

If the sweet counter sugared the senses, then the delights at the cake counter drew them out as slabbers to the chin. It was truly hard to take in. Like the sweet counter, the cakes were laid out in compartments on a slight slant so you could see the full range of them. Huge, square chocolate cakes of different varieties with chocolate cream in the middle and cream piped along the edges, sponge cakes with jam and cream in the middle and a dusting of icing sugar on the top. Swiss rolls over two-foot long, covered in chocolate, or just brown without the chocolate, so you could see the flash of the white cream on its rounded end, and ordinary Swiss rolls with the cream and jam oozing out.

Seeing the look on my face as we passed by, me ma said,

'Don't worry, son, we'll get a slab o' cake on the way out,' and with these reassuring words, I happily traipsed onwards with her to get the messages.

'Hi, Ma, look at this! It's a dog-food called the same as our Brandy!' I loved calling Brandy, 'our Brandy', as it was great having a dog. I held up the red tin with a sheepdog on it for her to see.

'Oh God, so it is. Grab a tin o' that and we'll see if she likes it,' me ma said.

'Was there no dog-food dumped out the Line?' she asked and I said naw but I'd look again the next time.

We were passing the café at the back of the shop when me ma said, 'Will we go in for a wee bite, Tony?' and I said 'Aye', and in we went. I sat down at a square, white table on one of the orangey-brown chairs, and me ma joined the queue and chatted to the women and girls behind the counter. I remember wondering how she knew everyone when we were up the town, as all you heard was 'Ach, yes Eileen' or 'What about ye, Eileen?' and me ma would say 'Yes, Susie, aye, grand, Susie,' or 'Not so bad, Mary. What about ye, yerself?' and then they would turn their backs to me and continue a whispered conversation, presumably about her and us living after me da dying.

Both of us got fish and chips, and tea, bread and butter. She brought it down on a tray and we sat down to eat. I finished mine, but me ma didn't finish hers. She just sat looking around her, eating her white bread and butter and drinking her tea. I was worried about her not eating her fish and chips. I was worried about her living without me da.

The café was buzzing with mothers, grannies and young wains at tables.

'D'ye see that wee woman there with the wee brown hat?' me ma asked me, nodding to somewhere behind my head.

I turned around and saw a wee woman with a wee brown hat and a brown overcoat, sitting with her back to us a few tables down.

'Aye, what about her?'

'She's a store detective; she works for Wellworths,' she said.

'What's a store detective?' I asked her, smiling and thinking she was taking the hand, like me da used to.

'She walks up and down the aisles lookin' out for people shop-liftin'. She thinks nobody knows her, but everybody does. She'll get up now in a minute. Wait to ye see.' And, sure enough, up she got with her wee straw shopping bag, dandering back into the aisles, where my eyes followed, and her not lifting any messages, but just walking up and down the aisles, now and again letting on to be interested in something but always looking around her at the other shoppers.

Me ma was true to her word about the cake, as we got a slab of Victoria sponge and a bag of assorted biscuits. These would be devoured as soon as we got home by the hungry

Dohertys. We went up to the till and packed the messages into Wellworths' white plastic bags with navy blue polka-dots and the Wellworths name on in large, orangey-brown writing, and headed home through the same checkpoint we'd come in by. The whole of the city centre was ringed off by checkpoints by this stage; you couldn't get in without going through one of them to be searched. On the odd occasion we crossed over Craigavon Bridge to go to the Waterside, you had to pass a sandbagged checkpoint sitting squat in the middle of it, the soldiers and RUC men stopping and searching cars travelling in both directions.

'We'll see if we can get a Sticky Taxi out to the house,' said me ma as we walked up William Street with the packed shopping bags.

'There's me granda, Mammy!' I called out, excited to see the tall, burly figure of me granda appearing from the red-brick terrace of Chamberlain Street, carrying a handful of pale-yellow bookie dockets. He approached us with a broad smile, and me ma said, 'Yes, Daddy, were you over at the bookies?'

Granda said aye he was, and that he was heading up to Tracy's Bar if she fancied passing the hour. Me ma said 'Aye, surely,' and we turned around and headed back up to the end of William Street, past all the large-windowed shops, towards the bar, just across from the BA checkpoint. There was a queue of women and wains on the street waiting to go through and be searched. The barrel of an SLR rifle pointed into William Street through a wooden frame built into the sandbags.

I loved the odd occasion when I would be taken into Tracy's. The last time was a few months before with me granda, when he took me down the town for my birthday and bought me black Gola football boots with golden stripes on the sides. I carried the orange McLaughlin's Shoes bag with the black writing on it into the bar, and the men, me granda's friends, asked me to show them the new boots. I took them out and put them on the bar, where they stood proud on their rubber studs beside the brown bottles of Guinness stout and small whiskey glasses, to be admired by one and all. Me da was still alive then.

We went in with me granda and the bar was packed. There was a radio on for the horse-racing and some of the men were gathered round it with their bookie dockets clenched tight in their hands. 'What d'ye fancy, Eileen?' asked me granda as we sat down.

'I'll take a wee brandy wi' ice 'n' water, Daddy,' she said.

'A wee coke for you, Tony?' asked me granda, and I nodded back to him.

Apart from the few men gathered round the radio at the end of the counter, all the other men in the bar were looking in our direction and a few raised their thumbs at me and smiled. One came over, a tall man with long, curly hair, a beard and a brown suit, who me ma called John Keys.

'What about ye, Eileen?' he asked, sitting down beside us on one of the hard wooden stools.

'Aye, grand, John,' said me ma. 'I have to get on wi' it.'

'Patsy Doherty was a great man, Eileen. The best there is,' said John.

'I know he was, John,' said me ma. 'I know he was.'

'And how are you, big fella?' he said, putting his hand on my head and ruffling my short, dirty-fair hair.

I reddened in the face, mumbling that I was OK.

'Are ye lookin' after yer mammy?' he asked, and I smiled and nodded back to him, still embarrassed.

'Oh, he's good to me, that boy. They all are. They're a credit,' said me ma with a smile, showing her perfect white teeth, a beautiful feature in her now often sad face. She still kept her dark brown hair long and straight and parted in the middle, the way it had been for years.

'Here ye go, Eileen,' said me granda, as he placed me ma's brandy down on the table and handed me a bottle of Pepsi and a straw.

He sat down with his bottle of stout beside me and me ma and John, and me ma told them about the soldier searching me at the checkpoint.

'I told them,' she said, 'that he was only a wain but they didn't take me on.'

'What did they do, Tony?' asked me granda.

Embarrassed, I said, 'He told me to lift me hands up and

then he searched me coat and rubbed down the outside of me trousers.'

'Imagine that,' said John to me ma and granda, 'searching the wee boy. They're a shower of English fuckers, I swear to God!'

'Aye, sure, what can ye do?' said me ma, and after a short pause, added, 'Hi, there was a house blown up around the corner from us yesterday, where the Slavins and the Hales used to live. The army had the house sealed off when we left the street this mornin'.'

Éamonn Slavin was in my class in school. They had moved from the house which was now blown up to a new housing estate called Carnhill, down near Shantallow, out in the country. When we went home a few hours later, carried across Rossville Street and Lecky Road in a Sticky Taxi which, after dropping us off, was bound for Creggan, me, our Paul and Dooter McKinney went round to see the house. As well as the Slavins, Snooks Hale, who was a year older than me and in our Patrick's class at Long Tower, used to live there but the Hales had moved to Creggan. Most of the roof and front wall had been blown out by the bomb. It looked like a doll's house: from the street you could see right in and out the back windows, which were all blasted out, and you could see the ends of the ceiling and floorboards and the gap in between, facing out into the street.

The BA had gone by this time so we were free to go in

for a look. When we went in, the front room was not as bad as the upstairs. A huge statue of Our Lady leaned against the wall beside a display cabinet with red velvet shelves, on which were china cups and teapots. There was a thick layer of dust on the top and on most things but it looked much like anybody else's front room with its fanciness of furniture and good carpet. We couldn't go upstairs because it was blocked by rubble from the bomb. We didn't lift or take anything because it all still looked as if it belonged to somebody, and it even felt strange going in through the wrecked downstairs.

When we went back home later I told me ma we were in the bombed house and she told me that all the furniture still belonged to someone and not to go back in, that it wasn't our house and it could be dangerous.

'What d'ye mean – another bomb?' I asked, and then there was a knock at the front door and when I went out to answer there was a priest with a broad smile standing there.

'Is your mammy in?' he asked, and I thought he was there to complain that me, Dooter and our Paul had been over at the blown-up house around the corner. I went back in and told me ma there was a priest at the door and she told me to bring him in.

Father Tom O'Gara came in that early evening and spoke to me ma in the scullery for a while and then came in and sat with us in the sitting room and had our fry with us as we watched TV. He started coming to the house for visits and often brought his guitar with him. Father O'Gara was from Moville in Donegal, but was one of the priests serving at the Long Tower Chapel. He had a mop of browny-red curly hair, a kind face and a pleasant way about him. He was with me ma a lot of the time. He'd call for her in his navy-blue Hillman Avenger to take her out for runs. Sometimes some of us would go as well. He kept his guitar in the boot and when he played it in our house, we'd sing 'Bridge Over Troubled Waters' and 'Moon Shadow' in the sitting room. He'd play anything you asked him. Uncle Eugene and Father O'Gara got on very well together.

Me ma said that there was an 'Inquiry' into the killings on Bloody Sunday, and that she'd have to go up to Coleraine every day to attend. I wasn't sure what an Inquiry was. I'd never heard the word before, but it sounded like someone was going to do something about me da's death and the deaths of the other twelve men that the BA had shot dead. I think she did go nearly every day. Father O'Gara took her up in his car most days, when we were at school. Me granny Sally or me aunts would watch Glenn and Colleen for her when she was away at the Inquiry. In the evenings it would be dark by the time she came back, leaving Karen in charge of making the dinner. Me and Patrick helped out and, between us, we kept the house clean and everyone fed. Maisie McKinney called in often from up the street to make sure everything was all right.

It was Aunt Geraldine who encouraged me ma to learn

to drive. One evening there was a knock on the front door and me ma got up from her chair, saying excitedly, 'That'll be Junior McDaid for me,' and we all went out to the street to see. Sure enough, it was Junior and he put me ma in the driving seat. After a few minutes she started the car and drove down the street towards Foyle Road. The car shuddered and jolted a few times on its way towards the corner before going smooth. Me and our Paul ran after it for the craic, following it down to the end of the street. We saw the indicator light come on to go left and the car turned the corner and disappeared down Foyle Road. She went out driving with me Aunt Geraldine as well in her wee white, two-door Vauxhall. Very few families in our street had a car, and no other woman in the street could drive. Me Aunt Geraldine said that me ma was a natural driver and that she took to it like a duck to water.

On our way to school we passed the Sticky headquarters: a house on Lecky Road not far from ours and just across the street from the Lourdes Hall. The Stickies used to set up checkpoints outside it and stop and search cars travelling into our part of the Brandywell. I don't know if they ever found anything but they searched a lot of cars and delivery vans. We used to sneak over from Hamilton Street to watch them standing around outside the house with their .303s, .306s and Thompson sub-machine guns. They wore green combat coats or denim jackets, jeans and masks. When a car approached, one of them would stand out on the road with his gun pointing upwards from his hip and his other hand held out to stop the car. All the cars stopped and gave the Sticky their licence, even if they just lived down the street, and the Sticky would read the licence, sometimes look in the boot and then let them go again. The Sticky would sometimes call the drivers by their first names and sometimes the driver would call the Sticky back with their first names as they drove off: 'Churrio, John', or 'Churrio, Joe'. The Provos also mounted foot patrols and checkpoints.

Our Hamilton Street gang was often divided as to who we supported, or should support, and our loyalties, or lack of them, were based on a range of sources: older boys like Terry McKinney, Thomas Starrs and Davy McKinney, who all knew more than us; and talk in the house among parents and aunts and uncles, often repeated in the street, as to who was in the Provos and who was in the Stickies, and which was thought to be the best or most active. This information was supported by a body-count of British soldiers, and who was thought to have killed or injured them.

Gun-battles happened almost every night. Sometimes they'd be very brief, with only six or seven shots, while others could go on for fifteen minutes or longer. We heard the shots in the street, at school, when we were in bed at night or when we were at Mass on a Sunday. Following a shooting, the news would emerge, vague or accurate, that a soldier had been shot on Lone Moore Road or at the bottom of Bishop Street. The boys in our class who lived in Creggan brought in stories of soldiers being shot on New Road or Southway, or other streets I didn't know.

All the dogs in the streets around us barked fiercely at the BA vehicles as they drove by on Foyle Road, the soldiers sometimes swinging their boots at the dogs for a laugh. There was a wee dog on Lecky Road called Provo, and a big black-and-tan brute of a dog in Quarry Street called Rebel.

From the day me da was killed on what people now call Bloody Sunday, the BA were rarely seen on the streets in the Brandywell, but would patrol in their Pigs, Saracens and Jeeps around the outside of the area, using only the main roads. Sometimes, though, they would take a chance and come up the street on foot to be met by dogs, large and small, who barked and snapped in packs at them. The soldiers sometimes swung at them with their varnished wooden batons, or threw axle grease at them. Axle grease was very hard to wash off, so a dog who was 'greased' ran around for days with a dark green patch on it that looked like a disease of some kind. The noise of the barking dogs was often drowned out by the clatter of women down on their knees, blowing whistles and banging their tin dustbin lids on the pavement in small groups outside their houses. This warning noise almost always accompanied the BA when they came in.

The soldiers were a mix of cocky, cautious or simply scared of their arses, as they walked the streets with their SLRs held in both hands in front of them and their faces, even the black ones, covered in black camouflage paint. You could tell the scared ones by the look on their faces and the glassy fear in their eyes, and while they looked old to us, most of them were probably in their late teens or early twenties. Their uniforms were immaculate and they kept their shin-length black boots in a high order of shininess. The badges on their berets told you which regiment was 'in'.

We threw stones at them in the street, running for our lives up through the waste ground to hide behind Paddy Melaugh's pigsty, or up to the top of the bankin', where we lay flat on the grass, out of sight of the streets below. After a while we realised they didn't always run after us so we became a bit more confident at the stone-throwing, and practised our aim by throwing them at the rusty old cars that lay almost buried in horse manure in the quarry. We had to be careful, though, not to hit people's good cars or windows, and sometimes oul boys would call to us to 'stop peggin' stones' in the street. But mostly we had a free hand. On Foyle Road there were no such obstacles, so we'd wait at the corner of Hamilton Street or Moore Street for hours for a BA vehicle to come along, and throw hails of stones or bottles, which smashed noisily against the dark green metal before scattering harmlessly on the road. Sometimes you could hear the soldiers inside laughing their heads off at us and shouting stuff as they drove along. If the Pig or Sixer stopped suddenly there would be a scatter of young rioters up the street into the relative safety of the back lanes, or up towards the high bankin'.

***

'Alla balla! Alla balla! Who's got the ball?' Teresa McKinney called out. She stood with her back to the rest of us, her dirty-fair, curly hair unmoving, facing the gable wall of the end cottage across the street from our house. It was a spring evening and the day was darkening towards night.

'Alla balla! Alla balla! Who's got the ball?' she called out again. Calling twice was the rule of the game. She'd just thrown the wee ball over her shoulder, which we scrambled for on the dusty ground at the bottom of the lane while she continued to face the wall. Dandy McKinney had scrambled for it as well. When she got the ball in her jaws, it was nearly impossible to get it back out of her slabbery mouth. Whoever captured the ball hid it behind their back while the rest of us stood with our own hands behind our backs as well. Teresa, who was 'on it', had to guess from the faces presented to her who had the ball. After her second call, she spun around to face the scattering of boys and girls facing her with their hands behind their backs. She scanned the smiling and suspicious faces of me, Dooter, our Paul and Patrick, Johnny Barbour, Hughie Barbour, Jacqueline McKinney, Donna O'Donnell and Gerard Starrs, also known as Starrsy. If she guessed right she remained 'on it', but if she guessed wrong, whoever had the ball would be 'on it' for the next throw. Dooter had the ball behind his back and had a broad grin on his face. His face could hide nothing. Our Paul was the same. She scanned each of our faces and after a few moments she said, pointing her finger in the right direction, 'Alla balla! Alla balla! Our Dooter has the ball!'

Dooter's role was then to slowly chant, 'I've got the ball in my pocket; Alla balla! Alla balla! I've got the ball!' while presenting it to Teresa like a trophy for her to repeat the exercise.

'Ye couldn't miss that big simple Gransha grin anywhere!' said our Patrick, and everyone laughed.[2]

'Right, are yis ready?' called Teresa again. 'Aye' we all called back and she threw the ball again over her shoulder. The ensuing scramble, involving pushing, skidding and grunting on the dry dirt, resulted in me gripping the wee red bouncy ball in both my hands and tearing away from the scrum. Once you had the ball firmly in both hands, it was yours and the struggle was over. Teresa sensed from behind her that it was indeed over and that someone had won the ball.

'Yis ready now?'

'Aye,' we all said.

'Alla balla! Alla balla! Who's got the ball?'

---

2   Gransha was the local mental hospital in Derry.

'Alla balla! Alla balla! Who's got the ball?' she repeated and leapt in the air and swung herself round to face the crowd.

She'll never know from me that I've got the ball, I thought, as I rolled it in my fingers and Teresa scanned the faces.

'There's a soldier doll tarred and feathered outside Sweeney's shop!' called Davey Barbour as he came around the corner towards us. We abandoned the alla balla, dashing the short distance up the street to see what had happened. Sweeney's red-brick shop was on the corner of Quarry Street so we had to be careful about the Quarry Gang, especially the Blisses, who would rip your head off in a fight. But Davey was with us and no one could tackle Davey. The soldier doll had been tied to a lamp post, had her hair shaved off and had black paint thrown over her head. When we got there, she'd been untied and was being led away screaming, not words, just screaming. Small crowds of people had gathered around outside the shop to see 'the bars' and some of the women called 'Soldier doll!' and 'Serves ye right, ya blone ye!' to her as she was being led away, and they stood smoking in the darkening evening, chatting and looking around them in their bright headscarves and cardigans. A sign, written in black marker on a sheet of cardboard, saying simply 'Soldier Doll', lay in a shiny pool of black paint on the pavement. Clumps of hair were strewn on the pavement too and some had stuck to the ornate cast-iron lamp post.

The next morning, we took the same route up to school,

past Sweeney's shop. We saw that the pool of shiny black paint had congealed thickly on the pavement below the lamp post. Clumps of hair lay matted through it, breaking up its otherwise smooth surface. The cardboard 'Soldier Doll' sign had skidded to one side of the black pool but was still stuck to the ground, with a small black shoe print over the letters as if some wain had slid on it. From head-height down to the ground, there were lumps of long, mousy-brown hair stuck to the lamp post by the shiny black paint. Neither our Paul nor me touched anything but just passed by on the roadway and headed on up towards the Folly to school.

Some women were tarred and feathered because they were accused of 'soldier-dolling'. 'Soldier dolls' were Irish women who were going out with British soldiers. How or where they went with them none of us had much of a clue. Patrick Brown said one day that they were tarred and feathered because they allowed soldiers to put English spunk into them. We were sitting on the footpad near our houses: me, Patrick, Gutsy and Johnny Barbour, when Patrick said this.

'What are ye on about, Patrick?' said Gutsy.

'The soldiers put their English spunk into the women. That makes them a soldier doll,' said Patrick with great authority.

'Aye, but what's spunk? What are ye on about?' I asked.

Patrick reddened in the face and wouldn't or couldn't answer the question. 'I jist heard men saying it in me da's garage this morning. A man said they deserved it "because they took the spunk of an English soldier".'

Each of us knew that, whatever spunk was, it wasn't a question we could safely ask.

I was very confused about soldier-dolling, as you would often see photographs of Derry women in the pages of the *Derry Journal* in their white wedding dresses marrying British soldiers, and them in their uniforms standing outside St Mary's Chapel or some other chapel, with another soldier or sometimes a line of them, all in their British Army uniforms, peaked caps and broad white belts. If marrying a British soldier wasn't soldier-dolling, I wondered, what was?

***

At night rumours went round that there was a prowler in the Brandywell or a prowler in Bishop Street. None of us, not even Gutsy or Terry McKinney, knew what a prowler was exactly, or what he did, so we had to rely more or less on our imaginations. At night when I lay in bed I imagined the black-and-white scene of a man changing into a hairy werewolf with sharp teeth, sneaking around the back lane of Hamilton Street, crouching in the dark on the wall in the yard looking into people's windows while panting heavily like a dog in heat. The Vigilantes were out looking for whoever the prowler was, and everyone was told to be on their guard. The Vigilantes walked and drove around Free Derry, mostly at night but also during the day, and sat at the street corners smoking and taking all in. They were the only police force we knew at the time, and they would warn us about playing football and causing annoyance to old people. You never saw the real police force in our streets any more after Bloody Sunday, but you would see the odd grey police Jeep driving between two army Jeeps or Sixers on the Foyle Road, heading to the Mex or the checkpoint further out the Letterkenny Road. One evening, as me and Dooter came out of Sweeney's shop, someone said that the prowler had been 'kneecapped' in the dark alley across the street. As we stood to see what we could, an ambulance zoomed up the street, stopping opposite us. The ambulance men disappeared into the alley and helped the prowler hobble out into the streetlight where we could see the dark-red patches of blood on each trouser leg.

***

One spring morning, a few months after me da's death, me and our Paul were walking up the Folly towards school. At the time, they were erecting huge concrete pillars along the new route down into the Bogside from Abercorn Road. It was called the 'Flyover', someone in our class had said. A lot of houses had been knocked down around the school to make way for this new Flyover, which was a lot broader than the old roadways around the school. Whole streets had been tumbled and the place looked more and more different every day. The area changed from streets to wasteland in a very short time. We called into wee Lorny Quigg's shop for sweets. There were a few other wains there being served by Lorny, who wasn't much taller than any of us and was as broad as he was tall. Daniel McDaid and Peter 'Kinker' O'Donnell from my class were there, and as we left together they told us of a fierce gun-battle down the Bog the previous night, near their houses.

Daniel McDaid was a boxer. He pulled up his sleeves to show me his hard muscles and talked about boxing all the time. In the schoolyard at the break he showed me how to stand properly, how to duck and dive, how to throw punches and how to protect my face with my fists. I didn't fancy being a boxer as I didn't like getting hit and didn't have any muscles, but I went along with it because Daniel talked about it that much, and because I liked him and looked up to him. Daniel always came to school with Kinker O'Donnell, who lived in Cable Street and had bright red curly hair; he boxed as well, in a local club.

Daniel said they were up all night because of the gun-battle, and that there was blood everywhere.

'D'yis fancy taking us down for a look?' I asked them. They agreed and we headed down past the high Gasyard wall into Stanley's Walk. The street was completely deserted; not a person or a car moved and there was a smell of gas in the air; not CS gas, but a thick, chemical smell like house gas. Sometimes when you walked up or down the Folly on the way to school you would get that smell wafting up from behind the high stone walls of the Gasyard. It had two vast green gasometer tanks, which one day would tower high up in the air and the next day would have almost disappeared back into their huge black metal bases. At the bottom of Stanley's Walk there was a row of cottages and further up a row of terraced houses; a gap in between was the entry to Cable Street. Daniel and Peter started walking up Stanley's Walk; this was their territory, strange to us, so we followed the leaders. As we passed the open doorway of one of the cottages, Daniel pointed to a pool of blood in the tiled hallway and said, 'There was someone shot there last night; I think it was a soldier.' The round pool of blood covered most of the small hallway. The pool was deepest in the middle and shallower along its edges. There was also a splatter of blood on the brown, yellow and orange wallpaper. The windowed and netted vestibule door to the cottage was closed and I wondered why nobody was out cleaning up the blood.

Daniel led us on up the street, and just before the gap for Cable Street there was a similar sight. In another cottage with an open front door, there was another pool of blood. On the footpad just outside this cottage, though, there was a piece of metal which I recognised as the twisted handle from an SLR rifle, and a piece of wooden casing from an SLR lay on the road nearby. They must have been blown off by an IRA bullet during the gun-battle, and the blood on the tiles must have come from the soldier who was carrying it or shooting back with it. We didn't touch anything but simply stood around for a few minutes looking at the blood in the hall and the pieces of broken rifle on the street before turning to dander back up in the direction of school before the bell rang for class.

Me, Daniel and Kinker were the centre of attention as we told the rest of the boys about what we'd seen on Stanley's Walk. Boys were guessing how many British soldiers had been shot dead and at one stage someone had the body count up to eight, which I thought was over-the-top.

'OK, wains, after we do the roll-call, we're goney do a poster competition about smokin',' said Mr McCartney, through his sandy, bushy sideburns and big hairy moustache. He started the roll-call: 'Beales – Carlin – Cooper – Curran – Doherty – Donnelly – Doyle – Goodman – Griffiths – Healy, Damien – Healy, Martin – Kelly – Martin – McDaid – McGarrigle – McLaughlin – Mooney – O'Donnell – Ramsey – Slavin – Vail – Wade.'

'Wade' was Barry Wade, from the Bog. 'Present, sir,' he said from his chubby, smiling face. Barry had a head of brown hair, cut short, but it grew out into a ball of curls between haircuts.

'Sir, there was a wile lot of shootin' down in our street last night,' said Barry to the teacher.

Mr McCartney looked up from marking his roll-call and said, 'I know. I heard it too.'

'I think there was BA killed in Stanley's Walk,' said Barry. Mr McCartney looked back at him, but didn't respond.

'There's pools of blood everywhere on the street, sir,' I said, to put myself in the story.

'Sure, you don't live in the Bog, Tony. How did *you* see it?' he asked.

'We went down for a jook, sir, before comin' into school,' I said. 'There were pieces of an SLR lyin' broke on the street. Beside the pools of blood, sir.'

Mr McCartney didn't say anything else. He put the roll book away in his drawer and then got up and walked up and down the rows of desks, giving us each a single white sheet of paper, then passing around a few tin boxes of crayons for us to pick our colours. 'If yis want another colour, just put your hand up and I'll sort ye out,' he said. 'Yis are goin' to do a poster about smokin'.'

The whole class stared blankly back at him. *Sure everybody smokes*, I thought to myself, *what's the big deal?*

'Doctors now reckon that smokin' isn't good for ye and that it causes cancer and other diseases that can kill ye,' said Mr McCartney. This was the first time I'd heard the word 'cancer' said out loud. I'd heard it many a time in me granny Quigley's house, but it was usually said in a different way, almost in a whisper.

'Ruby McCallion's not a bit well,' me granny would say to me ma.

'God, poor Ruby; what's wrong wi' her?'

Me granny would mouth the word 'cancer' without saying it.

'Cancer' me ma would mouth back to her in a similar fashion, shaking her head, while both of them sucked on an Embassy Red each, filling the room with smoke.

'So the poster is about givin' people advice about why they shouldn't smoke,' said Mr McCartney. 'There's a wee prize for the winner,' he added, causing a buzz of excitement among the room full of nine-year-olds with their crayons, their white paper on their varnished wooden desks and their heads down in thought over their busily moving hands.

I drew a picture of a row of slated rooftops with chimneys that had fags coming out of them instead of the sandy coloured funnels. I drew the outline of the roofs and the slates in black crayon and then, turning the crayon on its side, I shaded in the slates so that they came out a light grey colour. The brickwork of the chimney stacks was also black and I used a red crayon to fill in the many bricks in each of them so that they all looked the same. Black and grey smoke billowed out of the row of fag chimneys and wafted up into the light-blue sky. A few birds sat on the rooftops, taking it all in. In bold letters, I wrote along the bottom of the page: 'SMOKING IS FOR CHIMNEYS, NOT FOR YOU'.

When we came back into the classroom after the break, Mr McCartney was sitting behind his desk with his back to the blackboard, and in front of him he had a sheaf of some thirty smoking-posters.

'Well, wains,' he said, looking round the room after we were seated and the noise had died down, 'I showed the posters to some of the other teachers during the break and this wan here is the winner,' he said, standing up and holding up the poster. 'Who drew this wan?' he asked. It was mine!

'I did, sir,' I said with my hand in the air, as if seeking permission. Everybody was looking from the poster to me and back.

'Well done, Tony,' he said, still holding the poster up for all to see. 'C'mon up to get your prize.'

I walked to the front of the class, where he reached into his drawer and brought out a 'Bar Six' in its bright orange wrapper and said, 'Congratulations, and well done again. Give Tony a wee clap, boys.'

I took the Bar Six as the whole class clapped their hands and I walked back down to my desk feeling happy and embarrassed at the same time. Mr McCartney pinned the smoking-poster onto the wall beside the blackboard, where it stayed for a long time.

At lunchtime, Danny McDaid asked me to go to his house for a bite to eat and I agreed. Between me, Danny and Kinker we ate the Bar Six on the way down. Each of us got two of the wee chocolate-covered wafer fingers as we dandered down past the Gasyard. Danny's house was in Abbots Walk in the Bog, just over a bit from Stanley's Walk. The houses in Abbots Walk were newer than ours but had flat roofs. Danny turned the key in the front door, and when we went into his scullery his ma, Anna, was there putting chicken soup out into bowls on the table, next to a plate of white bread cut into triangles. Danny told her who I was and that I was from Hamilton Street.

'I knew your father,' she said. 'You're very welcome in this house, son. Sit down and take some soup and bread.'

Danny had four or five brothers, all steps of stairs and all boxers, and they were all back from primary school to get their lunch. I felt like one of the family, sitting at their table in the Bog, dipping the triangles of white bread into the blue-and-white striped bowls half-filled with creamy chicken soup. It was my first time being in someone's house in the Bog as it was considered too far from our house. As we ate the soup with our bread, Mrs McDaid stood by the sink and told us how bad the gun-battle had been the previous night.

'Jesus, Mary and Saint Joseph but the shooting was desperate. There were two young fellas shot dead down the street by the army and there was wile shootin' over at the Gasyard and Stanley's Walk,' she said, as if she was talking to the woman next door.

'The whole house was on the floor for nearly an hour, it was that bad,' she said as we dipped our bread and slurped our soup at the table.

'Was there shootin' over in your street, son?' she asked me and I said naw, there wasn't, feeling a bit guilty and somewhat left out. I hadn't heard a thing the previous night, which was strange because the Gasyard wasn't that far from our street.

When we were finished, Mrs McDaid gave us each some bread and jam, then we put our coats on again in the hall and dandered back down past the Gasyard to go up the Folly towards school. When we were on the Folly we could look down on Daniel's part of the Bog, at the squat, square, red- and yellow-brick houses, which always looked to me as if they had no roofs.

'They call it Jerusalem – wi' the flat roofs,' said Daniel, and I wondered what he was on about.

When we reached the schoolyard we linked up with other boys from our class and played tig. The green metal poles that held up the long shed roof where we would go when it rained were 'parley', and you could stay touching the poles with both hands and not get tipped as long as you didn't stay there too long and spoil the game.

Me and Joe Mooney had our hands wrapped around the same green pole when I noticed the student teacher. She had long, shiny brown hair and was wearing a dark brown jumper, a fawn-coloured skirt down to just above the knee, whitish tights and dark, strapped shoes. More importantly, she had bright red lipstick and, even more importantly, she was smoking a fag as she patrolled the yard, walking up and down in a straight line in the company of Mr O'Kane, another teacher, who was tall, dark-haired and spoke with a country accent. She walked, talked and smoked and I followed the movement of her hand as she brought the fag up to her red lips, sucked in the smoke and blew it out of her mouth into the spring air of the schoolyard. As she turned to my left to come back up the yard again she flicked the fag butt away from her and I could see that it landed in an alcove, set back a bit from the yard. My mind was made up.

'C'mon wi' me, Joe!' I said urgently. There was no time to waste.

'What? Where are we going?' he asked as I sprinted across the yard, dodging bodies playing tig, into the alcove, Joe following close behind. The fag butt lay on the clean concrete ground with the smoke still coming out of the quarter inch of white left in it. I picked it up and saw that there was a band of bright red lipstick on the cork tip. Not put off, I raised the fag butt to my lips, sucked on it and felt the warm smoke come through into my mouth. I didn't inhale. I took the butt away again, blew out and handed it to Joe, who put it to his own mouth, dragged on it, and blew the smoke back out through his smiling lips. I took another drag from it and blew the smoke back out again without inhaling.

'It's finished now, look,' I said, showing him that there was no white left and flicked it away again into the corner of the alcove. For many weeks afterwards the student teacher with the white tights and bright red lips became our fixation as we watched her walk, talk and puff her way through break time and lunchtime, hoping she would leave a healthy band of white on her fag butt before scooting it away.

***

One day, Daniel McDaid told me in the classroom that someone had painted me da's name on a flagstone down the Bog. 'It's down at the Rossville Flats, in front of the shops.'

I knew where the flats were, as I'd passed them a few times with me ma as we headed down the town for the messages.

'What does it say?' I asked, taken by what he said.

'I canny mind exactly, but it says something about your da being killed.'

'Ye fancy takin' us down, me and our Paul, after school the day?' I asked, knowing me ma wouldn't be back until after five.

'Aye, sure, me an' Barry an' Kinker'll take a scoot down to show yis.'

In the end, only Daniel, Kinker and me made the journey down past the Long Tower Girls' School, where our Karen and Jacqueline McKinney went, past the Long Tower Chapel and the white marble statue of Christ lying wounded on a marble block, down the high-walled stone steps that led to rows of terraced houses, and down towards the three blocks of high flats, built as three sides of a square, which we could see in the distance. The Bog was strange territory to me and we were often warned about going there in case we got battered. I felt safe, though, with Daniel and Kinker as we dandered down past the rows of houses and cottages in various stages of decay, some still lived in and others being knocked down, until we reached the more modern end of the Bog, the houses with flat roofs and gardens at the front. At the front of the flats we walked along the row of shops at the bottom until we came to the long set of stone steps held in by high concrete walls. The green flagstone was right in front of me. We were all careful not to put our feet on it, the way you would avoid walking on a grave in the cemetery.

On the single flagstone slab, written in black letters on a bed of olive-green paint, it read: *PATRICK DOHERTY WAS KILLED ON THIS SPOT ON 30TH JANUARY 1972. RIP.* There were four wee black crosses painted in each corner of the flagstone. Each of us blessed ourselves almost at the same time as we read the words to ourselves.

We didn't say much, but stood looking at and reading the words again and again until there was nothing more to be done. I looked around me. We were standing more or less in the front court of the flats beside the gable end of the first or last house on Joseph Place. This was the house that me ma had mentioned that day when me Uncle Michael had brought Brandy in for the first time. Joseph Place, where me da's cousin lived. What had happened to me da was beyond my understanding. Everything around me seemed safe and normal, and I wondered how a man could be shot and killed here, in Rossville Street, with cars driving along it. We went into one of the shops and bought a few hard treacle dainties which we chewed soft as we walked back towards their part of the Bog, near the Gasyard, and then I dandered on, passing its high arched walls and the Sticky headquarters in the wreck of a house on Lecky Road where the Stickies were out stopping cars with their .303 rifles and their Thompson machine guns, towards No. 15 Hamilton Street.

***

The Wilsons lived in Moore Street. They'd moved into the waste ground between Moore Street and Hamilton Street and lived for a while in a long caravan. We called them gypsies but we knew they weren't. Mr Wilson was a thin, swarthy man with black hair, who rarely smiled. He sold sticks and blocks from his wee blue van around Derry and had asked me, Dooter and our Paul to sell sticks for him around the doors in our part of the Brandywell. He gave us an oul pram, which was boggin' with dirt, to wheel round the doors selling the sticks in bundles.

One day he asked us to go with him in the wee van to sell his sticks. So away we went, the three of us in the back of the van, which was stacked up with large bundles of sticks in clear plastic bags, tied at the top with cord. The three of us sat in a gap near the back doors. Mr Wilson smoked as he drove, rarely speaking except, when the van stopped, to tell us to go down there, or around that corner, to sell the bags of sticks. They were heavy but we carried one in each hand. It was a relief to sell a bag, which meant you only had one left to carry. That was until you brought the money back to Mr Wilson, smoking at the back doors of the van, and then you were away again with two more heavy bags. We were down in Carnhill, where all the houses were brand new and built in squares, not streets like our street. When we finished the squares in Carnhill we piled back into the van and looked out the back windows as Mr Wilson sped along the main road to another stop.

'Right, boys; out yis go!' and out we got again with two heavy bags each to start going round the doors.

'Shantallow Crescent' the sign read as I ran around the back of a block of shops, knocking on the first door. Between no one being in and others not wanting sticks I ran back after a few minutes around the front of the shops with the heavy bags of sticks pulling on each arm in time to see Mr Wilson's wee blue van disappear back onto the main road and away. *He'll probably stop around the corner to do more houses*, I thought, as I followed the path of the van on the footpad. When I reached the bend where the van had gone, I looked down the long, tree-lined road but there was no sign of Mr Wilson or the van. I kept going along the road, expecting him to pull up beside me any minute for me to jump in the back.

The bags of sticks were getting heavier as I walked along, so I put them down beside a low wall and sat on top of one for a minute to see what would happen. Nothing happened, so I got up again with my cargo and began walking a bit further. It was a bright day with a bit of heat in it, so I wasn't cold in my trousers and t-shirt. The sticks eventually became too heavy again for my thin arms so I sat down again in front of a row of houses for a few minutes, still expecting to see the wee blue van pull up with the smiling faces of Dooter and our Paul in the back. But nobody appeared. I got up again. *I'll have to ditch these effin' sticks*, I said to myself, after starting to walk again. I drew level with two tall gateposts with bushes and undergrowth behind them. I carefully stashed the two bags of sticks behind one of the gateposts so that I could show Mr Wilson where they were later on.

Later that night, when I got back to the house in Hamilton Street by some unknown means, Mr Wilson came round. Me ma brought him in to the sitting room where we all were. 'Here's two bob, Tony,' he said, handing me the silver coin. 'I thought you were in the van when I drove away the day,' he said, looking shiftily at me ma, holding his huge hands up each side of his swarthy face. 'I drove back round a few minutes later but I couldn't see you.'

'You're lucky, Mr Wilson, that Paddy Doherty isn't here to greet you,' said me ma. 'He would have thumped you first and asked questions afterwards.'

'I know, Eileen. I'm really sorry.'

'That's OK,' she said, looking at me and smiling. 'The last time he got lost we lived up in Moore Street. He just put his foot on a scooter, pushed himself and kept going and didn't look back, and ended up outside the courthouse away up in Bishop Street. He was only about three. The whole street was out looking for him. Two policemen picked him up and brought him back to the house in their big black car, and when they brought him in he was wearing a policeman's hat, eatin' a doughnut, the snotters trippin' him and the sugar from the doughnut stuck to the snotters. And ye shoulda smelt him wi' shite,' she said, laughing as she remembered something I had no knowledge of at all. 'He was cacked to the nines and it all down his legs! Their da was mortified that the big policemen had been in our house and the whole street was around their big black car. We had to take him to the yard to clean the cack off him,' she chortled, and Mr Wilson and everybody else laughed.

It was funny for me too, to hear about something that happened to me before I had any memory of my own.

***

Me da's absence from our family became final and forever as the moments surrounding his death became clearer, and his belongings were returned to us at 15 Hamilton Street. One day me ma came back very late from the Inquiry. She looked tired and pale, and her eyes were dull. I began to notice these things about me ma as, in my own way, I was worried about her being left on her own with us six wains and without me da. She came into the sitting room, sat down with a sigh and took a small blue booklet from her handbag.

'It's a total whitewash, a sham,' she said, her voice weak. I couldn't see the connection between paint for the back walls and us. 'We're not goney get justice. He described your da as a gunman. They were all described as gunmen and bombers ...'

She seemed to steel herself before saying, 'May God forgive them' as she stood up, walked to the hall and left the wee blue booklet on the telephone table. It sat there untouched for days. I picked it up one day to have a look. The following words were on the pale-blue cover, which, apart from the black script, could have been a schoolbook:

Report of the Tribunal
appointed to inquire into the
events of Sunday, 30th January 1972,
which led to loss of life
in connection with the procession
in Londonderry on that day
by
The Rt. Hon. Lord Widgery, O.B.E., T.D.

And at the bottom of the cover, in smaller letters, it read:

LONDON

HER MAJESTY'S STATIONERY OFFICE

36½p. net

Me ma's photo appeared in a newspaper, along with some other relatives of the men who had been killed on the same day. I knew me da wasn't an IRA man. He just wasn't. He was in the house with all of us when the gun-battles were raging outside. I remember me ma told Maisie McKinney a story about him as they stood in the street outside our house smoking, months and months ago. I just sat on the edge of the footpad and listened.

'Jesus, Maisie, ye missed the bars last night,' said me ma.

Maisie's eyes widened and she said, 'What, Eileen, what?' to speed the telling.

'Aw, Jesus, there was near murder, so there was,' said me ma, serious but nearly laughing at the same time.

'What, Jesus, tell me what happened!'

'We were sitting in Mailey's enjoying the craic, me and Paddy, when Tony Cooley came in,' she said as she puffed on her Embassy Red. 'He had a jar in him. And didn't he sit down across from us and didn't he put a wee gun down on top of the table, beside Paddy's Carling bottle!'

'Oh Jesus, Eileen, what did he do that for?' said Maisie.

'I dunno, but wait to ye hear. Paddy said to him "What are ye at with that, Tony?" And your man Cooley said, "It's my army issue revolver, Patsy," and Paddy said, "Well, take you that away with ye to fuck. A fuckin' bar's no place for a gun and well ye should know it!"'

'Aw Jesus, Eileen, your Patsy's a wile man!' said Maisie, puffing on her fag. 'And what happened?'

'Aw fuck, Maisie, didn't Tony Cooley lift the wee gun and bang it down on the table!' said me ma. 'The whole bar was watchin'. "It's my fuckin' gun and it stays there!" Tony Cooley roared into Paddy's face across the table. Ye know Paddy, Maisie; I thought he was goin' to explode!'

'Oh dear, Eileen, don't be telling me any more for Jesus' sake, ye must've been shitin' yerself!'

'Jesus, Maisie, don't talk; didn't I see Paddy rubbing his hands on his legs underneath the wee table and the next thing he had Tony Cooley by the throat wi' wan hand and he had the wee gun in the other. He just lifted him out of his chair by the throat! The look of shock on Tony Cooley's face is a sight I'll never forgit, Maisie, for Paddy walked him out the door backways by the throat, put him to the street and came back in, reached the wee gun down behind the bar and sat down again! Hughie Mailey didn't know where to put himself!' said me ma, laughing out of her.

'And what happened then, Eileen? Jesus, Mary and Saint Joseph but your Patsy's a wile man.'

'Nothin', Maisie, he just sat down wi' me and took a drink of his beer. Nothin' else happened,' said me ma, and Maisie just stood with a look of wonder on her small, beautiful, film-star face.

Near the end of April someone brought a copy of *The Sunday Times* newspaper into the house. I took it to the front room, spread it out on the good carpet and bent over it to look at the photos. The photos were of me da in the minutes and seconds before his death, with a white hankie up over his mouth and nose cowboy-style to protect himself from the CS gas. He was wearing his black-and-white speckled overcoat with the black fur collar and was with a group of other men, all on their hands and knees or down on their hunkers with the look of fear in their eyes. Behind them was a high concrete wall with white-painted graffiti on it saying 'Join the Provos'. This was the first time I'd seen me da's face alive since that Sunday a few months back when we last ate our dinner together. The final picture in the set of photos was of a group of men gathered around me da as he lay on the ground with his eyes half open, seeing nothing.

He has no gun! I thought to myself. He hadn't. Here he was, a few seconds from his death, and you could see both of his hands. He had no gun. Our Paul came into the front room and we both knelt down, poring over the photos in silence.

After a while, Paul said, 'Did he have a gun, do you think?' and I said, 'Naw, sure he wasn't in the IRA. He had no gun, Paul. He was shot dead for nothin',' and we went on looking at the pictures of him wearing his coat, and looking so alive and then the last one of him lying with his eyes half shut and staring, dead, into space. After Paul went out again I folded the newspaper up neatly and left it on the sideboard beside the record player.

We had a short stack of LPs, mostly rebel songs. On one cover the title, *Rifles of the IRA*, was graffitied in large white letters on a wall of an abandoned cottage, alongside which the four Wolfe Tones stood in a bunch, a couple of them with shotguns in their hands, wearing dull green combat coats with belts strung across their chests and waists and green fedora hats.

I tilted the sleeve of the LP so that the record slid from it into my hand. Easing it carefully over the upright chrome spindle of the record player, I pushed the lever across the top to secure it. When I turned the knob at the front, the record player came on with a hum, then I pulled the smaller lever to spring it into play. The LP dropped into position and began its spin on the turntable as the needle arm clicked, slid and hovered over the edge and then landed silently on the record. The first sound you ever heard from our LPs was the light crackling as the needle negotiated its way over mostly invisible scratches before it hit the circling groove and the music started.

The familiar lyrics about the British bombarding Dublin in 1916 and the Black and Tans running from the IRA in 1921 rang out. I'd heard these words many times before from this record player or sung in the street, but they'd never meant as much to me as they did that day as I sat on a fancy green chair of the fancy green three-piece suite that helped to make the front room in our house in Hamilton Street the 'good' room, along with the carpet and the intricate embossed wallpaper. On the wall was a shiny brass shield with two metal swords criss-crossed behind it. This was the room me da was waked in. Someone took all the furniture out to make room for the coffin and the wake-goers.

I wondered why me da hadn't joined the IRA when a whole lot of other men from around the Brandywell had. *It made sense to join*, I thought, as I sat and listened to the words of the rebel songs, sung with such power that they sent goose pimples up my arms, raising the hairs on the back of my neck. I shivered a bit as I sat there picturing men with fedora hats and flat caps like Paddy Stewart's putting flight to the Black and Tans on the streets of Dublin all those years ago. Not that I knew much about it, but you didn't have to be a history genius to grasp the basics of what had happened in Ireland before I came into the world.

We had a few other LPs as well, which weren't rebel songs. One of them was *Teaser and the Firecat* by a man called Cat Stevens. There was a cartoon drawing of a wee boy on the cover, sitting on a footpad, smiling and petting his cat. The songs were like rebel songs, though, in that some of them gave me goose pimples as well. 'Morning Has Broken' and

'Changes IV' called people to peace rather than war, but while I liked these songs and their effect, I felt awkward in their company, as if I was betraying the meaning of the rebel songs.

Glen Campbell's Greatest Hits had the man himself, smiling and tanned, on the cover. Me ma loved Glen Campbell so much that she named our baby brother Glenn after him. Glenn was born in June 1971 and was only now getting on his feet, running around bare-arsed with his big baldy head and a wee wisp of white hair on top. 'Wichita Lineman' reminded me of cowboy films that were usually on the TV on a Sunday. It wasn't hard to imagine myself on a horse, like Trampas from *The Virginian*, crossing the prairie in the heat of the Kansas sun, singing about being the lineman for the county, or leaving his wife and heading off to Phoenix and not calling her to tell her he was away with himself. I remember sitting on the sofa wondering why he left her all alone, and her crying in her bed waiting for the phone to ring.

The record player sat on top of a long wooden press that had three drawers and two doors with brass handles. The records were kept inside. As I poked about the dozen or so LPs, I opened the other press door and saw hundreds of mass cards stacked neatly on the shelf. I lifted a few out for a nosey. They were all signed by priests, and most had Jesus, Mary and angels on their fronts. Inside the cards was a place to write a family name, like 'From the Melaugh Family', 'From the Canning Family' or 'From Sister Assumpta' or 'From

Father Green', and they came from places I'd never been to, like Dungiven, Belfast, Limerick, Dungarvan, Dublin and Mullingar. There were hundreds of them, all shiny and new, carefully stacked in tall rows.

***

Not long after the day me ma brought the wee blue book into the house we came home from school to find that me da's clothes had been returned to us in a thick, see-through plastic bag with a smaller envelope taped to the top. 'M.O.D. Property of Patrick Doherty Deceased' was written on the bag, lengthways, in black marker. In the envelope was an unopened pay-packet which he must have got on the Friday evening before he was killed. I remember thinking that it was strange he went to a march with his pay-packet in his pocket. The money was in another small plastic envelope with his name on it, as well as the name of the Du Pont plant where he worked. You could see the green, blue and rust-coloured notes through the plastic cover and see, feel and hear the 50p piece and the 10p and 2p coins moving about inside. There were two rings: a plain gold wedding band and a silver band he'd made some years ago at work out of a two-bob coin. You could still see the distorted coin markings on the inside of the ring, while the outside was smooth and looked like silver. There was also a ten packet of Park Drive with a few left in it, a yellow and red box of Bo Peep Safety Matches, and a set of plain black rosary beads. Me ma laid all his belongings out in a straight line on the sofa in the living room for us to see and then collected them all up again and put them back in the thick plastic envelope without saying a word.

The large plastic bag with his clothes sat in the centre of the sitting room floor unopened. You could see the black and grey-speckled coat with the black fur collar pressing against the plastic. His boots were at the top and all his clothes were folded neatly underneath. His coat was too bulky to fold neatly.

***

Me ma came in one day waving a wee brown plastic wallet at us and calling out, 'I passed me test! I passed me test!' She was smiling from ear to ear. We were all really happy for her, and for ourselves, as it also meant we were going to get a car. And we did – a few days later she pulled up at the front door in a big, red Austin Maxi. She was giggling to herself as she got out, and called across to Lena Carlin, who was standing at her front door next to ours.

'Jesus, Lena, would you believe it? I was stopped by the boys over the street at the checkpoint, and me on me first run out in the new car!'

'Oh dear, Eileen, what did they say to ye? Was it the Provos or the Stickies?'

'It was the Provos. They must've taken over from the

Stickies. Ach, but it was only Willie … ye know, that lives up the Moor?' she said, leaving out his surname so we wouldn't know who she was on about.

'Oh aye, surely I know Willie. And what did 'e say?'

'He stuck his head in me winda and said "Hello, Eileen, did you get a new motor? Have ye your licence on ye?" and I said, "Aye, surely, Willie,"' and she and Lena laughed. 'He had a big sleeve of a jumper over his head with the eyes cut out,' said me ma, pretending to pull something over her head, and they laughed again.

I lost track of the talk as I took in the full glory of the new red Maxi. Me, Paul and Patrick opened the doors and got in. It was class! Our Patrick got into the driving seat, I got in the passenger seat, Paul got in the back and Brandy sniffed her wee brown nose around the tyres, wagging her tail. It was really class! We had a car at last: big, red and shiny with mirrors and everything. As we wound the windows down and wondered what all the knobs and dials on the polished wooden dashboard were for, me ma stuck her head in the window and said, 'Don't yous be futterin' wi' them knobs in case yis break somethin',' and then went back talking to Lena at her front door. The seats were yellow leather and the whole inside smelled like furniture polish. There was a tape player underneath the radio for playing eight-track tapes. Our Patrick put me ma's new sunglasses on and sat back in the driver's seat, gripping the steering wheel as if he was driving the car.

'Will we go to Buncrana?' he said, and me and Paul said, 'Aye, Buncrana; let's go!' and we made car noises as Patrick tried to turn the steering wheel but it wouldn't move.

'We'll go for a wee run in a minute up to your granny's to get Colleen and Glenn,' said me ma after Lena went in. 'Jist wait to I grab a wee drop o' tay.'

It was great seeing me ma happy, even if it was only about passing her test and getting a new car. We continued on our journey to Buncrana beach until me ma came out again, pulled the green front door shut behind her and opened the driver's door of the car.

'Git you into the back,' she said to Patrick as she stood with the keys in her hand.

He turned to me and said, 'Git you into the back, I'm the oldest.'

'Naw, I was here first! It doesn't matter about age!'

'Tony,' said me ma, 'g'won jist git into the back, would ye?'

The only reason she was saying this was because our Patrick was thran and would huff for ages if he didn't get his way. Not wanting a row, I pulled the wee handle on the door and stepped out. By the time I opened the back door and got in, our Patrick was sitting in the front seat, having climbed over the gearstick and handbrake.

'Hi, Ma, will we bring Brandy?' said our Paul.

'Aye, Ma, c'mon we'll bring her,' I said in support.

'Naw, she'll have hairs all over me new car,' said me ma, putting the key in the ignition.

'Ach, g'won Ma, look at her sittin' all on her own,' I pleaded. 'Sure we can put her in the boot.'

'Aye, I suppose so,' she said and we all whooped and cheered. Me ma got out and opened the boot, calling 'C'mon wee Brandy!' and Brandy sauntered over, sprang up on her back legs and landed right inside the boot. Me and Paul turned to pet her and she sat with her wee paws up on the edge of the back seat and licked our hands.

'Don't let her slabber all over me new seats now, boys,' said me ma, checking behind her and the car started with a hum and we took off – well, nearly – as she did a full turn on Hamilton Street to head over the Lecky Road. Chesty Crossan had come out of his cottage and smiled when he saw the new red Maxi. Me ma stopped beside him and said out the window: 'D'ye like me new car, Chesty?'

Chesty, in his white vest with his dark braces up over his shoulders, said, 'God aye, Eileen, it's a great big motor. May ye git the good of it!'

Me ma said, 'I'm away up to Sally's to git the wains. See ye later, Chesty!'

As we drove along Hamilton Street I waved out the back window to Chesty and he waved back with a broad smile on his face.

Away we went on our first journey in our new red Maxi.

We waved as we passed the McKinneys, who were all out in the street, and they waved back. Other people waved as we went along Hamilton Street and we waved, and me ma beeped the horn a few times at them. When we passed the Provo checkpoint on the Lecky the boys weren't stopping cars but were leaning back smoking against the wall of the empty house. They still had their masks on and me ma beeped the horn at them as we passed and they waved back. Their rifles were lined upright against the wall beside them. Turning left, we went up Brandywell Road, past Eddie Carlin's and Tony Martin's cottages, past Bluebell Hill Gardens where there were tribes of wains out playing, passing 'The Cottage' near the top of the road and the long, red-brick wall of Brandywell football ground on the left. We went right at the T-junction to go over Lone Moor Road, past the black-painted wrought-iron gates of the cemetery on the left and the sometimes-used Celtic Park, where Gaelic football was played.

Gaelic football is very different from soccer, or football, as we called it. Me da took us to Celtic Park one day to watch a match. The two teams were in red and blue, like Manchester United and Everton. The referee was sending off a red-rigged player nearly twice his size for fouling someone on the blue team, when the player punched the ref right in the face and knocked him clean out. The ref was carried off the field unconscious before being left on the ground near where we were standing. The player who knocked him out came off the field as well and stood, with a look of desperation on his face, comforted by his wife and daughters. The match continued and the ref eventually came round. I loved recalling memories of me da and, even though he was dead only a few months, I was determined never to forget him. His smell was gone from the house, though, and I didn't know if anyone else had noticed but me. Me ma kept his Park Drive, matches and other things up in the press in the scullery and every now and then I'd sneak out and reach up to lift the wee red-and-white, fancy-lettered fag packet, pushing its cardboard end up through the sleeve to open it and sniff the tobacco. 'It's good tobacco' it said on the flap when you pushed it up, revealing the five fags inside. I breathed the smell of the good tobacco deeply into my lungs. This had been the main part of me da's smell and was now the only one left.

We drove across Lone Moor Road, turning right to go up Bligh's Lane towards Creggan. Our Patrick turned on the radio and David Bowie's new song 'Starman' came on. As the spell of the song was cast, the smell of CS gas came into the car and we rolled up all the windows and rubbed our slightly stinging eyes. We were used to it by now.

'Turn that up, Patrick,' I said and he turned it up for us to hear the line about the starman waiting in the sky. I imagined, or knew, that this song was about me da and that he was waiting for us all to meet again someday. The new red Maxi took the steep hill of Bligh's Lane with ease. *It was a song of hope and it's for us*, I thought to myself, but didn't say anything to anyone else. 'Starman' was special to me and me da. There was even a line in it about not telling your da because he'd be so afraid he'd have you locked up.

As we came out of Bligh's Lane to get onto New Road and into Creggan, the road was littered with bricks, broken paving stones and bottles. There were crowds of teenage boys and girls gathered on the green slope overlooking the huge BA base located midway between the Creggan and the Bog. The base was called Essex. There were around a dozen BA vehicles parked along the New Road, and squads of soldiers were grouped behind them drinking tea and sitting on the ground. There was no rioting going on as we passed. We all laughed as our Patrick said they must be on a tea-break! Me ma steered the car round the worst of the rubble on the road and Brandy had to lie down because she staggered with every turn till we came to the roundabout at the top, passing St Mary's Chapel and then up Fanad Drive towards No. 26 Central Drive. 'Starman' had finished on the radio.

Central Drive, like most of Creggan, was composed of square, white-painted, semi-detached houses. Situated near the top of the hill, there were steep steps down to the houses on the right where me granny lived and steep steps up to the houses on the left as you headed towards the grassy circle of the Cropie at the end of the street. All the houses had small, steep gardens at the front, mostly bordered by hedges and bushes, and their front doors were at the side, facing each other across low fences.

When we reached the house we got out of the car and me granny, granda, Siobhán with Glenn up in her arms, Joe, Lorraine and Colleen came up the steep steps onto the street to look at and feel the new car.

'God, it's a great-lookin' motor,' said me granda, 'I have to get back down; there's a race startin' on the TV.'

We all laughed, as nothing came between me granda, his horse-racing and the bookies. Everyone stood around the car, touching it and saying how class and great it was. Joe and Lorraine got into the front seats.

'Aye, and wait till ye hear,' said me ma to me granny and Siobhán. 'Wasn't I stopped at the Provo checkpoint down the Lecky on me first drive and me only after buyin' it!'

'Did they not know ye, Eileen?' asked Siobhán.

'Aye they did, sure it was Willie … ye know, from over the Moor,' said me ma, nodding to them as if the nod would improve the recognition.

'Willie who?' asked me granny.

'Willie round a sheep's arse, Sally!' said Siobhán, laughing. 'What's the point in you askin'? Sure, you'll only forgit in a minute anyway!'

Me granny laughed too and said, 'Ach, sure I know; I've a head like a pot. Sure, didn't I meet wee Suits down the town the other day, and says him to me, "Yes, Sally, what about ye?"

and says I to him back, "Ach, hullo there, ahm, Clothes!"'
and she laughed in her high, squeaky pitch at the memory. 'I
couldn't mind his name an' there was me walking up William
Street wi' me shoppin' to git the bus and me nearly peeing
meself in a fit of gigglin'! Ah dear, people musta thought I was
away off me head,' she laughed, wiping the tears from her eyes.

'The Stickies and the Provos are checkpointin' up around
here all day the day,' said Siobhán, looking over towards the
shops. 'They're steady at it, firin' away at the soldiers all last
night as well. The helicopter was up all night with the big
searchlight out. The boys were blastin' away at it too.'

'Did ye git a new motorcar, Eileen?' a loud voice boomed
from across the street. It was Mary Stewart coming down her
steps with her huge chest bouncing up and down under her
flowery apron. 'Ach, dear God, isn't it great for ye love, God
look to ye,' she said as she approached with one arm under
her chest and the other with an Embassy Red in it.

'D'yis want a wee fag?' she asked, having crossed the road
to join the gathering around the car. She held the box open
and flashed the Embassy Reds around. Mary had a long,
straight nose, a square jaw and eyes that never seemed to
settle on one thing at a time. She was in her curlers, pink
and blue, all held in by a flowery scarf tied under her jaw. Me
granny, me ma and Siobhán took a fag each as Mary Stewart
scratched a match, holding it cupped in her large hands for
each to dip their heads for a light. A plume rose above each

head as they dragged to get their fags lit right. The women held their fags near the tips of their middle and index fingers and gave them a prim kiss each time they took a drag. Me da used to hold his fag below the knuckles of the same fingers so, when he took a drag, his hand covered his whole mouth, chin and jaw-blade. The sounds were the same though, the kiss, the deep intake of smoke and air, and the rush of the smoke as it fumed back out the mouth and nose.

'How're ye keepin', Eileen?' Mary asked, all eyes.

Me ma smiled back and said, 'Grand Mary, I'm keepin' grand. How's Mickey?'

'Mickey's all right,' she said, lowering her voice to a loud, gravelly whisper. 'He's over there at his winda. The eyes and ears of the street! He's never out o' that chair o' his. He could tell ye what time the next gun-battle's goney start!' she bawled out of her and everyone laughed.

I looked over and sure enough there was Mickey Stewart sitting with his baldy head and bulging eyes, half out the window, taking all in. He waved over when he saw everyone looking over at him.

'Jesus preserve us, but what was that shootin' last night, Sally?' said Mary. 'I thought the roof was goney come in roun' us. The whole house was on the floor nearly the whole night saying the rosary. I had every wan o' them leggered in holy water. I'll have to git down to the parochial house for more for the night. I've run out.'

'And then in the middle of it,' said me granny, her low-hung chest and her shoulders heaving, and her laughing again, 'wasn't Willie Edgar out in the street, and him full as a po, shoutin' "I'll drink to Murry and the wains!" and didn't he nearly tumble down the steps!'

The Edgars were a large Protestant family whose front door was just opposite me granny's. Mr Edgar kept greyhounds out the back garden and walked all four of them on long, brown leather leads over past the Cropie three times a day. We used to pet the greyhounds' long noses and give them biscuits and bits of bread through the thick bushes out me granny's back garden.

The sound of an electric guitar came from the open upstairs window of the Fords' house up the street.

'There's Paul an' the boys at it again,' said Siobhán, looking over towards Dozey Ford's house. 'Come hell or high water, them boys'll rock 'n' roll away any day.'

'Is Paul still in King Rat?' asked me ma.

Siobhán said, 'Aye, sure they're doin' a bomb. Playin' nearly every night somewhere or other.'

Just then a few shots went off in the far distance. They were too far away to need to duck, and the group of mothers and daughters went on talking and smoking in the street beside the new car.

'They must be at it down the Bog,' said Siobhán, blowing rings of white smoke out of her circled mouth. Like Indian smoke signals, they faded into thin air after a few seconds. That was how teenagers smoked.

'Aye, there's a riot down the New Road. There's crowds everywhere,' said me ma.

'Anyway, I must go: I've a treacle scone on!' said Mary, and she turned to cross the street. 'See yis later!'

'Oh God, haven't I got scones in as well! They'll be burnt black,' said me granny, turning to go down the steps.

'Ye have a head like a pot, all right!' me ma called after her.

'Sure, c'mon on in, and we'll have a sup o' tay and some treacle scone,' called me granny as she carefully descended the steps.

'Treacle scone!' I called out in delight. 'Me granny has treacle scone ready! Yes!' and we all hung around the car, taking turns in the front seat, till we were called in a few minutes later. The steam rose off the hot treacle scone, the butter melting into it as it lay in thick-cut slices on the drop-leaf table in me granny's scullery. The teapot was simmering on the gas cooker and me ma had the cups on the table, ready for the pouring. Our Paul had let Brandy out of the hatchback boot and she hung around the open front door. Me granny didn't want her in the house in case she set Uncle Joe's asthma off.

'Can we have high tea, Ma?' asked Paul, and me ma brought the huge teapot over with both hands and poured the tea from about eight inches above the already milked cups. The browny-red tea splashed and bubbled and frothed in the cups, leaving a head of shiny bubbles near the rim of each.

High tea is what me da used to do, I thought, feeling the last remains of the strange hunger in my gut. It wasn't as bad now. There were days I didn't feel anything at all. The taste of the hot treacle scone, mixed with the high tea and the familiar comfort of me granny's house, had made this day a happy one. I looked around the sitting room as the Quigley and Doherty wains slurped their tea and ate their treacle scone. Me granda sat with his back to us, his big yellow chair pulled forward so as not to be interfered with as he watched the racing on the TV, which was turned up loud.

Brandy smelled the treacle scone and melted butter from just outside the front door where she sat, nose in, looking at us eating, with the slabbers tripping her with hunger. I went out and gave her a piece of scone, which she swallowed without chewing, then licked the butter and smell of scone off my fingers. Paul Ford's electric guitar filled the air in the street and the horse-racing commentator was frantic on the TV behind me.

3

FANCY FALLS

Uncle Eugene was the oldest of me ma's brothers. He was round our house almost every day. Eugene had jet-black hair, a crew-cut like me granda, and wore American clothes, like checked trousers and bright sports shirts. He had spent a lot of time working in Canada, then came back to work in Dublin, and only recently returned to Derry to stay.

One day I went into the house crying, as Patrick Brown was hitting and pushing me around near our front door. He was a better scrapper than me so I didn't push or hit him back. I was too scared about what he might do.

'What's wrong wi' ye, Tony?' asked Uncle Eugene, standing in front of the fireplace where me da used to stand, with his back to the heat. Me, Patrick and Karen had taken over clearing and lighting the fire since me da was killed, using the half-burnt cinder coals from the night before, sticks and newspapers. We even used the large double page from the *Derry Journal* or the *'Tele'* (*Belfast Telegraph*) to 'draw' the fire, with the smoked-glass door to the sitting room open to let the air in. You had to be careful with the paper as it could easily catch fire if the air sucked it in too far.

'Nothin'. I'm OK,' I said through my tears.

'Is there somebody botherin' ye, Tony?' he asked, looking down at me.

The silence was broken only by me blubbering and rubbing my snottery face with my hands.

I said, 'It's that effer, Patrick Brown. He won't leave me alone in the street,' I replied, feeling a bit ashamed for not standing up for myself.

'Patrick Brown? What does he look like? Is he bigger than you?' asked Uncle Eugene.

'Naw, he's the same size as me. He lives down the street beside Gutsy. He's a better scrapper than me.'

'How do ye know?' he asked, and it struck me that I didn't know at all if he was a better scrapper than me or not. 'Ye don't know, sure ye don't?' he said, reading my face.

'Naw. I don't, Eugene,' I said, a bit embarrassed.

'Git you out to the street, and if he comes near ye, jist remember that he's only a loud-mouth and a slabber, and most loud-mouths and slabbers couldn't beat Casey's drum,' he said, and put his hands on my shoulders. I giggled a nervous laugh at the mention of Casey's drum, as me granda said this all the time when we boxed with tea-towel-covered hands in the big sitting room in Central Drive. Out I went to the street. Patrick Brown was with Gutsy down outside his house. They lived next door to each other. Gutsy and Patrick came up to me as I stood near our green front door. I knew that Uncle Eugene was behind me in the hallway.

As soon as they reached me, Patrick Brown came up to me and pushed his skinny chest into mine and began pushing me back against Lena Carlin's front door next to ours. I allowed myself to be pushed against the door until my back felt the hard prod of the brass doorknob. Using the support of the door as a base, I reached up and pushed Patrick with both hands in the chest, and what did he do but fall over onto his arse on the footpad, losing his breath! *He's as effin' light as a feather!* I said to meself, but he got up in a ball of anger and rage and made another grunting go for me with his hands. He tried to push me in the chest the same way, but I grabbed him by his skinny throat and tossed him backwards and again he fell back on his arse on the ground.

'Right ye fucker ye, Doherty, I'm goney kill ye for that,' and in another grunting rage he pushed himself up before making another go for me. But my tail was up at this stage. There was nothing to him, he was like a whippet pup! I pushed him back, harder this time, and as he fell back he banged his head on the ground with a thud and began to cry, calling me a 'fuckin' bastard' through his tears and snotters as he ran down the street towards his front door.

'Ye can eff off now back to your effin' smelly house,' I shouted after him. 'Ye couldn't beat Casey's drum!' and I looked over towards our doorway and saw Uncle Eugene standing in so as not to be seen, with his thumb in the air and smiling broadly at me. Me and Gutsy headed up the lane towards Moore Street. Patrick Brown never bothered me again.

***

A young, male student teacher was filling in for Mr McCartney. He was thinner and taller than Mr McCartney and had short, brown hair and short sideburns on his fresh, pink face. He began the roll-call: Carlin, Cooper, Curran. When he came to my name, he said 'Oh, Doherty, Anthony 'Dutch'?' Everybody looked from the teacher to me as I sat, red-faced, wondering what he was on about.

I put my hand up saying, 'Present, sir.'

'Well,' said the student teacher, 'has anyone here ever heard of another Anthony Doherty?'

The boys in the class buzzed and hummed around asking themselves and those next to them about another possible Anthony Doherty, and you could tell from their faces that they hadn't heard of another one.

'No one? Not even you, Anthony?' he asked, looking in my direction.

'Ye call him Tony, sir,' someone in front of me said.

'Naw, I don't know, sir,' I said.

'Anthony "Dutch" Doherty is a famous IRA man from

Ardoyne in Belfast. He was arrested earlier this year in Dundalk but got out again. He's a comrade of Martin Meehan, from Ardoyne as well. Has anyone ever heard of Martin Meehan?'

A few boys put their hands up and mumbled 'Ayes' or 'Yes, sirs', but it didn't sound convincing.

'God bless us and save us, what sort of crowd are yis?' said the student teacher. 'Anyway, let's get on with the roll-call here: Doherty, Anthony "Dutch"?' he called out again and everyone in the class laughed.

'Present, sir,' I repeated with a smile. From that day the nickname stuck. It began in the yard at break-time as word went around about the student teacher and the roll-call. The teacher himself was on yard duty and when he passed us as we were playing tig he called over, 'Hello, "Dutch" Doherty!' and everyone laughed again. I liked the nickname and, it appeared, so did everyone else.

When we got back into the class the student teacher asked us to pass up our exercise books. Even though Mr McCartney had only given us the new ecker books a few weeks back, their covers were all drawn on. I drew Ferrets, Sixers and Pigs on mine, with their huge, black, rubber wheels and metal hatches with machine guns sticking out of them. I also drew British soldiers with their helmets and riot batons. I preferred drawing the vehicles, though, as most of the lines were straight. Nearly everyone drew on their books; mostly the green, white and orange tricolour flags and IRA men in dark glasses shooting at British soldiers across barricades, their rifles held by matchstick hands.

The teacher looked through the stack of about thirty mustard-coloured ecker books on the desk in front of him. 'Mmm hmm, mmm hmm,' he noised, or 'God Almighty, who drew this?' holding up a book belonging to someone or other.

'Yous'll all have to get these books backed at the weekend. They're a wile mess and the artwork is atrocious. Have them back on Monday morning, all neatly backed. OK?'

***

There was always shooting at the Mex army base. We would often hear it as we lay in bed. Sometimes I would stay awake for as long as I could, just to make sure I heard the shots so that I could tell the boys in class the next day.

One evening we were in the sitting room watching TV when a loud shot rang out and we all dived to the floor. When no shots were returned, we got up and went out to the street to see what had happened. A crowd gathered on the corner of Hamilton Street as a green army ambulance drove by on its way to the Mex. A few minutes later, the ambulance came back out the gate and squealed up Foyle Road with two Sixers as an escort, one in front and one behind. Nobody threw stones or anything, because we knew that would be wrong, but people shouted 'English bastards' as the army vehicles sped by on their way to hospital. Dandy and Brandy and other dogs barked and snapped at the huge tyres on the Sixers, and ran after them until they disappeared down the road.

Brandy had learned to bark at the soldiers as soon as she was let out to the street, copying all the other dogs. She had grown a short mane from the top of her brown head down her neck, which disappeared into her brown coat. It looked really class. It was great to have a dog. She was trained to sit and give you her paw. She licked all our faces and hands. Me and Dooter had taken Brandy and Dandy out the Line a few times to see if we could catch a rat, but there were none. She did get really excited though when you hissed, 'Rats, Brandy, rats!' and she would run around, following Dandy as she poked her nose among the heaps of building rubble.

After the Sixers left we decided to head out the Daisy Field to play Fancy Falls, shouting abuse at the soldiers through the tall, black metal gates of the Mex as we went.

'Fack off, you Paddy bestuds!' they called back, laughing.

There were always stones and broken bottles strewn on the ground where they'd fallen short or bounced off the Pigs and Sixers as they left or entered the Mex. Patrick Brown lifted a stone and threw it at the gates, making a huge bang as it struck, and we all ran for our lives out towards the Daisy Field in case the BA came after us.

The Daisy Field was a strip of land lying between Letterkenny Road and the River Foyle, bounded by a low wall along the road on one side and by bushes on its three other sides. It had a carpet of white-petalled daisies with their wee yellow suns in the middle; bright yellow, almost orange, pish-the-beds, many with white, rounded seed-balls ready for blowing to make a wish and for the wind to carry to another place; and the low-lying yellow buttercups competing for attention through the long grass and rushes.

When we got to the field we played a bit of football, with jumpers for goal posts. I loved playing Fancy Falls and couldn't wait to get the football over, so I shouted 'First to five!' before someone else got a 'First to ten!' shout in before me. The grass was long and it was difficult to control the ball, especially with our Brandy chasing it at the same time. Dandy, who was older and wiser, didn't waste her time chasing about. We eventually stopped playing, as we didn't want to hurt Brandy with a wild, swinging foot. Having survived the football, she sniffed in and out of the long grass and the rushes for a while, before falling asleep on the grass beside Dandy.

Football over, we set the jumpers up on top of one another beside a thick clump of rushes. The first lucky machine-gunner, Johnny Barbour, lay behind it with a sturdy stick to his shoulder as the rest of us lined up about thirty yards away. One by one, we charged the jumper-protected outpost holding a make-believe rifle, bayonet out in front, or a machine-gun across the chest, shouting at the tops of our voices and getting shot about four or five yards from where the machine-gunner lay.

The contest in Fancy Falls lay in the name of the game; whoever fell the fanciest won, and it was up to the machine-gunner to decide. Patrick Brown was the first to go, making a quick dart from our queue of waiting soldiers. The machine-gunner opened up on him as he sprinted like a whippet, throwing his arms in the air, rolling over a few times before lying still.

'My turn now,' said our Paul, and he took off, zig-zagging across the deadly gap between us and the line of jumpers. On his final zig-zag, a rat-a-tat-tat sound of bullets, produced by Johnny's tongue, rang out from behind the jumpers. Paul let a yelp out of him, stumbled, fell and rolled over a few times, landing near the body of Patrick Brown. Dooter was next, taking off in a beeline towards the outpost before being cut down as he almost reached its woollen wall. It was Michael McKinney's turn. He was a great runner, darting from side to side through the long grass until he got too near the outpost and was cut down in a hail of hot lead, where he fell with a series of injured groans, holding his gut and rolling and writhing. Brandy woke up and stuck her head in the air every time someone shouted, but Dandy just lay on sleeping through it, offering the odd open eye every once in a while before going back to sleep. Our Paul had opened his eyes as Michael approached and I shouted to him that he was dead and that he needed to keep his eyes closed until the game was over. That was the rule.

Gerard Starrs was next. He took off and ran straight for the outpost, accepting his fate but keen to make the best of it. He opened up with his imaginary rifle as he neared the growing number of bodies but the machine-gunner simply cut him down with a quick burst. Gutsy went next, his wee, dark-red head bobbing up and down as he dashed out towards the outpost, his legs going like mad through the grass in a straight line and then a zig-zag as he veered away from the machine-gunner, until he was caught from the side and had to jump over several bodies before he too fell beside them, after he'd stopped writhing and holding his side and gut for the pain.

I was determined to go last to make the best impression on Johnny, the machine-gunner, so I said to Terry McKinney, who was older than me by two years and wiser to the world, 'Will you let me go last, Terry?' and he said 'Aye, OK,' and away he went, his bulkier figure ploughing through the field with his hands out in front of him holding his rifle with the bayonet fixed, ready to stab it right through the machine-gunner if he got the chance. But that wasn't what the game was about; it wasn't a fair fight. There was no fight at all. It was all about staging your own death and making the best of it. Terry made the best of it, as he squealed and rolled several times, even over the body of someone else, before coming to a stop. I thought to myself, *Geembeddy God, Terry's goin' to be hard to beat.*

At last it was my turn to perform and, with my hands holding my machine-gun across my chest, I took off in a straight sprint towards the outpost with its pile of boys' bodies strewn in a range of fancy contortions. I could feel the warm wind as I raced the short distance, and saw the dead bodies tensing and some opened their eyes to watch as my final moments neared and the mouthed shots rang out from Johnny's outpost. I threw my arms in the air, releasing my machine-gun, jumped, holding the pain in my chest, over several bodies and fell with a forward roll right into the outpost before coming to a final halt at Johnny's crouching feet.

'Right, up yis git and stand in a line,' said Johnny.

We picked ourselves up, eventually forming a line, as each of the Fancy Fallers looked Johnny eagerly in the eye, hoping for victory in defeat.

Johnny scanned the line before announcing, 'Terry won and Dutchie came second.'

'Who's third, who's third?' they all asked.

'Patrick's third,' said Johnny.

'Aw, for fuck sake!' cried Michael McKinney. 'Sure he's fuckin' useless,' and began walking away in a huff.

'Michael, stall a boat,' shouted Terry, his older brother, after him, 'we'll get another game of football.' But Michael kept going, jumping over the low stone wall onto the road. It was clear he wasn't in the mood for taking his oil. Dandy and Brandy had woken up again and were writhing around in the grass. We all sat down, picking the seed-balls from the pish-the-beds, blasting them with gusty blows in one go to make a wish. If you failed to blow off all the feathery seeds, you couldn't make your wish. So you picked another one and drew a deep breath and blew with all your might until the full ball was torn apart and the seeds had turned into single tiny parachutes or floating white clouds on the breeze. We all blew like mad, making a new wish every time we finished one off in sharp gusts of breathed wind until the sky around us was filled with flotillas of seeds drifting around the field and descending slowly to the ground. We kept our wishes to ourselves.

Kicking the seed-balls as we went, we dandered on up towards the far end of the Daisy Field. Two teenagers, a boy and a girl, lay on the grass. The girl had dark-orange hair, parted in the middle. The boy was on top of her. They'd been courting. When they realised we could see them they sat up and looked in our direction.

'Go on ya boy, ye!' we shouted to him, before running a bit, and she took red in the face as he smiled.

'We know ye now, we know ye now!' we shouted, before running again, hoping he'd give us a cheevy, but he didn't. He just stared at us with an awkward smile on his face and remained on his knees as we retreated back down the field. When we reached the other end I looked back and couldn't see either of the two for the long grass, so we kept going on down past the Mex towards Hamilton Street.

Jangly loud music filled the air as the poke van came up Foyle Road and stopped in front of Morrisons' house. Brandy and Dandy began howling, their heads held high, until the chiming notes from the poke van stopped. No one had any money, so me and Dooter walked to the open window and said, 'Hi mister, have ye any broken pokes?' The poke man reached below him into a box and brought out a handful of broken pieces of cones and wafers, dropping them gently into our cupped hands. At the same moment, I felt a sharp pain shoot right up my arse and felt myself falling forward, almost hitting the side of the van. 'That's what ye git, ye wee fuckin' skitter!'

'Jesus Christ!' I shouted, holding my almost impaled backside, swinging round to see the teenage girl from the Daisy Field marching off at a quick pace in her white, grass-stained-at-the-arse mini-skirt and denim jacket, around the corner to Hamilton Street, her high-heeled shoes click-clacking on the pavement. It was the worst and by far the deepest steever up the arse I'd ever received in my life, and for a long time to come. Her partner was nowhere to be seen, so we took off after her, eating our dry, broken pokes, with me, hobbling a bit, calling out, 'We know ye now, we know ye now.'

Then Patrick Brown called out, 'G'won ya oul ginger blone ye!' Suddenly, everyone stopped in disbelief. Patrick had called the girl a blone!

'Jesus, Patrick, ye canny say that,' said Terry McKinney with a look of disgust on his face.

'She's an oul ginger-snap fuckin' blone, lyin' out there wi' her legs in the air!' said Patrick, a bit hurt, in his own defence.

'I don't care, don't call her a blone, all right?' Terry was right in his face.

'Aye, all right,' said Patrick, 'keep your drawers on!'

By this stage the red-headed girl was almost out of sight, her mini-skirted backside jiggling away in a mix of huff and satisfied retribution at having stuck the pointed toe of her high-heel up my backside.

I felt the pain of it for days after. Me ma said to me, 'Have ye a bee at your arse, or somethin', Tony?' but I didn't tell her what happened. And later on she asked, making a laugh of me, 'Have ye a wee scourge in your backside, son; d'ye want me to put somethin' on it for you?' I said no, I was all right because I didn't plan to explain to her how I got injured.

My arse was still sore, right up inside, so I rubbed it with one hand while taking the scissors and a roll of Sellotape from the scullery drawer into the front room to back my ecker book. Me ma and da kept rolls of wallpaper left over from the decorating. They used to do all the painting and papering in our house between them. Always on a Saturday, when they were off work. They were well-matched, working as a team when it came to decorating. From our point of view, the painting and papering was not a good time, as we were usually chased to the street and told to keep out of the way for hours at a time. The pale-blue drop-leaf table in the scullery was used for pasting, with the activity taking up almost all of the downstairs as they manoeuvred between the scullery and the front hall or the sitting room or the good room at the front. Me ma scoured the front window with circles of Windolene so people couldn't see in. Me da kept a Park Drive fag butt behind one ear and a short pencil behind the other as he worked on the ground or up on a kitchen chair with the sheets of patterned paper for the sitting room and front hall, or with the heavier embossed paper for the good room. We were barred from the house and told to take turns pushing Colleen up and down the street in her pram.

We starved for the day and were handed out biscuits or pieces and jam every once in a while instead of our usual meals. The smell of wallpaper paste filled our lungs and bellies every time we went to the door, only to be shouted at to get out again. Me ma brought us in near the end of the decorating day; me da was down on his knees finishing off the papering in the good room, cutting in with a pair of scissors around the light-brown, tiled fireplace and then smoothing the paste-sodden, embossed paper down onto the wall so that it looked neat and tidy. There were wrinkles and wee bubbles on the newly covered walls but me da said that it would smooth out flat when it dried overnight.

The reason we were brought in was to help 'red up' by picking up the cut pieces of wallpaper. We were all good cleaners-up. The pieces of cut wallpaper oozed with paste, making our hands slimy, then quickly dry and then slimy again. 'Don't put your hands in your mouths wains, for that paste is poisonous,' said me da, as he wiped his scissors with the dishcloth in the scullery, before proceeding to wipe the drop-leaf table with the same cloth dipped into warm, soapy water in the scullery sink. Wallpaper paste had a strange smell. Even after cleaning it off your hands you could still smell it and it left them feeling really dry.

When all the redding up was done, the smell of the Saturday night fry was never more welcome as we sat in the newly papered sitting room, our fry on our knees and drinking our mugs of tea from the floor, the smell of the paste mixing with the rissoles, sausages and fried eggs. The whole house smelled of paste for days afterwards. I came downstairs the next morning to see if the wrinkles and the bubbles had disappeared from the good room wall. They were gone. It was a professional job.

Backing my ecker book was a professional job too. There were a few half-rolls of wallpaper in the press but I took the creamy-white embossed roll they'd used for the good room. As I picked up the roll and put it on the carpeted floor to cut it, I realised that the last person to handle and cut this was me da. Me da was a neat worker, the scissor-cuts on the end of the thick wallpaper barely visible. I ran my fingers over the cut edge before placing the opened book down on top so I could measure how much I needed. I bent the wallpaper over and creased it with the palm of my hand, the way me da used to, cutting along the creased line until I had the piece I needed for the job.

The emboss ran up and down the ways on the wall in thick ridges, like the bark of an ancient tree. That was how it would look on my ecker book too. Backing books was simple: I placed the book in the centre of the reverse side of the embossed wallpaper, made two cuts with the scissors to meet its spine, so that the paper would fold neatly at the top and bottom of the thick, yellow, heavily-illustrated cover-page, before Sellotaping it to stay in place, bringing the edge of the wallpaper over the end of the page in a neat fold, then Sellotaping again. I did the same with the back cover, and when I'd finished I had the neatest-backed book in the whole street. It was hard to believe it was the same book. I was very pleased with myself and went out and sat on the doorstep in the sun.

***

John Starrs returned home a trained sniper, having spent several years in the Irish army. I had no memory of him leaving but there was great excitement when he returned to his house, a few doors down from us, in his Irish army uniform. His younger brother, Gerard, who was in our Paul's class, said he was back to join the IRA – the Provisionals, not the Stickies. *Having him as a trained sniper would make a lot of difference to the battles on the streets with the British Army*, I thought. He was the first definite member of the Provos in our street, though the Brown brothers across the street were all in the Stickies, me ma told us.

While I sat petting our Brandy on our doorstep that day, I saw John walk past our house. As he disappeared from view I wished I had a big brother like him.

Later that day word went around that he'd been shot dead in a gun-battle over in the Bog. We were playing in the street when small groups of people started to gather round the Starrs' front door. Me, Gutsy and our Paul sat on the pavement outside our house.

'He was shot down at the new Flyover,' said Gutsy, 'and there was another boy shot as well.'

'Who's the other boy?' I asked, and he replied, 'Nobody knows; they opened up on the BA and the BA fired back at them.'

Later we found out that it was actually in William Street that he was shot, after they opened fire on the British Army checkpoint. Gerard Starrs came out to his front door, crying into his hands and into the chest of his older brother, Thomas.

The next day me ma took us all down the street to the wake. Almost all the houses in our street had small, square black flags hanging from their top windows. They fluttered in the warm breeze as we joined the queue of people outside. John Starrs' coffin was in the front room next to the street, the same place as me da's had been. A man in an IRA uniform, wearing a beret and dark glasses, stood behind the coffin. It was the same type of uniform that John Starrs wore in his coffin. Me ma left a Mass-card in the coffin as we all stood in a line, blessed ourselves and said a few silent prayers.

When we turned to leave, we had to squeeze past other wake-goers as they filed in through the house from the front street. When we got outside, I remember seeing James Brown and his English wife standing across the street on their own looking across at the wake house. James Brown was connected to the Browns in our street and was sometimes called Seamus. He was a small, stocky man with black hair, a tanned face, buck teeth and black hair on his hands. There was always something about James Brown that made me a bit nervous and I wanted to keep away from him if we passed in the street. I didn't know what it was about him; just a feeling that I was scared of him. When I thought of the Prowler, the face of James Brown always came into my head.

On the day of John Starrs' funeral, the street was packed with people, right from the bottom of the street at Foyle Road up to as far as we could see at the other end towards Lecky

Road. We stood in a group outside our front door and I could see the Barbours, the McGonagles and Patrick Brown's family standing outside their doors to our right. There were also a lot of people I didn't know and had never seen before. Everyone was wearing their Sunday clothes. Across the street, I could see Chesty Crossan standing, looking across towards Starrsy's house with his sad, serious face and his boxer's nose. A line of Provisional IRA men stood to attention on each side of the road outside. Me and our Paul sneaked away from me ma down towards Gutsy's to get a better look.

'Do you know which wan's Martin McGuinness?' asked Gutsy. I knew he was testing us because he already knew. We'd heard the name mentioned many times in the house and in the street as the leader of the Provisional IRA, but I'd never seen him before. At least, I didn't think I had. The Provisionals used to drive around the Brandywell in cars, mostly Ford Cortinas, and sometimes they would stick their guns out the car windows. We would stop to look as they passed, and a few times someone had said, 'There's Martin McGuinness in the back seat,' but they would be gone up to Moore Street or somewhere before I got a good look.

'Naw, Gutsy,' I said, scanning the lines of uniformed men in their berets and dark glasses, standing silent and unmoving in our sunny street.

'I don't either,' said our Paul. 'What wan is he?'

'He's that wan there,' he said, pointing across the street

to the far side. At that very moment there was movement at Starrsy's front door and all the family came out of the house in suits and ties: Gerard, Thomas and Patrick, followed by their ma and da, their eyes red and swollen from crying. Oinky O'Donnell, the oldest of the O'Donnells from up the street, came out as well. They were quickly followed by the coffin of John Starrs, covered in the green, white and orange tricolour flag. Four men in dark civilian clothes held the coffin high on their shoulders. Someone called out something in Irish and the funeral procession began to move. I was still curious about which one was Martin McGuinness, so I simply stood and scanned the uniformed men in the hope of some type of recognition as they passed by on their way to the Long Tower Chapel. None came. Hamilton Street was burying its first fallen IRA man.

4

BUTLINS 1972

As the school holidays approached it dawned on me that me ma's head was straying. I'd lost my favourite pair of trousers for a few months and then I found them again and put them on. They were black and grey tweed with a back pocket that buttoned and I loved keeping things in it. They felt a bit tighter now around the waist and, while they didn't go all the way down to my shoes the way they did before, they were still comfortable enough and I was glad I'd found them again.

When me ma saw me later that day coming in from the street she laughed and said, 'Hi boy, you're like Half Hung McNaughten in them there trousers! Ye can nearly see your whole socks.'

I looked down and realised from the flash of red at my feet that she was right.

'I know, Ma, but these are my favourites.'

'Well, they're too wee for ye now. Paul can have them. I'll get ye new ones later up the town.'

'Can I come up wi' ye?' I asked.

'Naw, not the day Tony, I've too much to do.'

When she came back later that day in the red Maxi, she had the messages in the boot. She also had a brown bag of mixed biscuits from Wellworths. A biscuit during the week was a rarity unless someone was sent to the shop of an evening for a packet of Morning Coffee or Rich Tea.

'I got ye new trousers the day, Tony,' she said, lifting an orange and black plastic bag from the boot and placing it into my hands. 'Two pairs. Here ye go.'

I looked into the bag as I took the single step into our hall. Jeans! She'd got me two pairs of jeans! I ran upstairs to try them on. They were identical blue jeans, so I grabbed a pair and put them on and, not having a mirror to look at, ran downstairs to me ma, who was in the scullery putting the messages away.

'Look, Ma, at me new jeans!' I said, and when she turned to look at me, I thought her movements were a bit delayed and awkward.

'God, they're nice on ye, son. May ye get the good of them,' she said in a frail, resigned voice that I'd heard a few times since me da died. As if she'd been crying, or was just really fed up and couldn't be bothered with things. Our Patrick came into the scullery.

'What did *I* get, Ma?' he asked.

'Aw, nothing the day, son. Sure ye've a pair of jeans already.'

'I got two pairs,' I said, rubbing it in.

'What did he get two pairs for and me wi' only wan?'

'Because he's hardly a stitch, Patrick, that's why!' snapped me ma. 'G'won away the two of yis and give me head peace!'

Patrick turned to leave the scullery and muttered, 'Aye, he got two fuckin' pairs and me wi' nothing,' and me ma shouted after him, 'You stop that fuckin' cursin', boy; all the age of ye, ye cheeky article!' Patrick went out into the street, still muttering to himself.

When she had the goods all put away, she came into the sitting room where I was watching TV and said, 'And by the way, Tony, ye'll have to wash your new jeans in the bath, as they canny get washed wi' other clothes.'

I just said, 'That's all right, Ma,' but I was wondering why it was me who had to wash me own clothes. I'd never done this before.

'You're getting bigger now, son, and I'm not fit to be doing everything for yis all,' she said, reading my mind. 'By the way,' she continued, a smile breaking across her face, 'we're booked for Butlins Mosney in August for two weeks.'

'Butlins? We're goin' to Butlins?'

'Aye,' she said, with a broader, toothy smile. 'All of us – your granny, granda, Eugene, Siobhán, Joe and Lorraine.'

I ran into the street where our Paul was playing with a few other boys and shouted, 'Hi, Paul! We're goin' to Butlins in August!' and he ran over to me and squealed, 'We're goin' to Butlins?'

'Aye! Me ma has it booked an' all!' For weeks, if not months, afterwards we chanted, 'We're goin' to Butlins! We're goin' to Butlins!' After school, on the way down to the house, after our tea, out in the street, after our prayers before bed and when we got up again in the morning, we'd give each other the look and recite together, 'We're goin' to Butlins! We're goin' to Butlins!'

Or Paul would say, 'Tony?'

'What?'

'We're goin' to Butlins!'

Or I would say, 'Paul?'

'What?'

'We're goin' to Butlins!'

We'd never been on a family holiday before, except for the odd Sunday to Buncrana on the Lough Swilly bus. I also vaguely remember me da taking some of us on a boat from Derry to Moville on a grey, rainy day, and there were small pools of rainwater inside the boat and me feeling that this couldn't be right; water *inside* a boat? When I lay in bed at night I thought of me da all the time and was determined never to forget him, forcing myself to remember things about him in as much detail as I could muster.

We'd gone to Buncrana the previous summer on the bus with me ma and da, all eight of us, as well as me Aunt Lorraine, with flasks of tea, sandwiches, Custard Creams and McVitie's Digestives. The heat was fierce and all the wee sliding windows were opened to let the sea air in and all the wains who had plastic tricolours stuck them out the window where they fluttered loudly as the bus headed up the road towards Derry. As we approached the BA checkpoint on Buncrana Road, the bus slowed in a long line of traffic. The bus jolted forward every minute or so as the queue shortened bit by bit. Then the slow movement turned to no movement and wains started crying in the heat, and someone said, 'This is a bloody disgrace.' Our Glenn started crying as well, and me ma jiggled him about on her lap to keep him quiet. He was usually a quiet wain, but when he *did* cry he bawled out of him like a child possessed.

As we got nearer the checkpoint, the busman got out of his seat, stood up at the top of the aisle and called out, 'Can yis all make sure there's no flags flyin' from here on in? And if yis want to git home the day, don't give the soldiers any oul guff when they git on. I'm only askin', OK?' Several people murmured in agreement.

Me da took the tricolours off Karen and Patrick, placing them upright in the corner of the seat beside him as the bus started moving slowly again towards the checkpoint. We could see the sandbagged sangars with their shiny, corrugated tin roofs, and rifles sticking out of the wide horizontal gaps, pointing down the road. There were soldiers out on the road, some carrying rifles, others without, checking cars, opening boots and bonnets, and searching long-haired teenagers on the roadside before packing them back into their cars and letting them go on their way back to Derry. When we reached the checkpoint, a young soldier with a spotty face came onto the bus, said something to the driver, then walked slowly up the aisle, pushing past several men who'd been on their feet the whole journey. Everyone was hushed except for a few whimpering wains. The young, spotty soldier looked at faces and jooked under a few seats. As he passed us, me da didn't even look at him, just stared straight ahead. The soldier turned at the bottom of the bus, making his way up the aisle again, where he caught one of his shiny black boots on something and stumbled and almost fell. The whole bus erupted in laughter. He turned to say something, but realising the futility of it, beat his retreat down the few steps, nodding to the driver to go on. As soon as the bus started up, all the wains who had tricolours got up on their seats and stuck them out of the windows and we all let out a huge roar as the bus took off. The green, white and orange fluttered and flapped in the wind on the narrow road to Derry.

We were all a healthy, pinky-red colour by the time we got back home to Hamilton Street that sunny evening. When we came in from the street later, our pinky-red condition had taken a turn for the worse, though, as we were all shifting and scratching around under our clothes. After we'd been put to bed the sensation got worse, eventually turning into a burning pain all over our chests, bellies, backs, shoulders, arms, necks and faces.

We cried with the pain as we lay in bed, all four of us, as well as Aunt Lorraine, who was staying the night, eventually going back down the stairs moaning and gerning to me ma and da. Me da brought us all back up again, lifting the bedspreads from the two beds, leaving only a sheet covering us.

'Yis'll jist have to git to sleep. The sunburn won't be as bad the marra,' he said.

'Da, I've a dirty big blister on me shoulder. Look!' said Patrick, sitting up on the bed and thrusting his shoulder forward to show a bulbous blister about two inches wide. 'Will I jist bust it?'

'Aye, that's what ye do. It'll be full o' water,' said me da.

Patrick prodded the blister with his finger and then he nipped it and it burst and water ran down his arm and chest. We eventually got to sleep under a single white sheet after much moaning and crying. In the morning, which came painfully early, everyone was covered in huge water blisters, all over our shoulders and backs and bellies. We spent the morning, before me ma and da got up, bursting them with our nipped fingers and safety pins, mopping up the water with clumps of toilet roll. Me and Paul had blisters on our cheeks which we had to burst as well. When we were all finished we looked like a sick, miserable and dying family, covered in clumps of saggy skin. We walked around the house still moaning with the pain which, despite what me da had said, was as bad as it had been the night before.

A few days later, our skin had dried out, fraying at the edges of the blisters, so we began to peel it off. Small strips at first, then Patrick pulled a long strip from right across his shoulder and held it up like a trophy.

'Look at the size of this wan!' he called out.

The competition started. I pulled at the dry edge of my shoulder-blister and mine too came away from my body in a single strip of floppy grey skin. Pulling sunburnt skin from your body is a strange and addictive sensation. You can't stop once you've started. We nibbled at it as well, just wee bits of our own skin, to see what it tasted like. It wasn't unpleasant. The bits we didn't eat, which was most of it, we threw into the hearth.

When me da came downstairs he took one look at us and called up the stairs to me ma, 'Jesus, Eileen! We have the whole Karloff family down here! It's like *The Curse of the Mummy's Tomb!*' He laughed out of him and we all laughed, despite the pain and misery of the sunburn, which lasted for another few days.

***

Not long after hearing the news about going to Butlins in August, me ma told us we were going first to Dublin for ten days in July. Me and Paul were going to stay with the Randles family, while Karen and Colleen were staying with a man called Enda Wymes. Patrick was to stay with the Goldens, somewhere in Dalkey. I'd never heard of anyone called Golden before and reckoned they must be loaded. Millionaires, at least! Dublin was a place beyond our imagination. We'd never been there, and our only knowledge of it came from rebel songs:

> And we're all off to Dublin, in the green in the green
> Where the helmets glisten in the sun
> Where the bayonets flash and the rifles crash
> To the rattle of a Thompson gun.

We met Enda Wymes in Dalkey on a day of squally showers and the odd flash of the sun's warmth. He took us to a chip shop and bought us all fish and chips, or hamburgers and chips, and tall glasses of Coke. Me ma had given us all our own spending money, but he was happy to pay, so we let him.

Afterwards, we were split up into three groups: two twos and a one. As it turned out, me and our Paul weren't going to Dublin at all, but to a place called Navan, which we'd never heard of. I was glad I was with our Paul, as it meant that I'd be the leader without question. 'Navan' turned out to be a huge, white country house owned by the Randles family: Paddy and Mary, their three daughters Sandra, Mary and Susan, and one son, also called Paddy.

We were mesmerised by the house, with its 'French' doors and beautiful rolling gardens with tended flowers and plants galore. They all spoke in what we called a 'snobby' accent. Mrs Randles was amazed at how much we could usefully do around the house. We described the scullery chores as 'doing the dishes, doing the drying and doing the floor', which made the girls laugh, especially Sandra, who had long, blonde hair. I liked her the most for some reason and wanted to make her laugh.

Once, when we were about to eat ice cream after dinner, there was a spoon short so I went to the drawer and took one out. The girls were almost in a tizzy, drawing their ma's attention to the fact that 'He took a soap spone!' At least that's the way we heard it. In our house we had big spoons and wee spoons. Needless to say, 'He took a soap spone!' became the secret holiday anthem between me and Paul for the remainder of our stay.

I had our Paul warned not to show us up by pishing the bed, so at night I'd get him up out of his sleep and walk him down the hall to the toilet like a zombie. He never fully woke up, so I had to steer him in his vest and underpants out the door and down the hall to the toilet. Luckily for me, he had the instinct of all boys and men, no matter what their state of mind, to pull his own dickie out and pish for himself. He never pished the bed once when we were there, which I was glad of.

The bathroom had a shower in a glass cubicle. We'd never

seen such a thing before. As we'd always taken a bath together, me and Paul used the shower together as well. It was a wee bit cramped and after the first one we realised it was better to take turns! Not that we showered much anyway.

To impress them, but especially Sandra, we told them stories about our street, the British soldiers in their Pigs and Saracens, the shootings at night, the men in the street with guns, and the effects of CS gas. They sat, their mother included, wide-eyed, looking at us as if we were from the moon. The da, Paddy, was a surgeon in Dublin. Each evening when he came back the girls gave him a full update of everything we'd said and done that day. He just laughed at us and called us the 'crazy Dohertys from Derry City'.

Our bedroom was easily the size of our whole upstairs in Hamilton Street. It had only one bed in it. We had French doors as we were on the ground floor beside the garden. One evening, near the end of the holiday, both of us were luxuriating in the wide expanse of the huge bed, dozing off. Paul was nearest the French doors and I was nearest the bedroom door. We were lying in silence when, suddenly, we heard three distinct knocks on the glass, with a brief gap in between each knock. Three knocks meant death we always believed. Our Paul slid over to my side, almost on top of me, both of us lying there petrified for hours until eventually we trembled off to sleep. We hadn't the nerve to get up and look out through the curtains. When we told the ma, Mary, in the morning as we ate our cornflakes and drank our orange juice at the high table of the 'breakfast bar', she said it must have been a branch banging in the wind. Later that day, me and Paul went round the outside of the house to investigate. There was not a branch anywhere near the French doors. After that, we were glad to leave for Butlins.

I didn't really know what to expect when we were told we were going to stay in a 'shalley'. It had the ring of the makeshift about it. It could have been anything from a tent to a Nissen hut. We met me ma, Glenn and me granny and granda at the entrance to Butlins. They were all really glad to see us and gave us hugs. Glenn was a year old now, had a deep voice when he laughed and cried, but still had hardly a hair on his huge, baldy head. Me granda called him 'Mussolini'. We pushed him round for the whole two weeks in his pram, running him up and down the pathways between the shallies, and him bawling his head off laughing and squealing the faster we ran. The shallies turned out to be chalets, rows and rows of long, rectangular buildings laid out in grids with numbers and letters up on lamp posts nearby so you could keep your bearings.

We went to the huge canteen for our tea on the first night and stared in wonder at the gangly white legs, swimming trunks and bathing costumes writhing above us through the huge windows of the swimming pool. Me ma and granny Sally had brought our swimming gear in a huge bag, so after a tea of burgers, chips and Coke we all went and got changed for the pool: me, Paul, Patrick, Colleen, Karen, Lorraine and Joe. I could sort of swim and already had a 50m badge on my trunks. I couldn't wait to dive to the bottom to wave through the windows to me ma, granny, granda, Uncle Eugene and Aunt Siobhán in the canteen. I headed to the deep end, jumped in and put my head under to see through the glass panels, only to be disappointed that all I could see were blurry shapes and fuzzy pastel colours on the other side.

The Redcoats were everywhere. Me ma had arranged for me granda to take us to the Children's Talent Show in the huge theatre. The Redcoats, who were mostly teenage girls and fellas, took our tickets. When the children went up to perform they had to queue at the side of the stage and be brought up one by one and asked were they from: 'Hill of Tara' or 'Hill of Slane'. None of us had a clue what Tara or Slane were, and I was really glad that I wasn't in the queue to affront myself before the whole hall by not knowing.

Given it was the first night, all us wains were allowed to go out to Dan Lowry's bar with me ma and the other bigger ones. Dan Lowry's bar, like everything else in Butlins, was huge. All the tables had beer and brandy glasses, fag boxes, matches and ashtrays overfilled with fag butts. There was a band up on the stage who called for people to go up to sing. Many did go up and sang mostly country and western songs.

'Will ye go up, Eileen?' me granda asked me ma.

'Naw, not the night, Daddy,' she said, 'maybe another night.'

Me granda loved me ma singing. She was enjoying herself, though, and at times she was getting back to her old self. But other times she wasn't and would often walk way ahead of the rest of us when we were all out dandering on the long, flag-stoned pathways that ran the length and breadth of the huge camp.

A photographer came round with a giant plastic Guinness bottle to take pictures of people holding it above their heads. Me granda and another bearded man, who was sitting at our table, held it up and had their photo taken with it, and everyone laughed and smiled.

We must have been starting to annoy people later on in the evening, though, so me ma suggested that Aunt Siobhán should take us out to the discotheque.

'Why do I have to do it?' she asked me ma.

'Because you're the youngest,' me ma said, and me granny agreed, reaching for her purse.

'Here, take that,' she said to Siobhán, putting a note into her hand. Whatever she got, it brought her round a bit, and we sailed through the smoky haze out of Dan Lowry's bar into the darkening night towards the discotheque.

'We'll all come down later on for the craic,' called me ma as we left.

All us wains and Aunt Siobhán travelled in a single pack.

She led us under the streetlights that brightened the way along the straight pathways of the Butlins camp. As we walked we asked her what a discotheque was, and she said it was a place where records are played and people dance together. Like *Top of the Pops*. The discotheque eventually came into view. It looked like a white-painted mouth of a cave with the word 'Discotheque' painted in an arc above the doorway. There were plastic palm trees in half-barrels on either side of the door, and you could see flashes of light coming from inside, accompanied by the sound of pop music.

Inside, the music was beating out loudly and there were flashing lights on the ceiling and strange coloured shapes projected onto the walls, giving the place the feeling of floating. People of all ages, but mostly teenagers, were out on the floor dancing in their flares and jeans, high platform shoes and long hair. Some of the older people had on shirts and ties, with straight trousers and shiny shoes. They danced in circles, some holding hands with children, while the teenagers sort of bounced on their legs, jerking their arms in a slightly awkward fashion, while smiling at each other.

Siobhán led us all out onto the packed dance floor, where we copied the teenagers' movements, shuffling our feet and jerking our arms, elbows out, in a sort of circular fashion. It was great, this discotheque! We all loved it, and Siobhán bought us bottles of Pepsi with straws, and packets of crisps, which we sucked on and munched at a high table built around a pillar without chairs. Siobhán pointed out the disc jockey to us, up behind a large, open hatch on the wall. When he put Gary Glitter on we all went out to the floor and danced round in a circle punching the air to 'Rock and Roll', and then The Sweet's 'Little Willy', and then my favourite, 'Starman' by David Bowie. 'Starman' was my song for me and me da. It was great to hear it at first, but then I thought of me da and stopped dancing, heading over to the high table because I wanted to be on my own.

As I was standing there, I noticed another three children looking in my direction from the next high table. Two boys and a girl. The girl had blonde hair and the younger boy looked about eight – our Paul's age. The blonde girl looked about nine. Like me. The two boys were skinheads; the older boy looked ten or eleven. The boys wore black boots, jeans and white t-shirts, while their sister wore a pink and white checked frock. I had a pair of my new blue jeans on, and I felt really cool, despite thinking of me da. I smiled across and the older boy and the girl smiled back. The younger boy had a bit of a face on him.

Eventually, the older boy and his sister came over, while the younger boy stayed put with his Pepsi and crisps. As he approached, the older boy held out his hand for me to shake, something that older people always did but not wains like us. I shook his hand and then his really beautiful blonde sister reached out her beautiful hand and I shook that as well.

'Where yis from?' I asked.

'From Dooblin,' he replied, his gorgeous blonde sister nodding in agreement.

'I'm from Derry. We're all here for a fortnight. This is our first day.'

'We're in our second week tomorra',' he said.

'We've a full week left to go,' said the beautiful blonde sister.

'God, it's great here all the same, isn't it? There's everything!' I said and they nodded in agreement.

'What's yer name?' asked the beautiful blonde sister. She'd asked me a real question!

'Tony,' I said. 'We're from Derry, ye know.'

'Yeah, you said dat already,' she smiled and I thought, *Oh, gentle Jesus, I'm making an eejit of meself!*

'Oim Sharon, dis is me brudder Joe and de grumpy one over dere is James. We're all O'Briens.'

'Yeah, he's a grumpy bollix, so he is. Wid ya look at the fooker,' said Joe. James saw us looking and looked away with even more of a face on him.

'We're all here together, me ma, granny and granda 'n' all. There's a whole crowd of us,' I said.

'Yeah?' said Sharon. 'We're here wit' me mudder and fadder. Dey're up at Dan Lowry's bar wit der friends, drinkin'.'

'Ha! That's where all our crowd are as well!' I said.

'Did ya see the huge Guinness bottle doin' da rounds?' asked Joe.

'Aye, it came over to our table. Me Uncle Eugene let on he was goney drink it!'

'Yeah, me da too!' said Sharon. She was indeed beautiful, even better than Sandra Randles from Navan, and I could feel myself wanting to talk to her but not really knowing what to say.

'Yis fancy goin' to the baths the marra?' I asked.

'Yeah, we go nearly every bleedin' day,' said Joe. 'But our fookin' James got put out for tumpin' anudder fella in de pool. What de fook is 'e not loike, Shar?'

Sharon smiled and nodded her head. Just then, I saw me ma, granny, granda and Uncle Eugene coming in through the archway into the lights and music. By this time the discotheque was packed.

'That's all our crowd coming in now,' I said to them. 'Bet ye me granda's bluttered!' I added proudly, as they looked to see how bluttered he was.

The music changed from pop to slow dance and many of the older people started to waltz round the hall with their partners. Me granda took me granny out and our Karen went out with Uncle Eugene, and they danced round and round smiling and being careful of their footing. Me granda was wearing a shiny blue suit with a white shirt and a thin blue tie with a small knot, and me granny had on a navy blue dress with a white pattern.

'Spanish Eyes' was playing. This was one of me granda's

favourite songs. He loved Al Martino. Near the end of it me granny and granda stopped dancing close to where we all stood round the high table. Me granda got down on one knee and, with his long arms wide open, looked up at me granny, who smiled down at him, and sang along as the singer begged his girl to say that she and her Spanish eyes would wait for him. When the song ended he got up from the discotheque floor and hugged her and she hugged him, and then me ma started to cry. Me Uncle Eugene hugged her and then we all hugged her and we all stood in a huddle on the floor under the flashing lights as The Jackson 5's 'Rockin' Robin' 'deedlideed' around the room.

At the end of the night I went back over to where the three O'Briens were standing. Their ma and da had also come from Dan Lowry's bar and they were getting ready to leave the discotheque.

'Yis must think we're all mad wi' everybody yammin',' I said, and Sharon and Joe just smiled back.

'Me ma cries when me granda sings and me granda cries when me ma sings,' I laughed.

'Where's your da den?' asked Joe.

'Me da's dead. He was shot dead a couple o' months ago.'

'Who shot him?' he asked, a shocked look on his face.

'The BA. Or, I mean, the British Army, it was.' I felt my face go red. I didn't know why. This was the first time I'd had to explain to someone about me da dying.

Nobody said anything else, so I said, 'Sure, we'll be headin' to the baths in the morning at about eleven. Yis fancy it?'

Both Sharon and Joe smiled, and Sharon said, 'Yeah, we'll be dere. See ya, Tony,' and they left the discotheque with their ma and da and their grumpy wee brother.

5

Monopoly Money

It was 1973; being born on 1 January meant I was ten for every single day of that year. While I often thought about the family's survival after me da's death, by then it was clear that, bad as it was, it didn't mean we were going to starve to death on the streets: me ma had money. We weren't sure where she got it from but we knew it had something to do with me da's killing. We had a car and the first colour TV in Hamilton Street. Not that there was much to see on it as the only station available in colour was BBC2.

But there was an election in June, and for some reason they switched all the usual children's programmes from BBC1 to BBC2. Me ma was out and there was a queue of wains right out to the front door wanting to watch colour TV for the first time. Our Patrick charged them 5p each. Only those who could pay their dues got access to the floor or sofa in the sitting room, while the rest had to stretch their necks in the hall or contort themselves to jook round from the bottom of the stairs. When 'Scooby Doo' came on, our eyes popped and our jaws dropped as we stared agog at Shaggy and Scooby being chased by some baddie in brilliant Technicolor.

Later that summer we went to Buncrana for a two-week holiday, staying in a rented house in St Mary's Avenue along with me granny and granda, Siobhán, Joe, Lorraine, Aunt Mary and Uncle Jimmy. The holiday house was always packed with other aunts and uncles visiting and staying for a night or two. Most of the time we slept in beds upstairs, but we also spent nights on sofas and at least one night in a sleeping bag on the floor.

The women, including me ma, took charge of the cooking. The smell of food being prepared was always around us, no matter what time of day or night. We were fed in relays, either at the scullery table or down on our hunkers beside the coffee table in the front room. As was the custom in the Quigley household, the cleaning up was divided among all the boys and girls. When everyone had eaten, a small group was left in charge of the washing, drying and putting away of the dishes, while the others walked down to the beach or, in the evenings, headed into the town to walk the main street or to play the slot machines. The working party would catch up with them later, which, depending on how many people were around the town, could sometimes take hours.

The main amusement arcade was at the top of the street. It had two wide doors that were left open when the weather was fine so you could walk in and out as you liked, passing all the old women playing the machines. I loved the sound of coins slotting and falling, the crumping of the slot-machine as its arm was pulled forward and the magic of the bell ringing when someone won the jackpot, accompanied by a flood of two-pence coins crashing into the metal tray of the winning machine. Those who weren't playing, or only watching in passing as they searched for their parents, would gravitate towards the ringing sound to see the lucky winner being presented with a bucket to get their coins changed into Punts, as Irish pound notes were called.

All our crowd played the machines, including me granny, me ma and me aunts. They sustained themselves with fags as they stood, backs to us, feeding the two-pence coins into the slots. On some machines you could save up your winnings until you were finished, then press the 'Pay Now' button at the bottom to get your money. I'd never seen this done before. One evening a woman had won so much money on her machine that a small crowd had gathered around her to watch. She was a wee woman with long, blonde hair. She hadn't yet pressed the 'Pay Now' button, instead dispatching someone for a top-up of coins as and when her supply ran low.

It was during one such dispatch that I found myself standing right next to her machine, only inches away from the 'Pay Now' button. The button was a small red disk with a shiny metal rim, sitting just above the metal coin-tray. People were gathered behind me, whispering about how much money she'd accumulated, while the blonde woman smoked without using her hands and chatted to someone beside her on the next machine. Her fag moved up and down as she spoke, enveloping her head in a fog of silvery-grey smoke. As she spoke and smoked, she played her machine with her right arm, pulling the handle down hard. A few times her hand brushed my arm, I was standing that close. The 'Pay Now' button was just about level with my head, and each time she won her winnings registered on a numbered display right next to it. She must have been up to £40 by that time, and looked like she'd be planked on her winning machine for the night. When the blonde woman turned slightly to her left again to speak to her companion on the next machine, my hand shot up and my finger pressed the 'Pay Now' button! The two-pence coins came in floods rattling out of the machine into the metal tray, and the bell went off.

'What did ye do that for, ye wee fucker?' said the blonde woman with a fierce mixture of disgust and shock on her face. I didn't know why I'd pressed the button. It felt as if my hand had gone up of its own accord! I just stood there looking up at her glaring down at me, hating me. Others were looking at me too, but not hating me the way she did. Someone called the owner and, when the man came down, the blonde woman complained, 'That wee fucker pressed me button when me back was turned.' The owner grabbed me by the collar and marched me out like a criminal, through the staring crowd, towards the door, telling me never to come back.

The next afternoon, as we walked along Buncrana main street, the blonde-haired woman passed us with her husband and wains. As they passed, she caught my eye and said something to her husband. His eyes shot around him in every direction but the right one. I thought she was going to stop and say something to me ma or granny. Thank God she didn't.

We were bound for McGinn Park, to where a local Derry football team, Shelbourne, were playing a Buncrana team. Before the start of the game, me granda took us up to meet me great-uncle Digger, who was Shelbourne's manager. Uncle Digger had the same jet-black hair as me granda but was half his height, with a huge hump on his back and wee matchstick legs. Me granny said he got the hump having taken very sick as a child. He shook hands with me, Paul and Patrick before turning his attention back to the game. Two of me granda's big nephews came up to meet him at the side of the pitch and me granda gave them money. Both were living in Buncrana. Dozens of other young men and teenagers on the run were at the match, meeting their friends and families. I knew some of their faces from around the Brandywell, where we lived.

When we left McGinn Park, passing Porter's Bar further down the main street, me granda said 'Churrio' to us, and me granny warned him that he'd 'Better not be gettin' bluttered!' Porter's was a man's bar, me ma told us, which meant women weren't served drink. Me granda once told us they didn't have a women's toilet, so they couldn't be served drink. If me da was here, I thought, he'd be in Porter's with me granda, drinking beer and having a sing-song.

Me da was never far from my thoughts. Every night, me and our Paul would kneel by the side of the bed and pray for the repose of his soul. That's what me granny had told us to do. 'Repose,' she said, 'is peace of mind for the dead.' I wanted me da to have peace of mind so I prayed and prayed that he'd get into heaven. I couldn't think why he wouldn't be let in. But then there was purgatory, and he had thumped us a right few times. Mrs Radcliffe told us in Primary Three that you could be in purgatory for years and years before being allowed into heaven. The whole concept of purgatory sounded cold, bleak and fundamentally unfair. *As if death wasn't enough*, I thought.

At the end of the fortnight we drove home depressed in me ma's big red Maxi. It was a hot day, so it felt strange leaving Buncrana to go home so early on a Sunday afternoon. Me Aunt Siobhán was in the front seat with wee baldy Glenn on her knee. Five of us were squeezed into the back seat. Me ma sang along to Cat Stevens' 'Morning Has Broken' on the eight-track tape-player as we drove along Hamilton Street towards No. 15.

I saw him first from the back seat as we approached from behind; he was wearing a green army coat, jeans and a pair of black boots. He walked slowly, with a large rifle held downwards parallel to his leg, along the waste ground, disappearing behind Paddy Melaugh's pig shed. The street was deserted except for a Sixer halted at the bottom of our street. I heard later that day that the gunman had stood at the gable end of the row of cottages across the street from our front door and fired at the army Sixer crawling slowly across the gap at the bottom, on Foyle street. He fired around six shots, I was told, and, as he fired, the empty shells tinkled onto the footpad. I was raging I'd missed it.

Our car pulled up outside the front door. 'Nobody get out o' the car until it's safe!' me ma said sharply, so we stayed put to see what was going to happen. Nothing did, so after a few minutes we all piled out of the red Maxi onto the street, me ma and Siobhán going into the house with Colleen and Glenn. Me and our Paul went over to lift the shells as me ma and Siobhán came back out and stood at the front door looking down towards the Sixer.

'Hi, Ma, what age d'ye have to be to join the IRA?' I asked.

Siobhán laughed and said, 'Ye have to be sixteen, but this'll be long over by the time *you* reach that age!' Me ma laughed as well at the thought of it.

This is no laughing matter for me, I thought, as I fingered the bullet shells in the palm of my hand, looking down towards the bottle-green Sixer.

Just then we heard a yelp from the bottom of the street. It was our Brandy hobbling and yelping up the street with her front left paw held up from the ground. She ran over to me ma and Siobhán, and me ma rolled her over on her back to see what was wrong. There was a cut on her bony knee. It was swollen a bit, but there wasn't much blood.

'Them bastards must've kicked her,' said Siobhán. 'I've a mind to go down to them English fuckers!'

'Don't bother yerself, Siobhán,' said me ma. 'Sure they'll only take the hand out'o ye,' as she lifted Brandy into the house to let her recover from her ordeal. From that day onwards Brandy limped along with her left paw held off the ground, but she could still run like lightning using all four legs.

***

Hippies appeared on the street. I first saw them gathered in a bunch at the same gable end the gunman had fired from a few days earlier. They were big, tall English hippies. There were five or six of them. One was called Robin, with a beard and wee round glasses. Gerry was black-haired and well over six foot. John was smaller, with long, brown hair. They spent a lot of time in the Harps Hall, beside Paddy Melaugh's shop, where they ran a youth club for us wains. One Saturday morning they took all the wains from our street on a bus-run to Moville. It was raining so we had to go into a church hall, where someone had prepared trays and trays of chocolate spread sandwiches. We'd never tasted chocolate spread before and everyone thought it was disgusting – bread and chocolate!

– and began throwing the sandwiches at each other. The hippies tried to get us to stop, so we threw the sandwiches at them instead. Before long, the hall and everyone in it was leggered in brown chocolate. Wasps started arriving through the windows and the wide-open doors of the church hall, so we all had to run out to the street to escape them, where the rain was now pelting down. A few of the wains got stung and were yamming, so the hippies had to pile us on the bus again to take us home.

One weekend, the hippies, who were youth-workers more or less, told us they were taking us to a place called Corry-meela. We headed off in two cars; me and Patrick Brown in one, and our Paul and Dooter in another. John the Hippie drove us up, and Julie, his long-legged, dark-haired hippie girlfriend, sat in the front. Julie was English too. When they picked us up in Hamilton Street, Patrick Brown whispered to me with a half-smile, half-giggle, 'Ye see the raspberry ripples on her?' I hadn't a clue what he was on about.

During the drive, John jerked the gearbox so that the car bounced up and down several times for the craic, but Patrick, who knew all about cars, said to him, 'There'll not be much left of your clutch and gearbox if ye keep that up.'

'I suppose you're right, Patrick,' said John, looking a bit embarrassed.

While Patrick knew every car on the road and everything about them, I knew absolutely nothing on the subject. His da was a mechanic who fixed cars in his garage at the bottom of the back lane behind our houses in Hamilton Street. There was always a line of cars in the lane waiting to be fixed. Once, when I was younger, I'd gone round with Patrick to his da's garage for a message, and while I was waiting found myself standing head-height to a bench on which sat a big, black car battery. It had several holes on the top filled with clear liquid. *Oh, water*, I said to myself. *I must stick me tongue into this for a sup*, which I did, bending over and, before I had time for anything else like swallowing or something, my tongue went funny and I felt the grip of a big, oily hand on the back of my neck, spinning me around. Patrick Brown's da was standing in front of me with a black, greasy face on him shouting, 'Don't swally it! Don't swally it! What the fuck're ye at, wee boy!' and forcing a dirty mug of cold black tea into my mouth with his other hand. 'Rinch your mouth out wi' this, ye stupid eejit ye, and spit it out on the ground before ye fuckin' kill yerself!'

I had no choice in the matter and quickly 'rinched' my mouth with the black tea and spat it out on the floor of the garage as ordered, his big, grimy hand still on the back of my neck.

'That's battery acid, ye know, wee boy! It would kill ye if ye drunk it! Put out yer tongue for me to see.'

I stuck my tongue out, hoping that his mood would change for the better. His face relaxed and he said my tongue was OK, but that I should go home and tell me ma and da just in case. I went home all right but I didn't tell a soul. The slight numbing feeling I had on my tongue went away after an hour or two.

John and Julie took us to Coleraine University and gave us food in the huge canteen – a large plate of chips, beans and sausages, with a tall glass of Coke. Later, when they took us to the house at Corrymeela, Julie was standing at the front door in her jeans and denim shirt with pearl buttons. As Patrick passed her to go into the house, he reached up and pulled her denim shirt wide open. It was the first time I caught a glimpse of a real pair of doobs as they bounced braless from her open shirt. My eyes nearly popped out of my head! Julie didn't know where to put herself, grabbing her shirt together and stomping off in anger into the house.

Later in the evening, having watched a werewolf horror show on TV, me, Dooter, Patrick and our Paul went to bed. There were two beds, so I shared one with Patrick, which was a novelty compared to sleeping beside our Paul. After a while Patrick sat up and, in an urgent whispered voice, said, 'Right boys, folly me!' Up the three of us got, following Patrick out into the hall, where he stood listening at a bedroom door. The next thing, he swung the door open and we all piled through to discover both Julie and John naked on the bed! Worse still, Julie was sitting over the top of John! They were breathing heavily and had a look of shock on their faces.

'For fack's sake!' shouted John from the bed as Julie got off him and rolled under the blankets. All our eyes were drawn to his huge hairy dickie, which lay on top of his belly like a riot baton. 'Fack off out!' he roared and we all piled back out the door, running the wrong way down the corridor in our vests and underpants. We found ourselves back downstairs in the dark, so we searched the scullery for biscuits. Big Robin came down shortly after and led us back up to the bedroom with our hands full of Ginger Nuts, past John and Julie's door. It was closed again.

After breakfast the next morning Patrick said, 'Hi boys, c'mon and we'll search for spunk on their bed!'

So we sneaked back out into the corridor and into John and Julie's room, where Patrick pulled back the blankets so we could carry out a search for 'spunk'.

'What does it look like, Patrick?' asked Dooter as we scanned the off-white sheets.

'It's white. Spunk's white,' he replied, stretching the sheets out flat for inspection.

'What is it anyway, Patrick?' I asked.

'It's the stuff that comes out the man's dick when he rides the wife.'

'What d'ye mean "when he rides the wife"?' I asked, examining the sheets even closer.

'Ride!' he said, 'Ride!' and he got up on his hunkers on the bed, thrusting his groin forward a few times with a broad grin on his face, rubbing his underpants with his hand. 'Ride!'

'What's this here?' asked Dooter excitedly, pointing to something on his patch of sheet. We all scrambled over to where his finger pointed and, sure enough, there was a wee smear of white ointmenty spunk near the edge.

Patrick rubbed his finger in it, sniffed it and said: 'Yip, that's it boys. That's spunk all right!' and we went back to our bedroom with a weird sense of having achieved something.

***

One day in September a small crowd gathered outside one of the Brown's houses on the other side of our street near the corner with Foyle Road. A few of us Dohertys and Barbours were playing football outside our house when me ma came out and stood at our green front door and looked towards where the people were standing. She was almost jooking round her own doorpost as if she shouldn't have been looking at all. Our football stopped and we all stood stock-still, watching.

'What's goin' on, Ma?' asked our Paul.

'Seamus Brown's dead.'

'What? Dead?'

'Shush!' she whispered, with her finger up to her mouth, like we were made to do at school sometimes.

'What, Mammy?' whispered our Paul.

'He was shot for stoolyin',' she said, holding herself back from the threshold of the front door, out of view from down the street.

'Was he an informer?' I asked in a whisper, wide-eyed.

'Aye,' she mouthed, all eyes. 'His corpse was foun' down the Foyle Road last night.'

Seamus Brown, the dark-skinned, black-haired, buck-toothed prowler of my night-time fears was dead: he'd been found shot in the head a few hundred yards around the corner.

'Stay yous all up here the day!' she added, pointing downwards to our front step.

Hardly anyone from Hamilton Street or Moore Street went to the wake. There was no queue outside the house and no one took sandwiches down to the wake-house. People stood in small gatherings around their own front doors pretending not to be looking down the ways to the wake-house.

A white slate appeared on your roof when someone in your house died. This information came from Terry McKinney, so it must have been true. Me and Dooter, our Paul and Patrick, Terry McKinney and Brian McCool did a tour of the area one day to do a count of the all the white slates on people's roofs. We started at our house, beautifully painted in green and cream; but there was a light grey slate smack in the centre of the roof. It was clearly different from the rest, which were dark grey. 'It's turnin' white,' said Terry, pointing up. We walked a few doors down the street towards Gerard Starrs' house. They had a pure white slate up near the chimney. We headed on down the street towards Seamus Brown's house. There was a light grey slate overhanging the gutter.

Brian McCool said there was an oul boy died in Townsend Street a while back, so we marched up Foyle Road, past Moore Street and into his street. Sure enough, there was a pure white slate right in the centre of his roof.

'Will we play Hookey?' asked Brian, as we stood looking up at the mystery of the white slates.

'Aye, will we?' said our Patrick, wide-eyed.

'Naw, I don't wanny,' said our Paul, sounding a bit scared.

'It's OK, Paul. Head you on down home if you don't wanny play,' said Terry McKinney, and our Paul dandered round the grassy base of the high bankin' towards home.

'There's a wee shed round the back o' here,' said Brian. 'We can go in there: it's nice and dark.'

I'd never played Hookey before, but I had an idea what it was. We walked with Brian round the back of the houses on Townsend Street towards the wee corrugated metal shed.

'We'll all need a piece of coloured glass first,' said Terry, so we rummaged around the back lane until each of us had our piece of glass. Terry closed the door of the shed behind him so that it became pitch black, with only a few rays of light breaking through cracks by the doorposts. When our eyes got used to the dark we got down on our knees in a circle on the dirt floor and placed the pieces of glass in front of us.

'Bend over the glass and keep staring right into it and don't blink. If you blink you break the spell,' whispered Terry.

'Everybody say "Hookey, Hookey, come to me",' he said in

a ghostly voice and we all followed suit in a choir of ghostly voices: 'Hookey, Hookey, come to me' and then silence.

I bent over the bit of green broken glass in front of me, not knowing what to expect or what I would do if I saw something. Everyone else did the same; you could just about make out the shapes of the others and the glint from the circle of glass on the dirt. I stared at the piece of glass. There wasn't a sound in the shed, nor a sound outside. I stared and stared. I could see nothing except the odd bit of flashing colour, like when you open your eyes in bright sunlight. There was complete silence. Nothing but the sound of five boys staring at glass, searching for the dead in the dark.

Suddenly, there was a sharp knock on the door. Our Patrick screamed, 'Oh, Jesus Christ! Jesus Christ!' and I could see his outline with his hands over his eyes and Terry getting up in quiet panic to open the door, revealing our Paul standing in the bright autumn sunlight in his stripy t-shirt and shorts.

'See you, ye wee fucker!' our Patrick roared out of him.

'What?' said our Paul. 'I on'y knocked, ye know!'

'Git yerself a piece o' glass or yer not gittin' in,' said Terry, sending Paul up the lane. I looked around at the pieces of green and brown glass on the ground as we stood rubbing our eyes in the daylight. Paul returned with his piece of glass in his hand. Terry closed the door behind him and again we were enclosed in the cool darkness of the wee shed.

'Right, everybody down on yer knees again!' ordered Terry.

We all knelt, making room in the circle for Paul and his piece of glass.

'Ye have to stare at the glass and don't be blinkin'. If ye blink ye break the spell and nobody'll come,' he repeated, mostly for our Paul's benefit.

'Now, everybody say "Hookey, hookey, come to me",' and we all said in our ghostly voices, 'Hookey, hookey, come to me' and then silence again.

I stared and stared and stared at the wee piece of glass on the dirt floor. Nothing happened; probably because I was a terrible blinker. I even blinked in my sleep. All I could see were the odd flashes of made-up colour every now and again on the glass.

I hope I don't see that Seamus Brown, the prowler and dead informer, I thought as we stared and stared in the dark silence.

'Me da! Me da! Me da! Fuck! Me da!' screamed our Patrick at the top his voice. 'I saw me da! Fuck! Let me out! I saw me da!'

We all jumped back in fright in the darkness, falling onto bags and boxes lying around us. Terry jumped up and tried to push the door open but it wouldn't budge. He and our Patrick were rattling at the latch and pushing the door as Patrick screamed, 'Open ya bastard! Open ya bastard!' He launched his shoulder full force on the slatted door. 'I saw me da! I saw me da! Git me fuckin' out!' You could feel the whole shed shaking, the sheet metal groaning and shifting under the onslaught.

The force of his body eventually caused the door to spring back and open inwards, as it was meant to. Our Patrick yanked it towards him, knocking Terry into the corrugated metal wall behind him, which fell from its fixings onto the ground behind him with a clatter. It sounded as if the dead were shaking the whole shed to smithereens. Patrick took off running in full flight round the base of the bankin' towards Moore Street and down the lane to Hamilton Street, screaming like a maniac with his hands in the air and the tears tripping him. We followed at a safe distance until he screamed his way in through the green front door of No. 15.

***

Me ma packed us into the Maxi, telling us we were all going to me granny's for our tea. When we reached me granny's house we went in and made ourselves at home. Me ma was in the hall speaking to me granny, and whatever they were talking about, it sounded like an argument. Our Karen followed me ma out and up the steps towards the car. Me ma still had the car key in her hand. She got into the car and drove away, leaving Karen on the footpad. When she came back in she muttered something to me granny in the hall about 'her away gallivantin' wi' him again'; I wondered for a moment who *him* was before heading out to the street to see who was up for a game of football.

After we returned to Hamilton Street later that evening,

as we played tig in the cold and dark street, someone shouted, 'There's somebody shot over at Sweeneys!' We'd heard shots nearby a few minutes earlier and had all hit the deck while the shooting continued. In the near distance, we could hear people banging their bin-lids on the ground and blowing whistles, followed by an ambulance siren. Me, Dooter and our Paul ran over towards the shop and reached it in time to see someone being wheeled into the ambulance under a white blanket. The scene was lit by a single streetlight and the light from the shop window. There was a large group of soldiers with dark berets and darkened faces, and people, mostly women with coloured scarves over their hair, were screaming at them.

'Yis shot that wee girl dead, yis murderin' bastards!' one women shrieked into a soldier's face.

A man was shouting right into a tall soldier's face; I knew him as Danny Feeney from Quarry Street. Danny was a tall man with jet-black, curly hair, a black moustache and dark eyes. He had a grip on a soldier's rifle and was trying to take it off him.

'Leave the fackin' rifle alone!' the tall soldier was shouting, almost pleading. 'Leave the fackin' rifle alone!'

'Yis are nothin' but murderers!' screamed Danny into the tall soldier's face, and, at that, the soldier suddenly jerked his rifle in such a way that he sliced Danny's hand, the blood dripping onto his trousers and onto the pavement. This sent the women wild. They began to spit into the soldiers' faces, screaming more at them. Stones winged from a darkened alleyway across the street and smacked off the front wall of the shop, sending everybody ducking. Someone shouted, 'For fuck's sake, stop firin'. They're too close to the women and wains!'

Maisie McKinney, wearing a flowery apron, appeared from nowhere and said to us, 'Right yous, git yous over that street to hell's gates, for there's goin' to be more shootin'!' She guided us out of the melee at the shop towards the relative peace of her front door about a hundred yards away.

Kathleen Feeney, aged fourteen, died that night from gunshot wounds; Danny Feeney was her big brother.

A few days later, me ma was out up the town again. It was Friday in the early evening. We were playing football in the darkening street; me, Dooter, our Paul and Johnny Barbour. The goals, or 'nets' as we called them, were four jumpers acting as goalposts, rolled up and placed on either side of the road directly opposite each other. This meant that goals were often disputed and the disagreement frequently ended in someone sitting down in a huff. This usually brought the game either to a temporary stop to allow for negotiation and a bit of coaxing or, very often, to complete abandonment. Me and Dooter were playing against Johnny and our Paul. Dooter flicked the ball up to me and I connected well with my head – sending the ball straight towards two empty milk bottles sitting on next door's window sill. It hit the top of one of them and sent it cracking its way through the window before settling again on the sill unharmed.

'That was your fault, Dooter, ye were told to keep it low and ye flicked it up!' I said, in a bit of a panic.

'Naw, it wasn't, ye didn't have to head it!' he said, equally panicked.

'Well, what did ye flick it up for then? It was too high,' I said, as we examined the damage to the window. There was only a wee hole in it and a wee diagonal crack at the corner.

'Me ma's not in. It's only a wee tiny hole. Will we jist say nothin'?' I suggested.

'Naw, ye canny do that, Tony,' said Johnny. 'G'won in and tell somebody. It'll need to be fixed.'

'Me ma's not in, it's only Karen,' I said, hoping this would get me out of it.

'Naw, jist go in and tell her anyway,' said Johnny.

I went into the hallway. Karen was hoovering the front room and Jacqueline McKinney was shining the long press with a cloth in one hand and a spray tin of Pledge furniture polish in the other.

'Karen, me and Dooter broke the winda next door wi' the ball,' I said. Better to spread the blame. Karen put her foot on the knob on top of the Hoover, turning it off. 'What did ye say?'

'Me and Dooter broke the winda next door wi' the ball.'

'C'mon out to we see,' she said, and went out to the street with me in tow.

'It's on'y a wee hole, Karen,' said our Paul.

'I know it's on'y a wee hole,' said Karen, 'but a broke winda is a broke winda,' and she went over and knocked at the door. The door opened a wee bit and I heard our Karen saying, 'Our Tony and Dooter McKinney broke your winda wi' the ball. Me ma's out. I'll get her to call in to ye when she comes back.'

We couldn't hear what was said by whoever opened the door but I was glad that my version of events had been repeated. The door closed again.

'Git away now to hell's gates wi' that ball!' said Karen as she went into the hall and turned the Hoover on again.

The coalman's lorry heaved its way slowly up our side of the street, eventually stopping outside our house. The driver's face and hands were pure black but there were square white patches around his eyes behind his glasses. He had a blackened leather satchel slung from his left hip to his right shoulder, which was all bulky at the bottom with the weight of coins. He knocked on the open door. There was no answer but you could hear the Hoover going from the street. I walked over, slid past the coalman and went into the front room, where Jacqueline and Karen were still cleaning.

Over the noise, I said to Karen, 'The coalman's at the door.' She went into the sitting room, where all the Friday night 'debtors' money' was usually left in small piles along the top of the fireplace. Money for the coalman, the insurance man, the milkman, the Maine (lemonade) man, the bread man and Mr Veejee, who was also known as The Black Man. Mr Veejee owned a clothes shop in Waterloo Street.

Karen came back out to the front door empty-handed. 'I'm wile sorry mister, me ma musta forgot to leave ye yer money. Can ye call back the marra?'

The coal man flipped his open leather satchel closed and said, 'Aye, that's no bother love. I'll call again in the morning.' He got back up into his lorry and drove slowly up the street to his next stop.

I remembered him from me da's wake. Me ma had been talking to a man in the hallway for a few minutes and, when he left, I asked her who he was and she told me it was our coalman. It was the first time I'd seen him clean. He usually came through our front hall bent over with the huge bag of coal on his shoulder, heading straight through the sitting room, scullery and out into the backyard, where he emptied the coal into the block-built bunker opposite the back door, quickly closing the lid to stop the cloud of coal-dust blowing everywhere.

'Jesus, Jacqueline, me ma hasn't left a shillin' for anybody the night,' said Karen. 'They're all goney be callin' shortly. I'm affronted.'

'Don't worry about it, Karen. Sure they can all call back,' said Jacqueline.

We went back to our football outside in the street, keeping

it low and no headers. A few minutes later Mr Veejee's wee blue van pulled around the corner, stopping about six houses down. He got out and knocked at several doors further down the street, eventually rapping on the open door of our house. Karen came out and said, 'I'm wile sorry, Mr Veejee; me ma's away out and she musta forgot to leave ye yer money.'

Mr Veejee stood on for a few seconds and didn't say anything. Karen stood in the hall facing him.

'Can ye call back the marra?' said Karen.

Mr Veejee was clearly unhappy at not getting his money, and muttered something under his breath before walking further up the street to knock at another door. A few minutes later, the Maine man's blue-cabbed lorry trundled noisily into our street. The driver and a wee boy got out and started lifting bottles of Coke, Raspberryade, American Ice-cream Soda, Cloudy Lime and Pineappleade out of the wooden crates stacked on the back of the flat-backed lorry, leaving the bottles on doorsteps and knocking on the doors. The Maine man whistled a tune as he walked back and forth to the lorry. Women came out to their front doors with their money in hand and the Maine man gave them back their change from the shiny brown leather bag slung across his shoulder. When he came to our house, he was carrying four different bottles of fizzy drink. As he placed them on the doorstep, Karen came out.

'I'm wile sorry, mister, me ma's out and she didn't leave anything,' she said.

'Sure, don't worry about it, love,' said the Maine man, flipping over the flap on his leather bag, which, like the coalman's, was heavy and full of money. 'I'll leave you the four and ye can tell yer ma I'll git her next week. OK?'

'Aye, that's grand, we'll take the four,' she said, as the Maine man continued on his way up the street, still whistling.

Karen lifted two of the bottles into the house as me and our Paul took a bottle each. I loved Cloudy Lime and our Paul loved Pineappleade. We opened the screw-tops to hear the fizzy escape of gas and took a slug each, enjoying the pleasant sting in our throats as it went down. Johnny and Dooter stood watching and, as I held the bottle over to Johnny, our Karen came back out for the two remaining bottles.

'Yous have your oul dirty mouths all over them bottles. Gimme that off ye o' that!' I handed her the bottle of Cloudy Lime and saw the look of hurt on Johnny's face. Paul handed his bottle of Pineappleade over as well as Karen marched into the house with a bottle in each hand. A few moments later she came back out with a wee tumbler of the green lemonade in one hand and a tumbler of Pineappleade in the other for Johnny and Dooter, which they drank in one slug.

The next morning, we were watching TV in the sitting room when there was a loud knock on the door. I went out and opened the door. It was Mr Veejee.

'Is your mother in?' he asked.

'She's up in her bed.'

'Can you please tell her I want to talk to her?'

I went upstairs to me ma and da's room. She was asleep, her dark hair strewn across the white pillow. 'Mammy!' I whispered so as not to wake Glenn, who was in the bed beside her. She didn't move. 'Mammy,' I whispered again. She didn't hear me so I placed my hand on her bare shoulder, shaking her slightly, and said 'Mammy!' again. She opened her eyes and snapped, 'What d'ye want? I'm tryin' to git a sleep!'

'The Black Man's at the front door. He said he wants ye.'

'Tell him I'm in me bed, for Jesus sake!' she said, turning her face away.

I turned to go out of the room and she called out in a whisper, 'G'won ask him how much I owe him.' I ran downstairs and out to the front door to The Black Man. 'She said how much does she owe ye?'

'One pound, please, tell her.'

I ran back upstairs and said, 'He said ye owe him a poun'.'

'Jesus, a poun'? G'won gimme up me handbag.'

I reached for her handbag on the floor at the end of the bed. There was a half-bottle of Cream of the Barley Scotch Whisky sticking out of the top, its dark tartan bands running along the top of the label. I gave her the bag and she took out her purse, clicked it open and gave me a green pound note. I ran downstairs to where Mr Veejee was still waiting. I handed him the pound note and he said, 'Thank you,' before getting into his wee van and driving away up the street.

Later that afternoon, me ma was out the town. Karen and Patrick told me and Paul to take Colleen and Glenn out the Daisy Field for a walk. Karen put Glenn in his pram and the four of us made our way out towards the Daisy Field. Paul brought a ball. After a while we got fed up and headed back in towards the house.

As we went into the hallway our Karen came out of the darkened front room and, closing the door behind her, said, 'G'won take themins into the sitting room and put on some toast for them.' She went back into the front room and shut the door.

I knew she was hiding something, so I stood on between the doors of the front room and the sitting room. I heard Davey Barbour's deep voice followed by Jacqueline McKinney giggling. Then silence. Then more silence.

'What's wrong wi' ye?' said a boy's voice inside the room.

'Aw, nothin',' said Jacqueline.

Silence.

'What now?' said the boy's voice. I realised it was Tommy Barbour!

'Ach, nothin',' said Jacqueline again.

Silence.

'What's wrong wi' ye?' said Tommy.

'It's your oul breath, Tommy! It's like smelly oul onions!' said Jacqueline.

More silence. Then I heard the sound of someone weeping.

Not a loud cry but a low and soft weep, followed by the sucking up of snotters into his nose.

'What are ye cryin' for?' asked Jacqueline.

'Nothin',' snivelled Tommy.

'Well, g'won stop yammin' there like a wain',' she said.

There was more silence, then more weeping, louder this time.

'Me granny died last week!' cried Tommy, letting a bawl out of him and sucking up more snotters.

'For fuck's sake!' said another voice. It was our Patrick! 'This is like tryin' to have a fuckin' date in Gransha!'

The door opened and Tommy Barbour came out, his face a blur of tears as he rushed to the front door with his head held down. Next came our Patrick followed by Donna O'Donnell. When I put my head around the door for a nosey, our Karen was sitting on the sofa with Davey Barbour and their faces were touching!

'I'm tellin' me ma what yous are at!' I called out, slightly annoyed that Jacqueline McKinney had been kissing Tommy Barbour, and now Davey Barbour was kissing our Karen! Jacqueline was the same age as me and everyone said she was my girlfriend.

Karen leapt up from the sofa. 'I'm goney kill ye, ya sneaky wee skitter!' she shouted, as I bolted through the sitting room into the scullery, where she caught me by the jumper and hit me a number of hard punches on the back.

She was a girl. I had to stand and take it. Me da had often told us never to lift your hand to a girl no matter what.

When she stopped battering me, she said, right into my face, 'Don't you breathe a word of this to me ma! Right!'

I shouted, 'Aye, right!' in defiance at her. As she went to leave the scullery, I called after her, 'We know ye now, Davey Barbour! We know ye now!'

She made another go for me and I ran towards the bathroom door but she caught me again, hitting me a few more thumps in the back.

'What did ye say?' she shouted. 'What did ye say?'

'I said, "We know ye now!" Ye were kissing Davey Barbour! That's what!'

She was about to hit me again when her angry face took a turn for the better and she lowered her thumping hand. She was very strong for a girl. 'Look, Tony, I on'y kissed 'im the wance. He's not me boyfriend or anything.'

'I don't care. Ye were kissin' him, so ye were.'

'Will ye not tell me ma on me,' she said, pleading. 'I'll give ye something.'

'What?'

'I'll give ye money.'

'How much?'

'I've 10p up the stairs. I'll git it for ye.'

'OK. 10p it is.'

'Is it a deal? You'll say nothin' to nobody?'

'It's a deal,' I said, rubbing the soreness in my back and shoulders. I was 10p richer for being in the right place at the right time.

The next evening, when Glenn and Colleen were in bed, me, Paul, Karen and Patrick were in the front room playing Monopoly. The four of us sat round the coffee table, keeping our money stacked in piles. Laying out the board and distributing the money was a non-competitive ritual that all four of us had a hand in. I always wanted the car, a Rolls-Royce, from the collection of solid silvery metal tokens that travelled round the board from street to street.

We had started late for Monopoly and, with our Paul taking too much time to make his mind up about buying this or that property, me ma came in to say that she was going out and we were to pack the game in at nine o'clock and get off to bed. She had a key and would let herself in. Karen went out to the hall to her, closing the glass door behind her, but came back in a few minutes later.

'She's away gallivantin' again,' she said in a sigh, looking towards Patrick. No one said anything else, but you could sense from others what I already felt inside about me ma. She always looked distracted. Nine o'clock came; we agreed to keep the board where it was, stacking the piles of money on the coffee table in case Brandy came in and ran through it.

In school the next day Satch Kelly, the head teacher, came

into my classroom and called me out to the corridor to tell me that me, Paul and Patrick needed to go home. That was all he said. I met Paul and Patrick near the main door and we left together, each of us wondering why we were going home early. As we crossed over the road to go down the Folly I saw a long plume of dark smoke rising into the blue sky from the direction of the Brandywell. When we reached our street the first thing that met our eyes was a fire engine parked outside our house, and a crowd of people, mostly neighbours, standing across the street. A fireman was reeling the long hose back into the fire engine.

As we drew closer we could see that the top windows of our house were broken and the green and cream paintwork around them was scorched black with the fire. The front step and the footpad outside the house were strewn with the multicoloured Monopoly money, now sodden and tramped into the ground. Me ma was among the crowd of people standing with Glenn and Colleen across the street. I could hear her laughing at something along with Maisie McKinney and oul Chesty Crossan, who had a suit jacket on over his white string vest and whose face and hands were black.

Me ma was saying that when the fire started she was upstairs and Glenn and Colleen were downstairs. She smelled smoke and rushed down into the sitting room, only to see the room on fire and Glenn and Colleen standing petrified at the scullery door. She said she grabbed them and ran them out into the street to a neighbour who had a telephone, to call the fire brigade. When she came back a minute or two later Chesty was running through the smoky front hall and out into the street with his hands held high above his head, shouting, 'It's OK, Eileen, I've got your money, I've got your money!' before casting piles of Monopoly money onto the ground and running back into the front room for more of what he thought was me ma's money. Chesty's chest heaved and his blackened face ran pink with tears of laughter as me ma told the story.

We stood outside our half-burnt house, staring into its smoke-darkened hallway. It smelled of charred wood doused by water. We didn't fully realise it then, but the Doherty family would never again wake up to a Brandywell morning.

6

TO THE GREEN HILL
OF CREGGAN

I didn't completely believe me ma about how the house got burned. I found her story strange. Me ma told people that Colleen and Glenn lit it by sticking newspapers into the open fire and throwing them under our black plastic sofa in the living room. But I sensed she'd become very unhappy in our house and I've always associated its burning with her unhappiness. Did me ma set fire to it? To get out? To escape from her and me da's past in Hamilton Street? I shall never know, as she always stuck rigidly to the story of Colleen, Glenn and the burning newspapers.

The family was forced to split up. Me and our Paul moved to me granny and granda's in Creggan. Me uncle Michael, who was nineteen, aunt Siobhán, eighteen, uncle Joe, twelve, and aunt Lorraine, seven, all lived there. Me and Paul slept in the largest bedroom, which had three beds, a single each for Michael and Joe, and a double bed for me and our Paul, all covered in heavy patchwork quilts. There was a black and white poster of Rod Stewart on the wall above Michael's bed.

Michael also had a wee cabinet mounted on the wall with a lock on it. Its door had the same wallpaper as the walls: lime-green, black and silver parallel lines with a flowery pattern in between. The cabinet door with the wee brass lock on it fascinated me and our Paul, and we stared up at it, night after night, wondering what was in it.

Lorraine and Siobhán's room was directly across the landing from ours. On their bedroom walls there were coloured posters of Slade, with their long hair, standing with their hands covering each other's tight trouser-fronts. Gary Glitter stood next to Slade in his shiny trousers, big platform boots and his half-open silver shirt with the black chest-hair bursting out. There was a row of the Osmond brothers, with their perfect hair, sparkling white smiles and eager eyes. There was also a poster of David Cassidy taking a lump out of a shiny red apple; his teeth were snow-white.

Karen and Patrick moved to Aunt Mary and Uncle Jimmy's flat in Carrickreagh Gardens. Jimmy had a wee blue motorbike. He and Mary each had a black helmet. Jimmy had a ball of brown, curly hair, a moustache and sideburns, and always seemed to be happy, as he smiled a lot. Everything to him was 'shit-hot'. His motorbike was shit-hot and his dinner was shit-hot. He took me and our Paul fishing a few times, and when he put the worm on each of the fishing rods, he said that it too was shit-hot. As we sat beside the small, slow-flowing river somewhere in Donegal, taking the corned-beef sandwiches from their bread wrappers, he said 'shit-hot' as he took his first bite and 'shit-hot' as he supped his first drink of steaming tea. Me and Paul looked at each other and giggled into our tea as Jimmy looked at us, took another bite of his sandwich and said 'shit-hot' again.

Jimmy cast out for us as we'd never fished with rods before and it all looked very complicated. The three rods stood on the grassy edge of the water, a few yards apart, with us sat behind them, waiting for the fish to bite. Nothing happened. They just sat there with their almost invisible lines of gut forming a triangle with the rod and the grassy ground. After a while we got fed up sitting and waiting for the fish to do something and started throwing stones into the water. Jimmy got on to us and said that we'd scare the fish away, chasing us on up the river where we could throw all we wanted. Throwing stones when you're out fishing is not shit-hot.

Me, Paul and Patrick stayed at Long Tower School, even though it was more than a mile down the hill from Creggan. Each morning we walked down Fanad Drive, past St Mary's Chapel and down Bligh's Lane, where the BA had their Essex army camp, overlooking the wide, shining river in the valley below and the whole expanse of the city, then down Stanley's Walk, where the BA were also camped, both inside and outside the Gasyard. After school, we walked the same route in reverse, usually in the company of the Creggan boys: Joe Mooney, Paul 'Penya' Ramsey and Damien Curran. It was strange seeing the Brandywell boys at school, knowing that we wouldn't be heading down the Folly or Bishop Street with them towards home.

In the long approach to Christmas, my Aunt Lorraine was practising at school to play a fairy in what she called the 'panotmine', *The Wizard of Oz*. Each day she came home she dropped her schoolbag on the sitting-room floor, and through the gap of her two missing front teeth, launched into 'Thomeday I'll with upon a sthar, and wake up where the cloudth are far behind me', as she pranced in her imaginary costume around the sitting room in performance after performance after performance. In the morning, when she got up from bed for school, she waltzed downstairs in her white vest and drawers, singing 'Where troubleth melt like lemon dropth, away above the chimney topth, that'th where you'll find me …'

When she eventually got her costume it was only a pair of pink tights, a piece of pink netting for a skirt and a pink vest. She was delighted, though, especially after me granny painted make-up on her face, giving her a glittery complexion, two rosy cheeks and a pair of darkish eyes.

'The spit of Clara Bow,' laughed me granny as Lorraine did a full performance in the sitting room, while the fire blazed and the tinsel on the Christmas tree flashed and sparkled brightly in the corner. I wondered who Clara Bow was.

Me granny and granda had a party planned for Christmas night. The Iriscots Drinks Company deliveryman had brought wooden crates of Guinness, Smithwick's and Harp beer, which were stacked on either side of the front door.

My Uncle Joe had a tortoise that he fed with lettuce. He kept it in a box full of newspapers in the hall. It came out now and again and walked around the hall and sitting room. On Christmas Eve we lifted it out of its box, placed it on the hall floor and, in our stocking soles, proceeded to take turns jumping over it as it ambled happily on the oilcloth. When it was my turn to jump, my foot slipped on the oilcloth, clipping the tortoise and flipping it over onto its back. Its wee head and legs disappeared into its hard shell. Joe picked it up, like a broken toy, placing it flat on the oilcloth, and we all expected its wee head and legs to appear again. We waited and waited and waited. We even had a cup of tea and a slice of currant cake in the scullery, keeping one eye on the tortoise shell lying squat on the hall floor for any movement. We waited. There was not a thing. Not a movement. Not a head nor a foot! My heart sank each time Joe or me looked towards the tortoise for any sign of life.

Me granda came out of the sitting room, where he'd been watching TV, and asked what was wrong.

'That there gulpin kicked over me tortoise,' said Joe. I could see him getting a bit upset.

'Sure Tony didn't mean to kick it,' said me granda. I was really glad to hear him say that. 'It's only a wee bit afeared. It'll be back out in the morning.'

Joe lifted it and put it back in its box.

The next morning, when we came downstairs to open our Christmas presents, Joe was already in the hall looking at his tortoise with the pain of death on his face.

'Is it back out, Joe?' I asked, hoping for a happier response.

'Naw, it's fuckin' not back out! Your big fuckin' spla feet killed it, ye useless wee bastard!'

I felt really bad having killed his tortoise. I hadn't meant to, but that didn't seem to matter to Joe. He was about to throw a tantrum and throttle me when me granny came in from the scullery and said, 'Ach, sure we'll git ye another wan nixt week. And you stop that bloody cursin' boy, on this good Christmas mornin'!'

Joe muttered something under his breath as I went into the sitting room to see what Santa had brought me. Under the tree were a pile of huge boxes; one each for me, our Paul, Joe and Lorraine. I grabbed mine and tore the Christmas paper off it to reveal the 'Big League' football game, where you got to paint the teams in whatever colours you wanted. It was great! Leeds for Paul and Arsenal for me! Leeds would never win a game! Everything was packed into a green plastic tray: the huge green cloth pitch lined out in white, lines and lines of pink footballers, each with a wee sprung leg for kicking, just waiting to have their rigs painted on them, and a small box of thin paint jars – all you needed for the job. It was really class!

Our Paul opened his present. He got a large dumper truck with a red cab and a yellow dumper. It was that big he could sit on it and push himself round me granny's sitting room with his feet!

Joe got a really class wind-up train set, complete with tracks, tunnels, a red-brick plastic train station, farm animals and railway workers in flat caps. Lorraine got a doll of some sort or other. We got a Christmas stocking and a selection box each as well.

'Yis won't have time to put that stuff together,' said me granny. 'Away now and git yersels ready for Mass!'

Me ma had got us new clothes for Christmas. We joined the hordes of other perfectly dressed families walking down Fanad Drive towards St Mary's Chapel, where the white-haired and white-eyebrowed Fr Rooney said Mass, which seemed to take even longer than usual. The whole chapel smelled of new clothes. On the way back we sang 'Tutti Frutti! Father Rooney!' which we learned from our Uncle John:

> Tutti Frutti, Father Rooney
> Tutti Frutti, Father Rooney
> Tutti Frutti, Father Rooney
> Tutti Frutti, Father Rooney
> Tutti Frutti, Father Rooney.

But instead of 'Wop bop a loo bop a lop bam boom!' we sang, 'And don't forget Saint Vincent de Paul!'

Siobhán laughed and warned us not to be caught singing it within earshot of our granny, or there'd be murder in Central Drive on Christmas Day. When we arrived back, me ma, Karen, Patrick, Colleen and Glenn were in me granny's, all gathered round on the sofa and chairs in the sitting room. Me Uncle Jimmy was there as well, and when Joe showed him his train set he said it was 'shit-hot'. Joe had the tracks laid and the tunnels and buildings all set out, and was happily winding up the wee train and watching it take off at speed with its carriages in tow going round and round. I asked him for a go and he let me wind the train up, and I watched it go round and round the track again. It stopped right beside me so I felt free to lift the wee engine to wind it up again. I wound it up really tight, but when I placed it back on the track, hooking it under the loop of the lead carriage, it sat motionless, as if waiting for a signal or a push. Joe looked at me with mild concern. I gave it a gentle push to help it start along its way. It refused to move. Joe looked at me, then to me ma and granny who had come over to see the beautiful new train set. Joe lifted the engine and gave it a wee shake to see if it would start, then put it gently back down on the track. Nothing. The blood drained from my face as both of us stared at the dead train sitting motionless on the track it had shot around only a minute ago. Me in disbelief and shame, and Joe in anger and disgust.

'What's wrong now?' said me granny, squinting down at us over her glasses as we sat hunched on the floor.

'He broke me effin' train!' said Joe. He was about to cry.

'I didn't mean it, Granny. I musta jist wound it up too tight!'

Me ma lifted the wee engine from the track, shook it up to her ear and placed it back down again. Nothing.

'It's OK, Mammy,' she said, 'I'll send for another wan next week from the catalogue.'

'Aye,' said Joe, 'nixt week! Me whole Christmas is fuckin' nixt week wi' Tony Doherty!' and he began angrily stripping down the tracks and throwing them into the box that had a colour picture of a train on the front billowing steam.

'You watch that foul tongue of yours, boy!' shouted me granny.

Joe didn't say a word over the Christmas dinner. He was really browned off with me. He sat with a face on him. After dinner, as the December darkness fell outside in the street, we all had to give a hand redding up in preparation for the evening's Christmas party. All the toys were put back in their boxes and left in the space under the stairs. Me granny and granda were in the scullery slicing the remains of the turkey and ham.

'Can I do the door the night, Granny?' I asked from the hall.

'Aye, OK, son,' she said, not really taking me on.

'Great! Hi, Joe, will me and you do the door for the party?' I asked, in the hope that he might have forgiven me by this stage. He had had a face on him all day and clearly hated me for ruining his whole Christmas.

'Naw! Ye can fuck off! I'm doin' the door!'

'Ach Joe, wise up, would ye! I didn't mean to break your train set!'

'And ye murdered me fuckin' tortoise as well! I'm doin' the fuckin' door. It's my house! You can fuck away off!'

'Ach, Joe, g'won let me do it wi' ye,' I pleaded. I loved doing the door, letting everyone in and getting patted on the head.

'Naw,' he snapped.

'G'won, Joe.'

'Naw.'

'Please, Joe.'

'Naw.'

'G'won, Joe, I'll let ye paint wan o' the Big League teams as Man City the marra.'

He paused for a while. Joe loved Man City. He was the only Man City fan I knew.

'All right, but I open and you stay out o' me road. Right?'

'Dead on, Joe!' I said, relieved at his change of heart and glad that he didn't hate me as much any more.

Me and Joe camped behind the front door from early evening waiting for our first customer. At the first knock Joe opened up to let in big, burly Thomas Daly, with his jet-black, curly hair Brylcreemed back like a Teddy Boy. He had a red, bulbous nose, red cheeks, and under his arm a bottle of whiskey in a brown paper bag for the house and a box of Milk Tray for me granny Sally.

'There ye go, Connor!' he said, handing over the brown bag to me granda in the hall, before giving me granny a huge hug in the scullery and placing the Milk Tray on the table.

'Ye shouldn't've bothered, Thomas,' she said, smiling, and Thomas gestured with his face and hands to say, 'Sure, it's nothin'.'

'What d'ye fancy?' asked me granda, as they went into the sitting room.

'I'll take a bottle o' stout.'

Joe reached up and lifted a bottle of stout from the highest wooden crate and handed it to his da.

Another knock at the door. Joe opened it. Me ma, Aunt Mary, Uncle Jimmy, Patrick and Karen came in.

'Jesus, but it would skin ye on this good Christmas night!' said me ma. 'Ye'd need to salt them steps or somebody's goney slip and kill themselves on them!'

'Oh aye!' said Connor, 'I mixed some salt up wi' the ashes from the fire this morning. Would ye go out an' do it for me, Tony?'

'Aye surely, Granda,' I said, as he went into the scullery larder for the box and shovel.

'Spread it well, won't ye, son,' said Connor. 'Ye'll need a coat on ye. It's freezin' out.'

'I'll be OK, Granda,' I said, and out I went to the steps and immediately regretted not putting a coat on. The bitter wind, with a light skiff of snow in it, blew right up the steps and right up the back of my jumper as I hunched over the box of salt and ashes, throwing and spreading the gritty mix across the flat of each of the eight steep steps until I reached the top one at the street.

'Good man yerself, young Doherty,' said Eddie McKevitt, as he and his wife approached. Eddie the Fruit Man was bald as a coot and as pleasant as the day was long. Always smiling.

'Me granda asked me,' I said, with teeth chattering in the bitter cold.

'Jesus, son, ye'd better git down them steps an' into that warm house outa this coul!' he said, and I followed him back down the dark, crunchy steps and into the house.

A short while later, Joe opened up again to let Winkle and Mary McMonagle in. Winkle was a small man with a baldy head and gapped teeth. Mary, too, was small, had a mass of curly hair and she laughed, smiled and giggled her way from the scullery to see Sally, and into the sitting room, where she sat with Eddie the Fruit Man's wife on the settee.

The room was filling up rightly as the next knock on the door revealed the long-haired and bearded John Keys in his brown three-piece suit, and John Leonard, a tall man with reddish, bushy hair and sideburns that came right down to his chin. Each man was carrying a bottle in their hands for the house. Shortly after came Hugo and Eileen Crumlish:

Eileen was me ma's cousin. Hugo was the size of a bear, had hands like shovels and a booming laugh that would shake the windows of a house. He had the face of a boxer, but me granda used to say about him, 'He wouldn't hurt a fly unless the fly hurt him first.'

Me and Joe parked ourselves on top of a crate each to cover the door and after a while we got used to hearing the guests approach the door before we saw them: Aunt Siobhán and Ann Stewart – Mary Stewart's red-headed daughter – Josie Brown, Uncle Patsy and Aunt Geraldine, and then Uncle Gerard, who'd come back from Dublin for Christmas. Michael came downstairs to join in the craic.

Our role in the festivities changed as the night progressed. From covering the door we moved on to opening and supplying bottles of beer for the men, who sat around the sitting room talking loudly, telling jokes, laughing and smoking, while the women sat in groups on chairs or hunkered down on the floor with their glasses of vodka or Bacardi, smoked and giggled at themselves and their men, and the wains tried their best to keep out of the way, but remain involved and in earshot of the four or five conversations taking place at the same time and who was wise-cracking about what.

I kept an eye on the men's bottles resting at their feet to make sure they didn't run dry of beer, lifting the empties and taking them out to the wooden crates in the hall, where Joe would open more bottles, then send me back to deliver them to the feet of each drinker. Me granny had a tumbler of Babycham, a drink that came in tiny green bottles and looked like lemonade. She would drink no more than two or three of them the whole evening, while the other women drank glasses and glasses of vodka, or Bacardi mixed with Coke.

'Give us a wee song, Eileen,' I heard me granny say amidst the noise of the room.

'In a wee while, Mammy,' me ma mouthed back at her, nodding.

'Me ma's goney sing, Joe,' I said, out in the hall.

'Holy fuck, me da'll be starting the waterworks!' said Joe, and we both laughed because we knew what would happen.

A short time later, Thomas Daly, his face a beetroot red, bellowed out across the room, 'Eileen Doherty for a wee song!' The room fell quiet. We got up from our crates and stood at the sitting-room door. Everyone knew this was something to hear. Me ma coughed into her fist to clear her throat, sat forward on the double pouffe and closed her eyes:

> I wish I was in Carrickfergus
> Only for nights in Ballygrand
> I would swim over the deepest ocean
> The deepest ocean for my love to find
> But the sea is wide and I cannot swim over
> And neither have I wings to fly
> I wish I had a handsome boatman
> To ferry me over, my love and I.

At the mere mention of 'love and I' me granda, sitting directly opposite me ma, started his quiet snivelling. 'Beautiful,
Eileen', and 'Amazing voice, Eileen', murmured around the
room. Me ma continued, her eyes closed and her voice pitch-
perfect, singing into the Christmas-lit sitting room to the
clink of glasses, the suck of lips on fags and the exhaling of
smoke into the hot air. By the song's end me granda had to
be brought round with a glass of Bush, drunk straight, no ice,
no water, and me granny had a face on her because she knew
he'd be wrecked and bedridden in the morning.

Later in the evening, Uncle Gerard was asked to sing
'The Frog's Wedding', which he did, through his long, dark
hair, which half-covered his face and his thick, black-rimmed
glasses. Gerard had drunk his way round the folk scene in
Dublin for the previous two years and knew all the songs by
Planxty, the Dubliners and other folk bands. He ended the
song with the words 'And the cat ate the mouse and dat was
dat!' and everyone laughed and cheered.

'"Cuanto Le Gusta", Connor', shouted Thomas Daly from
across the room.

'Wait till ye see this here!' said Joe. All the wains were
gathered around the door and spilling into the sitting room,
taking it all in.

Me granda and Winkle McMonagle were in the corner of
the sitting room, bent over and talking. A few moments later
they spun around and began, half-hunkered and with an arm

around each other's shoulder, bobbing their knees up and down and singing. Connor led with a broad smile, his black, Brylcreemed hair shining in the Christmas lights. Winkle followed, smiling a gap-toothed grin as his wee baldy head bobbed in time with the lyrics. As the song says, they packed up their packs, took the train – an arm each around the other's shoulder, revolving their free arms piston-like in locomotion; they took the boat, both of them rowing their way along the short river of space cleared for them in the sitting room; they glided, an arm each, along the same short stretch of runway; they rode the goat, bandy-legged as the merry audience laughed and squealed out of them. They bobbed in unison snapping out a string of *Cuanto Le Gusta*s, both down on one knee, an arm across each other's shoulder, ending the song with perfect timing, even taking a bow before their grateful and ecstatic audience.

The next morning when I came downstairs me granny was already up. She had the radio on and was cleaning the sitting room, emptying the ashtrays and taking glasses out to the scullery.

'I'll have to git that carpet cleaned,' she said. 'It's stinkin' wi' spilt drink.'

'Granny, my throat's a bit sore,' I said, and she told me to come over under the big light to get a look. I opened my mouth wide and bent my head back to let her look in.

'It is a bit red, OK. C'mon out to the scullery and I'll git some salt and water for you to gargle.'

I followed her out and she put half a teaspoon of salt into a glass with some water and stirred it around a few times.

'Take you that into the bathroom and gargle it for a wee minute,' she said. I tipped half the salted water into my mouth and, before I knew it, I'd swallowed it right down.

'Uugghh!' I could feel my stomach turn with the salt.

'Don't swally it, ye eejit ye!' laughed Sally. 'Ye have to gargle it! Put your head back and keep it in your throat.'

I did it right the next time, but I could still feel the slight salty trickle in my gut. I gargled and gargled for a few minutes.

'Ye'll have to stay in the day. It's still freezin' out and it'll do your throat no good to be gallivantin' 'roun' the street.'

I spent the day reading the *Shoot! Annual* and feeling my throat get sorer. Me and Joe decided to paint the Big League footballers. Joe mixed the dark blue with the white to make a light blue for the Man City colours and I began painting the jerseys of my doll-pink Arsenal team in red with white sleeves, shorts and socks. We placed them by the fender so that the heat of the fire would dry them quicker, Joe's Man City on the left and my Arsenal team lined up on the right. We practised a longy with the subs who weren't getting painted, pulling back their sprung legs and shooting the wee white football in the direction of the opposite net. If you placed the ball right and pushed the base of the player down into the green cloth pitch, you got incredible shots the whole length of the five-foot pitch.

Later, as it was getting dark, me granny came in from the scullery and said, 'Yis have turkey sandwiches and a cup o' tae ready out in the scullery.'

I went out to the scullery and tried to eat the turkey sandwich; I chewed and chewed but could only swallow it bit by bit because of my sore throat. I drank the tea as well but everything tasted like salt. Later, as we were checking how dry the painted footballers were, I felt my stomach turn and saliva filled my mouth. I was going to be sick! I hurried out to the hall and into the toilet and threw up the remains of the turkey sandwiches and tea. My throat was burning and I felt really hot.

The next thing I remember was waking up in bed the next morning and not being able to move. There was no one else in the room and I tried to call me granny but I only managed a sandpaper-rough 'guughgh' that no one could hear. I woke up later in the darkened room. Me granny had come in with a small bowl of ice cream. Slade were singing 'So here it is, Merry Christmas' somewhere in the house. 'It's Chriiiiiistmaaas!' Sitting up, I held the bowl in my lap and slowly spooned the ice cream into my mouth. It felt cool on my throat but tasted of salt. When me granny left, the ice-cream came up onto the bedroom floor.

The next day I woke up on the settee in the living room with a crowd around me: me ma, Aunt Siobhán and me granny and granda. The doctor was on his way, me ma said. I wondered why. I only had a sore throat. I took a drink from a glass of water and felt it making me sick again so I got up to go out to the toilet. But I didn't make it and ended up on my knees on the sitting-room floor, vomiting up the water.

I looked up from the floor to the street, which was eye-level height to the sitting room, and saw tall Grenadier Guards walking across Central Drive on foot patrol. They waved and smiled down at the collection of people gathered around the sofa.

'Don't take them on, Siobhán,' said me granny. No one did.

As I was being helped back up I heard me granda crying out, 'Jesus, Mary and Saint Joseph! What are we goney do if that young fella dies this day!' I thought in a slow, fuzzy way, *Dies! What's he on about? Dies?* I tried to say back to him, 'Sure it's OK, Granda. I've on'y a sore throat,' but all I could manage was a long gravelly groan, which probably confirmed to him that I was indeed on my way to an early grave. Worse still, I tried again straight away, to get my point across, only to hear it come out as, 'Ughnngh ungh!' Me poor granda could only look down upon me with tears streaming from his reddened eyes.

The doctor came, asked me to open my mouth, took my temperature and left a prescription for tablets. He spoke to me ma and granny at the sitting-room door, but I couldn't hear anything except 'taking him in'. As he left the room, he told me ma to call him later if I got any worse.

I woke the next day back in bed. My throat felt a bit better, but I was still as weak as water. Looking up from bed I could see a doubled-up magazine on top of Uncle Michael's locked cabinet and I got up and lifted it down. It was a copy of *Time* magazine and there was a picture of a naked woman sitting in a red double-decker. I liked the look of her doobs and stared at them for a long time.

I was on the mend and spent the day sitting up on the settee, watching TV, eating ice cream, taking my tablets – wee white ones and coloured capsules – and drinking water. The next day I was back on my feet, playing Big League with Joe and our Paul, and eyeing up the street in the hope of escaping my cabin fever.

A few days later, me and Paul went across Central Drive to the junction with Fanad Drive, a steep hill which swept right down to St Mary's Chapel. We took his dumper truck with us and took turns flying down the footpad. We steered by simply pulling the cab of the lorry left and right with both hands to avoid hitting the hedges or flying onto the road. As I was about to take one of my turns, I saw me granny coming across Central Drive with her two shopping bags; one was straw and the other a fawn-coloured plastic.

As she drew near the junction I called out, 'Wait d'ye see this, Granny!' and took off down the hill on the dumper truck. As I flew down the hill, a number of loud shots rang out from the direction of the shops, further over on Central

Drive. I put my feet down to stop, dived for cover, and lay on the pavement with my head down. The shooting continued. It was loud and felt really close. I looked up to see me granny sitting in the middle of the crossroads amidst her shopping bags. She simply sat, putting her dark head down to her chest while the shooting continued. Paul too was lying on the pavement on the corner beside the high hedge.

Eventually I realised that, even though the shooting was continuing, there was nothing crossing the air above us, no whoosh from bullets above our heads. You know when you're in the line of fire and when you're not, but you stay down just the same if it's that close. I thought it was probably up around Piggery Ridge, just above Creggan Heights, where the BA had a large army camp. There was always shooting up there at any time of the day or night.

The shooting stopped. You usually stayed down for a bit longer, 'just in case' as me da used to say. After a while I got up and walked up to where me granny was still sitting in the middle of the road. A man had come across to her and reached her at the same time as me. As I approached I could see her eyes were still closed, but her lips hummed in prayer and her fingers moved too, as if she was holding her rosary beads. She didn't realise we were standing there until the man said, 'Sally, are you all right?'

Me granny opened her eyes, blinking. She seemed surprised to see us.

'Aye, I'm OK,' she smiled, 'I'm hardly fit to rise!'

'Here, give us your arm, Sally, till I lift ye up,' said the man. I grabbed the other one and we helped her up.

She picked up her shopping bags and said, 'Ach, thanks, Joe. God but that shootin's desperate!' as she walked on across towards the shops. Me and Paul returned to the plastic dumper truck.

***

One evening, me, Paul and Joe lay in bed, and Joe said he'd heard me granny and me ma talking in the scullery.

'Me ma asked your ma was she still seeing some boy called John,' he said.

'What d'ye mean? Is she goin' wi' him? Wi' John?' I asked.

'I think so,' said Joe, and that was the end of the conversation. I lay beside Paul, who had said nothing, and thought about who John was, was she really going out with another man, and what would me da think about it? I decided not to believe it, though the feeling in my gut told me it was true. I didn't want to believe it because I couldn't imagine me ma with a man other than me da, and I didn't want to think ill of her.

***

Me ma swapped the big red Maxi for a gold-coloured Ford Capri. A crowd of us boys were playing football on the grassy

Cropie one day when we saw her driving up Westway towards us. We were lucky she hadn't come five minutes earlier, when two Sixers had passed the Cropie and we'd thrown stones at them as they headed down Westway. Bigger boys in denims were waiting for them at the corner of Dunree Gardens and pelted them with paint-bombs as they drove by. They ran right up to them before firing. They had no fear. All the BA vehicles were splashed in a variety of paint. When a new regiment came in, they would come out of their barracks in brand new, bottle-green Sixers, Pigs, Jeeps and Ferrets. But within a few days they'd be as bad as the rest, all paint-bombed up! I saw a photo in a newspaper once of a soldier whose Sixer had been hit by a salvo of paint-bombs. His whole left-hand side was multicoloured while his right-hand side was a perfect khaki green!

When we went in later, me granny was talking to me Aunt Siobhán about me granda 'taking to his bed'. This meant that he stayed in bed for several days, or maybe a week, with me granny taking him up his meals and pint glasses of water. I'd never seen this side of me granda before. As far as I was concerned he was one of the happiest men I knew.

When he took to his bed, if me granda wanted anything, he'd bang on the floor with a shoe and me granny would raise her eyes to heaven, saying to me or Lorraine, or whoever was at hand, 'G'won up and see what he wants. I'm sick, sore and tired runnin' up them stairs after *him* the day!'

So one of us would go up to their bedroom at the end of the landing, and open the door to strong bedroom smells of farts, rifts and oul feet. Connor would be lying gazing at the ceiling, only turning his eyes slightly towards the person at the door.

'Ye all right, Granda?'

'Ach, I dunno if I'm all right or not, Tony.'

'Can I git ye anything?'

'Where's Sally; I knocked down for *her*.'

'She's hangin' out the washing. Can *I* git ye anything?'

'Aye, I suppose so,' he said, weakly. 'Can you bring me up two Eno's and a glass of water?'

'Aye, surely, Granda.'

'What's 'e want?' asked Sally, as I passed the sitting-room door.

'Two Eno's and glass of water,' I smiled. 'I'll git them.'

'There's a box o' Eno's on the high shelf in the larder.'

The larder was in the scullery and had a number of stone shelves fixed to the wall. You could walk inside it and hide, which was handy for hide and seek on wet days. There was a four-stone bag of spuds on the floor beside the vegetables on the bottom shelf. The next one up held me granny's pots, pans, baking tins and dishes. The third held the flour bags: plain, wheaten and self-raising, along with a square double tray of eggs, raisins, a large deep-red and black treacle tin, a bag of caster sugar and a range of smaller tins of various baking powders. The top shelf was full of white-labelled dark-brown bottles and white boxes – the medicines and tablets. The red, white and blue Eno's box was lined up as part of this display. I stood on a chair and took two sachets of Eno's out of the box, ran half a glass of water, grabbed a spoon and headed upstairs to me granda. This time I went right into the room and placed the glass on the wee bedside cabinet. I could see that me granda hadn't shaved for a few days. He looked grey and he needed a haircut. He opened his eyes as the glass clinked on the wooden surface.

'There you go, Granda,' I said, and turned to leave.

'Would ye open the wee sachets for me?'

I lifted the sachets of Eno's, tearing each one at the corner, then pouring and shaking the white powder into the glass. It fizzed and sparkled onto my hand. I gave it a wee stir with the spoon and handed it to me granda. He slugged it back.

'That you now, Granda?'

'Aye, thanks son.'

As I was closing the door he let a huge rift out of him and I giggled my way along the landing and down the stairs. As I went back into the living room, I heard the knock again on the floor above. Me granny raised her eyes to the heavens, cursed under her breath and said, 'G'won you back up and see what 'e wants.'

I sprinted back up, taking three stairs at a time.

'What d'ye want, Granda?'

'I need ye to do me a wee favour the marra.'

'Aye surely, Granda. What is it?'

'Will ye go to the bookies for me?'

'Aye. But Granda, I've never betted before, except up at the Lifford dogs.'

'Don't worry about you bettin', son; I'll tell ye what to do.'

'All right, Granda. Is that all?'

'Don't be tellin' your granny I asked ye,' he said, looking me in the eye through his own half-closed eyes to see what I would say.

'OK, Granda,' I said. I took the stairs down in three goes and went straight to the street before me granny could ask me what he wanted.

The following day I was upstairs on the landing when me granda called me in a whisper into the bedroom and beckoned me to the side of the bed.

'Here, take this over to Otto Schlindwein's for me and don't give it to anybody else.' Otto ran the chemist's shop.

I took a warm wad of rolled up pound notes from him. It felt thick in my hand.

'And here's two bob for yourself as well,' he said, with the 10p coin held between his finger and thumb. 'Away ye go! Otto needs it before the race at three o'clock.'

'OK, Granda,' I said, and made my way quietly downstairs, hoping that me granny wouldn't hear or see me. She was in the scullery with the twin tub out, doing the washing, so I was safe. I headed up the steps and across the street towards the Creggan shops. The shops were where everything happened – rioting, shooting, kneecappings, religious parades, the lot. There was a Provo 'Incident Centre' on the nearside of the shops and a Sticky 'Incident Centre' on the far side, beside Barr's sweet shop. A dark-haired woman in a perfect white coat was behind the counter when I went in to the chemist's.

'Is Otto in?' I asked her.

'He is,' she smiled with her perfect white teeth and red lips. 'D'ye want him for something?'

'Me granda sent me over.'

'Who's your granda?'

'Connor Quigley.'

'Houl on a wee minute,' she said, and went through the white door behind her to a back room. She came back out with Otto, a kind-faced man with glasses and greying black, curly hair. He too was wearing a white coat.

'Have ye somethin' for me, son?' he asked. The beautiful, dark-haired woman stood to the side, watching.

'Me granda sent ye over this,' I said, holding out the wad of notes. 'He said it's for the three o'clock.'

'Is there a note in it?' he asked as he took the wad.

'I don't know.'

'OK, son. Tell your granda I'll sort it out for him.'

'OK,' I said, and left the chemist's to head over to Barr's shop for a quarter pound of white bonbons. I loved licking the white, sugary dust off them before rolling them on my tongue till their hard shells softened. The door of Barr's shop was held open by a wooden wedge. I walked in and was heading towards the counter, where two assistants were standing, to buy the bonbons, when a huge explosion went off. Everything in the shop shook and I found myself crouched on the floor. I could hear things falling behind me, and when I looked round towards the door there was a pile of building rubble about three feet high, and a cloud of white dust billowing over it and in through the open door. I looked back towards the counter. The two women had disappeared underneath it. No one moved for a minute or two, until we heard people talking and moving about in the street outside. A man climbed over the pile of rubble and asked whether everybody was OK. The women had come up from behind the counter and said they were.

'What about *you*, son?' asked the man.

'I'm OK too.'

'Are ye all right, son?' said one of the women from behind the counter.

'Aye, I'm OK,' I repeated. 'I on'y want a quarter of white bomboms.'

The two women smiled at each other and the younger one reached behind her for the large glass jar of white bonbons. She measured them on silver weighing scales, then poured them into a wee white bag and handed them to me.

'Churrio, son,' they said as I left, climbing over the pile of rubble at the door to get out. The bricks still had their wallpaper on. When I got out to the street a crowd had gathered, all looking up above Barr's shop, where the bomb had gone off. No one took any notice of me. I too looked up to where the flat used to be above the shop, took a white bonbon out of my wee white bag and began licking the sweet, white dust off it as I turned and headed back towards the safer part of Central Drive.

As I walked across the street towards me granny's, I could see people out of their houses looking across towards the shops and some were making their way slowly in the direction of the explosion. Me ma's gold Capri was parked outside the house and me ma, Aunt Siobhán and me granny were up the steps looking over towards the shops.

'Were you over there?' asked me ma.

'I went to Barr's shop for sweets,' I half-lied. I couldn't say that I took a wad of notes to Otto Schlindwein's for me granda!

'Where was the bomb?'

'Over Barr's shop. I was inside when it went off. The door was blocked up wi' rubble.'

'Jesus, Mary and Saint Joseph!' me ma said, almost in a whisper, looking into the faces of her sister and her ma.

'Are ye OK, Tony?' asked me granny.

'Aye, I'm dead on,' I smiled. 'I got me bomboms. D'yis want wan?'

They took one each, except me granny, who complained about not being able to chew toffee because of her false teeth.

We were chewing away, standing on top of the garden steps, looking over towards the shops, when me ma said, 'We're gettin' a new house, Tony. Down in Shantalla, near Carnhill. We'll be moving in next week.'

My heart sank. I loved me granny's house and the craic with Joe and Lorraine. I'd never thought it would come to an end.

'D'ye not want to live wi' yer own mammy?' said me ma. She could see the reaction on my face.

'Aye, but I like it here too,' I said, trying not to offend.

'It'll be great. We'll all be back together again under the wan roof,' she beamed.

I didn't say anything, but inside my head I thought, *There's not an effin' chance of me moving down there, out to the effin' middle of effin' nowhere to a new effin' house!*

However, I knew my days on Creggan's green hill were numbered.

7

SHANTALLOW
HERE WE COME!

Our brand-new house in Brookdale Park was No. 15. Me ma thought this was lucky as it was the same number as our old house in Hamilton Street. We were among the first to move in, at the start of summer 1974. Brookdale was in a new place called Galliagh, on the very outskirts of the city. Shantallow and Carnhill were a couple of fields away. We were surrounded by the countryside. A half-finished road ran between the estates, while the road through Brookdale was half-finished as well. Brookdale had only two parallel rows of houses with families in them, but there were many more being built. There was no exit at the bottom. The houses were all a pale yellow colour and had gardens at the front and back, like the houses in Creggan.

I was now eleven years old. I was taken straight to Brookdale Park on the day of my capture: I'd already evaded me ma by hiding under the bed when she came up to me granny's one morning looking for me. The next time, I hid in the long grass on the Cropie, watching as me ma pulled up to the house in her Capri and went in. I waited for what seemed like ages until she left before heading across. I was having a bowl of chicken soup at the scullery table when she came in again. She'd only gone across to the shops so now I was caught! Our Paul had been snared a few days earlier.

'You'll love it, ye know. It's a gorgeous house,' said me ma as she drove us out of Creggan with my clothes in bags in the boot along with my Big League football game.

'I probably will,' I smiled, to keep her happy. I *was* looking forward to seeing everyone as well as our Brandy, who was still hobbling about on three legs with her other front paw held aloft.

As we drove along the road near Carnhill there were boys galloping piebald ponies bareback along the greenbelt, keeping up with the car.

'That's the gypsies and Neil McMonagle,' said me ma.

'Who's Neil McMonagle?' I asked.

'Ye wouldn't know him. We, ahm, I go to the dogs wi' his big brother Lorny.'

'Where do they keep the horses?'

'Neil keeps his in the backyard in Carnhill. Dunno where the Stokes keep theirs.'

The new sitting room was the fanciest I'd ever seen. It had a brand new white leather sofa and chairs, a colour TV and a white furry mat on the floor beside a vase of huge white plumes. We didn't have a fire. Instead there was a gas heater on the chimney breast, surrounded by a grey tiled fireplace with wee brass pots, mounted brass cannons and copper vases on the mantelpiece. We also had rubber bullets in their shells on metal mounts, which sat at both ends of the fireplace pointing in, making their own equilateral triangle. There was no carpet, me ma said, because of the muck and the dirt outside. We'd wait till the road outside was finished.

The new street, me ma said, was a home from home. Two doors up from us was Laura Ford from Central Drive, who was married to Jim Glenn. Further up from Laura was Anna McNutt, whose husband, Mickey, was interned in Long Kesh prison. Across the street was Winnie O'Brien from Central Drive, who was married to Mark Grocott, a big, tall BA soldier who'd served in Derry with the lanky Grenadier Guards. Next door to Winnie were Alan and Joan Nash; Alan's brother had been killed on Bloody Sunday, and Joan was English. On the other side of Winnie were Mickey and Dolly Bradley – Mickey had been shot in the arm on Bloody Sunday. Next to Mickey and Dolly, in a four-bedroom house, were the Coyle family, who'd been burned out of their Belfast home by loyalists. Near the top of the street on Winnie's side were the Duffy family, whose father had been shot dead by the Provos in 1973, having been accused of being an informer. There were a few families up near the Duffys who'd also been burned out of their houses in Belfast.

Me granny's house was soon forgotten as I took in our new surroundings in the countryside. There was a wee abandoned cottage about 200 yards in front of us, near where they were building a new row of houses, and a roofless and windowless farmhouse behind our house, with a chocolate-brown donkey still tethered to a tree in a garden with a few apple trees.

Led by Dozey Ford, Laura's young brother, we headed off one day down the field below our house. We passed cows and sheep wandering about as if they belonged to no one. We got stuck and mucked up in marshy land and leapt over streams, disturbing a green-necked duck out of the water followed by a string of seven or eight ducklings all scrambling and fluttering to keep up, the last of which, said Dozey, was the 'tail-end Charlie'.

On our way back we passed the abandoned farmhouse and saw a group of boys taking turns riding the donkey round the garden. They were all from Bloomfield Park, just up from us off the half-finished main road. Opposite Bloomfield was Fern Park; these were the only three estates built by the summer of 1974. One day when we went looking for the donkey, it was gone, but there was a black-and-white cow with a huge udder lying on the pathway outside the farmhouse. Its eyes were open but it was dead and it didn't react or anything when we tried to rock it with our feet. It lay there for a few days and then one morning it too was gone.

The field below us was level so we converted it into our football pitch, where we played for hours when the weather was good, or we had sling-shot wars in the old cottage opposite our house. For slingy wars you weren't allowed to aim at the face. One group went into the cottage and the other group sneaked and sniped among the rushes outside, trying to pick off those inside with a well-aimed shot. More times than not, someone would let a squeal out of them after getting hit in the neck, face or head by a slung stone or pebble. But nobody ever had an eye put out, which is what we were always warned about. After a while, both me and Dozey had a deadly aim with the slingies. We could even splatter bluebottles on the wall from across the room, we were that good.

One evening when we went home for our tea, there was a man in the scullery along with me ma. Somehow I knew this was John, the man Joe had mentioned a while back.

'This is John,' said me ma. 'This is Tony and Paul.'

'Hello, Tony and Paul,' said John with a smile, his hand outstretched. Both of us shook his hand. He was a tall man with shoulder-length brown hair, brown eyes and a white-toothed, smiling face.

'What's for tay, ma?' I asked, before going back into the sitting room in embarrassment, as they were making eyes at each other. We sat in subdued silence and could hear me ma and John whispering something in the scullery. Colleen and Glenn had been out in the car with them and were now lying on the furry white mat watching TV.

Brian and Janice lived across the street in a flat. They were fighting again, and Janice had thrown him into the street. Our front door was open, so we could easily hear her shouting, 'Git outa my house, ye useless bastard!'

Our Patrick came in. Patrick's black hair had grown long and there was a dark shadow on his upper lip. He wore a pair of black 'parallels', cut and stitched a few inches above his ankle, so you could see his black socks and his shiny black Oxfords. Patrick loved the style and I was beginning to think more about clothes as well.

'D'yis see themins at it across the street?' he asked.

'Aye, the whole street can hear them,' I said.

'John's in the scullery,' said Paul with a half-smile, all eyes.

'Sure I met him a whole rake of times,' said Patrick. 'No fuckin' odds to me.'

'He's back out!' said Paul, who was gawking out the huge front window. We looked over at Brian sitting on the mucky kerb just opposite our house, his face in his hands and his curly head bobbing up and down with his sobs.

'They met in Gransha, ye know?' said our Patrick.

'Did they right enough?' I asked.

'Mad as hatters, the two of them,' he said. 'He must have the heart of a lion married to thon – the size of her!' Janice was heavy-set all right and had a face on her as if she had been neglected since childhood. She spoke to no one when she passed by in the street, leaving Brian to mutter a shy, down-headed 'Hello' as he traipsed ten or fifteen dejected yards behind her.

Me ma called us out to the scullery. It was stew for tea, which was already in bowls placed at intervals around the table. There was a loaf of plain bread and butter in the middle of the table for stew sandwiches, as well as salt and brown sauce. Karen came downstairs, picked up her food and went into the sitting room without speaking to anyone. Patrick picked up his and went in as well. Me and Paul stood smiling and smirking at each other as we ate the stew. John didn't say much.

***

Our Patrick told us that John was already married with wains. We were sitting up in bed on a warm summer evening with the window open. Patrick had been out on a date with Jeanie Bradley from Bloomfield Park. She had beautiful red hair and, like Patrick, wore black parallel trousers, creased like a blade, with black socks and black Oxfords. She also wore a pink and white cardigan, though.

'He has his *own* family?' I asked, hardly able to take it in. Paul was staring, listening to the conversation with his mouth open.

'Aye, that's what I said. He's got a wife and wains up in Creggan.'

'Jesus, man!' I said, half under my breath. I couldn't take in why a married man with a house full of wains would want to go out with another woman with a houseful of her own wains.

'Aye, I don't know what me ma's doin' wi' him,' said Patrick. If Patrick didn't know, there was no point in me trying to work it out.

After a few minutes I nudged Paul to get up to say our prayers. We knelt at the side of the bed and said the Hail Mary and the Our Father and then asked God to look after us and me da in heaven. Patrick just lay in the other bed smiling across at us.

Me ma was spending a lot of nights out, presumably in pubs, as all she talked about was the Glue Pot, The Lion, Tracy's, Mailey's and the Bogside Inn. When she was out, I lay awake night after night wondering about her being out and driving home in the Capri with the drink in her. Many a night I didn't go off to sleep properly until I saw the car lights turning into the drive and heard the lonely turn of the key in the front door.

***

Our street had a few broad alleyways, which ran between the blocks of houses. The alleys led onto a green that sloped down to the main road. Soldiers often drove along the main road in their Jeeps, Pigs and Sixers, and ten- to twelve-man foot patrols often came through our estate. The height of the green was perfect for stoning the BA down on the road, which we did almost every night as they passed by, before running back through the alleys and hiding in the gardens. One evening, when we were stoning them, a huge barn owl surprised us by swooping down out of the darkness, under the streetlights along the road, and flew the whole length of it before rising again into the black sky.

A few times the Jeeps drove up the green after us, the soldiers banging their batons to scare us. But we were experienced rioters by now and weren't frightened. I loved the rush of running away and hiding until they retreated, then re-emerging with more stones. The grey Jeeps of the RUC sometimes accompanied the green army Jeeps, and now and again you would see the dark-green, almost black, uniforms of RUC men up top in an army Jeep beside a soldier. The RUC were always armed with handguns and rifles. Brandy despised both the BA and the RUC and, along with her new friend, Rusty Ford, who'd moved from Central Drive with Laura in No. 13, barked furiously at them when they appeared in the estate. No one banged their bin-lids any more as the normal bins had been replaced with wire-framed cylinder bins with fixed lids and a long, heavy-duty brown bag for the rubbish. Often we'd come out in the morning to find the bottom of the brown bag had been shredded by rats and mice, and the rubbish had spilled out.

One morning, as we were getting ready for school, I was in me ma's bedroom looking down over the back garden when I saw a rat's tail dangling out of the bin-bag, just under the lid. I couldn't help myself. There are some moments in every boy's life when pure badness is the only option; this was one of them …

'Paul! Me ma said you're to empty the scullery bin before we leave for school!' I called down from the top of the stairs.

'OK!' he called up from the scullery as I took up my viewing position again at me ma's window.

Paul came out the back door with the bag of rubbish in his hands and lifted the metal lid of the bin. 'Aaagh, Jesus!!' he screamed at the sight of the rat in the middle of its breakfast. He let the lid down with a loud bang and cleared out beyond the back fence! The rat, which had been hanging round the back gardens for ages, tearing bags open on a rotational basis, was left in such a state of shock that the binman later carted it off in its brown breakfast bag, never to be seen again. Our Paul didn't have the courage to take the rubbish out again until 1980!

***

Girls and boys from Brookdale, Fern Park and Bloomfield hung around in each other's estates. I'd never kissed a girl but had been wondering what it was like, especially since our Patrick started going with Jeanie Bradley. Donna Dalton, who was from Fern Park, had begun to hang around our street. She had long, light brown hair and was the same height and age as me. One day me and Donna found ourselves on our own at the concealed entrance to the bottom flat next door.

'D'ye want a kiss?' asked Donna, leaning against the orange door of the flat.

'Do *you* want a kiss?' I put back on her.

'Aye, I do,' and we found ourselves standing face to face. As she pulled me in, she planted a firm open-mouthed kiss on my lips. She pulled back when I didn't respond.

'What's wrong wi' ye?' she asked.

'What?'

'You're supposed to open your mouth and kiss me back, ye know,' and came at me again with her mouth. I met her halfway, open mouth this time, and we kissed, warm, light and feathery for a short while. We did it again. And again. And again. Our young bodies pressed together and I could feel her heart racing against my chest. Kissing was class! Although, for some reason, that was the first and last time I kissed Donna Dalton.

I made some new friends too. We were playing football down in the rushy field when two skinheads came down towards us, wearing red and blue parallel trousers and Dr Martens boots. I thought they were down for a scrap as they looked fearsome with their haircut and clothes. They only wanted to play a game of football, though, so we let them. They were Kevin and Seán Boyle from Bloomfield. The Boyles had left their house in the Waterside on 11 July 1972. The children had been threatened by grown-up loyalist neighbours, and Seán had a knife put to his throat in the street in the weeks before they fled. They moved straight into their new house in Bloomfield Park. They had two older brothers, Bobby and Joe, an older sister, Julie, who was gorgeous and in our Karen's year at Thornhill, and a small, nameless tribe of younger brothers and sisters. All the Boyle boys looked more or less the same, the only difference was their height.

Later in the game another skinhead came down the field towards us, also wanting to play. His name was Benny McLaughlin and he lived up in Fern Park. Benny's da was a Sticky. When they moved into Fern Park his da and a few other Stickies in the Jim Larkin Official Sinn Féin Cumann built a pathway from the main road below the field at Bloomfield up the steep, grassy hill to the first square in Carnhill. The new flagstone path was called the Sticky Pad. All the houses in Carnhill were built in a series of squares with only door numbers as identification. There were no street names, so each square became named after someone you knew, like Darby's Square or Hutchie's Square. It depended on who you knew.

Benny's ma and da, Mary and John, were both very small. After they married, they moved to Springtown Camp. It had been a US Navy base during the Second World War, and when the Navy moved out, hundreds of Derry families, who'd been living in overcrowded houses, squatted in the Nissen huts and stayed for many years. The McLaughlins' first three children, including Benny, had been born in a Nissen hut in the camp.

Theirs was one of the very few houses in Fern Park to have a phone. Neighbours would usually pay them 10p to call for a taxi or to call the doctor. Benny said his da reckoned that people were making more than one call at a time when they came in to use his phone, so he bought a dinger which went off in the sitting room each time the receiver was put down.

'But even when he heard the phone dingin' a few times, and then the wee woman come in wi' the 10p in her hand, he still hadn't the nerve to charge them the full amount!' he laughed.

It was Benny's idea to make the paint-bombs. He was a year older than us even though he was slightly smaller. We had a tin of white gloss paint in the back hall of the house which we'd stolen and, after gathering up some bottles, we crowded round on the pathway that ran along the backs of our houses to get the paint into them.

'We need a funnel,' said Dozey.

'What's a funnel?' someone asked.

'It's for pourin' things into other things,' he said, 'without spillin'.'

'We haven't got wan.'

'OK, but we have to be careful or there'll be paint all over the place,' said Dozey.

Being careful meant prising the lid open with a screwdriver, lining the bottles up in a neat row and pouring the paint into them. The paint came out quicker than we'd imagined, and some spilled on the pavement, but there was enough in each of the bottles to do as a decent paint-bomb. Before long there was a row of bottles, each half-filled with white gloss, sitting in a seeping puddle of shiny white paint on the pavement. Then the dogs appeared – Rusty Ford and Brandy Doherty. We shouted at them to get away but they thought we were playing and ran through it, getting their legs clattered in white gloss. There were white paw marks everywhere, all over the footpad. Brandy only got three of her paws clattered as she still held the injured one up.

'Jesus, we're goney git kilt!' said Dozey. 'Our Laura'll hang me for this.'

'We'll jist deny it, Dozey,' I said.

'We need newspapers to wrap round the paint-bombs, or we'll be clattered ourselves,' said Benny.

We tore strips from the huge sheets of the *Derry Journal* and wrapped them around the bottles before stashing them to throw at the Brits later. Graffiti had appeared around Shantallow saying *Brits Out* and *Freedom 74*, so we all began to call the BA by their new name of Brits and began wondering what month in '74 they would leave and give us our freedom back. We reckoned that, if the IRA kept shooting them and blowing them up, they'd simply have to leave Ireland to the Irish again, as the Paul McCartney song said.

That evening we waited for the Brit Jeeps to come along the road. We waited and waited but there was no sign of them and it was getting near the time when we'd be called in. Kevin and Seán, both nicknamed 'Boiler', were panicking as they were out past their time. The newspaper had stuck well to the paint-bombs. We held them, felt their weight and pretended to lob them like hand-grenades just to keep busy. Suddenly, from the direction of Bloomfield, headlights appeared out of the near darkness. Then we heard the familiar whine of a Sixer.

'There's the effin' Brits!'

My heart was thumping as we scrambled for the paint-bombs. We lifted two each and waited until the Sixer began to draw level with the alley above the bankin' before running out onto the green towards the edge overlooking the road and firing the white paint-bombs at its side. Some of them hit the thick metal, others missed and hit the road.

'Brit's out, ya Limey bastards!' we shouted in victory as the Sixer headed on down the road.

'Yes!' we squealed in delight, having inflicted in our minds heavy damage on the Sixer, and then headed home to try to remove the white gloss from our fingers. The next morning, when we went down to the road to inspect the damage, we could see that the ones that had missed had made an impressive white arc on the ground.

***

Our Patrick had mentioned 'the hop' up in Shantallow. It was a disco on a Sunday afternoon, where someone would play records and people would dance. Me, our Paul, Benny and the two Boilers decided to go to our first hop. We walked through the fields to Shanty, paid our few pence at the door of the community centre and sat at the back watching the girls out dancing in bunches on the floor. Benny knew all the Shanty boys our age from St Joseph's School in Creggan. There was no secondary school in or around Shanty.

When the hop was over we came out into the street to see the Brits driving about the estate in Rat Jeeps. Rat Jeeps were open-backed Jeeps like in the Second World War films. The teenage Shanty boys were throwing stones at them from alleyways as they drove by, the soldiers ducking behind their hand-held green shields as the stones bounced off. Benny said we should wait in a back square with a group of Shanty boys, gather stones and bottles, and hang around in the hope that they'd come back.

One boy said they usually came in the top of the estate at Drumleck Drive, and if we waited at Moyola Drive we could see them coming. If they turned left at the T-junction, we should run to the end of the alley on our right and pelt them. If they turned right, we could go left to another alley and pelt them from there. It was very exciting being part of a bigger group of eleven-, twelve-, thirteen- and fourteen-year-olds clinking the milk bottles together and feeling the weight of stones in our hands as we waited.

Sure enough, after a while someone shouted, 'There they

are!' and we hid behind cars to see which way the Jeeps would go. They turned right, so we ran left to meet them at the end of the alley, running onto the street as they sped past, throwing our stones and bottles at the soldiers in the second Jeep. We hit them a few times, but mostly missed, our milk bottles smashing on the road near the community centre. The Rat Jeeps pulled in further down the road and waved back up at us as we gave them the fingers.

There were girls our age hanging around in their Sunday hop clothes, watching us as we pretended not to watch them. One of them had long, brown hair and beautiful grey eyes.

'Who's she, Benny?' I asked, pointing her out.

'That's Kitty Gallagher; she's goin' wi' Mark Doherty over there,' he said, pointing to a thin-looking boy with long, fair hair who was sitting on the kerb smoking.

'She's a quare half,' I said.

'I know she is and I fancy her too, so you keep your eyes off her!' he laughed.

'Has she any sisters?'

'Aye, wan, but she's fourteen and too oul for you!' said Benny.

The Sunday hop became a weekly excuse to go up to Shanty for a riot and get a look at the girls who hung around the back squares. Me, Benny and Kevin Boiler got to know every inch of Shantallow as we moved around the estate in a pack, waiting for the soldiers to arrive.

One Sunday, as we walked up towards Shanty, Benny said, 'Kitty's finished wi' Mark Doherty.'

'Aye?'

'But I'm goney try and tap her up after the hop.'

'OK,' I said. It was only fair, as Benny had told me he fancied her first.

Later, after the hop, Benny made his way over towards Kitty and began talking to her. I'd never tapped a girl up before and didn't know what to do or say. They were doing a lot of talking and laughing, I thought, as I stood on my own outside the hall. After about ten minutes, Benny came back towards me and said, 'She's goney think about it and I have to see her here nixt week.'

By the time next week came she'd made up her mind she wasn't going to go with Benny.

'She said she doesn't wanny go wi' anybody so soon after finishin' wi' Mark Doherty,' said Benny, having met her again outside the hop. She'd been looking in our direction at the hop and I wondered, red-faced, if she was looking at me? I'd let my fair hair grow a bit over the summer and parted it in the middle. I thought it was class-looking. She was definitely looking in my direction now as I was still standing with the rejected Benny outside the hop. He wanted to leave but I wanted to stay and, after a few minutes, he could tell what was happening.

'Mark Doherty's a quare scrapper, ye know,' he said, hoping to put me off my notion. 'He'll kick your balls in.'

Mark and the gang of young rioters were beginning to gather to head off in search of bottles and Brit Jeeps. I decided to take the bull by the horns. I headed straight across to him, and told him I was going to tap Kitty up. He said that was all right. Kitty was still standing outside the hop with her friends as I approached.

'Yes, Kitty,' I said.

'Yes, Tony,' she replied.

'Ye fancy meeting up during the week?' I asked.

She hesitated, looking around red-faced at her friends. 'Aye, OK,' she said. We'd made a date!

On the way home Benny hardly spoke to me, and when we reached his house he didn't ask me to come in and we didn't arrange to meet later.

'You're some friend,' he said as he closed the front door.

For our first date I'd arranged to meet Kitty in the square behind her house in Drumleck Drive. When she came out of her backyard she looked gorgeous in a pair of red parallel trousers and a red-and-white checked shirt, which was tied in the middle.

'I'm babysittin' in me aunt's flat over there in Moyola,' she said, pointing to the blocks of flats. 'Come you over in about twenty minutes' time.'

I dandered around the top of Shanty wondering about the things I should say to her during our first date. I needn't have bothered. Kitty's aunt must have smelled a rat as they came back within half an hour and I had to slink out the front door to the street to wait for her. When she came out, she told me that her aunt had chewed the bake off her for bringing a boy into the flat. We walked up to her back square and hid in behind the brick shed of a corner house where we kissed for a while before her ma came out to her back gate and called her in. When I saw Kitty again a few nights later she told me her ma had seen me walking down the street with my shirt hanging out and said, 'Look at 'im. He's on'y the size of a wee skitter!' And there was me thinking I was a growing lad!

***

One cold Sunday afternoon I met two older teenagers, Liam and Seán, outside the hop. They asked did I want to join the PLA (People's Liberation Army)? They told me they had hand-grenades and stuff for making bombs in a shed near their house. The PLA sounded like my type of army and I couldn't believe my luck that they even had hand-grenades and all!

'We're planning to plant a landmine near the Shanty Shops on Wednesday evening after school,' said Liam, who appeared to be the brainier of the two. 'We'll meet at five, OK?'

On Wednesday I walked the whole way up on my own, wondering what a landmine looked like. The Shanty Shops was a square block with large-windowed premises on the ground floor and a row of flats above. From left to right, the shops were: a post office, an off-licence, Owens's grocery shop and a bakery. When I got to the shops, our Patrick was standing there with some other boys his age. They all wore Wranglers cut up below the knees, black Crombies with the red breast-pocket pulled up to look like a hanky, and oxblood Dr Martens or black Oxfords. They looked like hard men, our Patrick as well.

Liam and Seán came out of the alleyway at the side of the shops.

'It's all on the night. The landmine's in place,' said Liam.

'Where is it?' I asked.

'It doesn't matter,' said Seán. 'Ye don't need to know. Let's go!'

We headed back up the alley, through Shanty to near the top of Drumleck Drive, where we sat on the footpad, keeping dick for the Brits. Liam got up after a minute and said he had to go and see the other boys about the landmine. 'Remember,' he said to me and Seán, 'the minute yis hear anything, run down to the shops where I'll be waiting.' He disappeared into the darkness.

Liam and Seán appeared to have everything under control. It seemed very simple to me to become a member of the PLA. We sat and waited to see if the Brits would drive up Steelstown Road and into Shanty. Seán didn't say much. It was a bit boring keeping dick, just sitting there waiting under the streetlight. There weren't many cars on the road so we could easily hear if a Brit vehicle was coming. Suddenly, we heard the familiar sound of Brit Jeeps from further down Steelstown Road. They were coming in our direction. Seán took off running, down through Shanty towards the shops, with me close behind. When we reached the shops, there was no sign of Liam or anyone else. Our Patrick and some of the bigger boys were dandering across the road and he saw us puffing for breath. Later in the evening, as I walked alone back down towards our house, our Patrick caught up with me and asked me what I was doing with Seán and Liam. I told him what I had been doing and that they wanted me to join the PLA.

'Themins are two Walter Mittys. They wouldn't know a landmine from a bag o' paralysed jujubes! It should be called the CLA, the Cowboy Liberation Army,' he laughed, 'but I'm telling ye this for yer own good.'

As well as attempting to join the PLA in Shanty and going to the hop on a Sunday, football was still a major preoccupation. A boy Yank was staying at his aunt's house in Brookdale. We were teaching him to play football down the street in front of the new houses when Mrs Ferry came out to us.

'Hi boys!' she called from her front door along the length of her garden. 'Yis couldn't move up the street a wee bit? Our Gareth's sick in bed wi' his asthma.'

'Aye, OK, Mrs Fer–'

'Put it in your tits, lady!' called the boy Yank.

Mrs Ferry's mouth fell open and her eyes near popped out of her head! I looked at her jumper-covered doobs to see what he was on about.

'What did *he* say?' said Mrs Ferry, her arms now firmly folded under her doobs.

'I said, "Put it in your fuckin' tits, lady!"' he repeated.

This time it was *our* mouths that fell open and *our* eyes that nearly came out of our heads!

'G'won ye cheeky wee article, ye! Away back to America where yis have no breedin' in yis!'

The boy Yank was about to go at her again, only Dozey Ford grabbed him by the arm and moved him up the street.

'It's OK, Mrs Ferry. We're away on!'

'Ye canny talk like that to a grown woman!' said Dozey as we retreated in shock. 'Ye'll git us kilt if she comes to our doors!'

***

Most of Brookdale, an estate of around 120 houses, was now full up with new families moving in as soon as their new homes were ready. One day near Christmas, our Paul showed up with a new boy, taller than he was, with curly, sandy hair and a strange English accent. His name was Seán and he had moved from Birmingham with his ma and his siblings. They'd just moved into a brand new house in a row at the top of

Brookdale. They were the Walkers from Birmingham. Me ma said that they had to get out of Birmingham after their da had been charged with bombings. There was a collection of money and food around the houses for them.

In the run-up to Christmas 1974 all six of us Doherty wains got new clothes. I got a blue jumper with blue and white checks on the front and two white stripes near the top of each sleeve – my first Gilbert jumper. I also got a pair of dark blue parallels, a Bay City Rollers shirt, a few pairs of hooped Bay City Rollers socks and a pair of platform shoes.

One day nearer Christmas a photographer came to the house to take a photo of us. He had a large, black camera slung around his neck. Me ma had told us earlier that she'd been given money by the British government because they'd killed me da, and that the *Daily Mirror* were here to take a picture.

'I'm not goin' into it,' said Patrick.

'Why not?' asked me ma.

'Jist, I'm not goin' in.'

I didn't want to go into the photo either. There was something I didn't like about the whole thing but I wanted to please me ma. I'd heard that the mother of Michael Kelly, who was only seventeen when he was killed on Bloody Sunday, had been discovered by her family during a snowstorm covering his grave with blankets to keep him warm. I had an image in my mind of the white-haired mother in the cemetery not accepting that her young son was dead. And here was me ma getting us to dress up for a photo.

The other five of us went upstairs to put on our new clothes. As we were dressing in the bedroom our Paul said that he didn't want to go into the photo either, but I told him it was for me ma and he carried on getting dressed. When we all went downstairs to the sitting room, Patrick sat in one of the white leather chairs with a face on him. Me ma sat down on the other white leather chair facing the sitting-room window, and we gathered round her in our new clothes for the photographer to take his picture of us, all smiling. It appeared on the front cover of the *Daily Mirror* a few days later, along with the story that me ma got money from the government. I thought my new Gilbert jumper looked class in the photo.

On Christmas morning I got two things: another box of Big League (there was a huge casualty list from the first) and a Bay City Rollers LP. Derek, Alan, Leslie, Stuart and Eric smiled happily on the sleeve as they sat in their lovely jumpers, checked shirts and perfectly parted hair. Having been forgiven for wiping his eye with Kitty Gallagher, me and Benny started hanging around the Walkers' house, playing the Rollers over and over again on their record player. 'Shang-A-Lang' was our favourite. The added attraction was Dawn Walker, who was the same age as me and had gorgeous round eyes. Her older sister, Veronica, was sixteen. She was tall and fair-haired and one of her hands was malformed, with only the tiniest fingers protruding from her wrist. Their mother, Teresa, was a small, dark-haired woman with a sharp Birmingham accent. She shouted a lot at her wains. Benny said she was bad with her nerves. Mr Walker had been jailed in England. His wains told us he was innocent, and they were heartbroken that the English police told him he would never be free to see his beloved Derry again.

We practised the words of 'Shang-A-Lang' until we got them right and then put on performances in the sitting room while everyone watched from the sofa and the floor. Me and Benny paired up, as did our Paul and Seán, practising our moves and words in the scullery, before performing with Veronica's and Dawn's Roller scarves tied to our wrists. Benny knew all the dances and moves from his da, who was still a Teddy Boy. My favourite was when he bent over and put his hands on his knees, moving them in and out, closing and opening, crossing his hands quickly from knee to knee. I copied him and learnt to do it very well as we swayed to the Rollers and boogied to Mud and Showaddywaddy.

8

TO SCHOOL
OR NOT TO SCHOOL

I'd passed the 11-plus to go to St Columb's College in Bishop Street, beginning in September 1974. Apparently me and Ciarán McLaughlin got the highest marks in the school. Me ma had heard this from someone in the factory. A lot of boys from our Primary Seven year at Long Tower ended up at the college, and it was good to see them all on our first day. That was all the good there was, because the older boys, mostly Second Years, ran around picking on us 'Yaps', or First Years, walking or dragging us into the toilets and trying to stick our heads down the toilet bowl. But I fought back and the Second Years moved on to other, more placid prey.

Bootsy, an old priest, was our form teacher and taught us history from a book called *Celts and Normans*. Fr McGarrigle taught us Latin from a small blue book called *Ecce Romani*. Mr Doherty taught us French using a tape-recorder, playing the same sentence over and over again: *Quelle heure est-il?* This became Mr Doherty's nickname, often shortened to *Quelle heure*. We thought *Quelle heure* looked like a Frenchman, with his baldy head, wee round glasses and blue Citroën car. Mr Kelly from Creggan taught us English and geography.

I made two new friends: Mickey Quigley and Malachy Bradley. Mickey had black, curly hair and the makings of a black moustache; Malachy also had black hair, but his was straight and shoulder-length. One day after school the three of us walked up Bishop Street in our new uniforms, heading towards Foyle Street to get the bus home. We sang pop songs as we walked, carrying our new brown-leather briefcases packed with books. As we passed the old jail beside the Fountain Estate, two older boys, who looked about fifteen, came out of a gate. One of them had a hammer in his hand. They walked towards us from the other side of the road. We knew they were Protestants as they'd come out of the Fountain, and we also knew that the hammer wasn't for straightening nails! Me and Malachy began to drop back as they approached but Mickey kept on walking towards Bishop's Gate. As the gap between us widened they went for him. The boy with the hammer swung it at Mickey's head and he dodged back like a boxer avoiding a haymaker. I started laughing. I don't know why I laughed. It wasn't funny.

'Run, Mickey!' we shouted.

Mickey stood his ground, and as the boy with the hammer swung it at him again, Mickey swung back at him with his briefcase. Both missed their target, but Mickey's swinging was a sign that he was up for the fight. The boy came at him

again with the hammer and missed again. The other Protestant boy hadn't joined in the attack but hung back, keeping
an eye on us. Mickey was swinging his briefcase in front of
him like a boy possessed, backing his way up towards Bishop's
Gate as he swung, eventually making a run for it up towards
the Gate as we called after him, cheering him on.

'We'll see ye down in Foyle Street, Mickey!' we shouted up
the street to him, and he gave us the thumbs up as he disappeared through the Gate.

Few of the college teachers appeared to like the boys
in our class. They rarely smiled except to be sarcastic and
used any excuse to slap us on the hands with heavy leather
straps. The worst thing was coming in late for assembly on
a cold morning and getting strapped by whoever was in
charge. There was always a line of late-comers blowing on
their cold hands to warm them up before getting strapped.
We had to hold our hands out straight and at a certain level
to get strapped, so that the teacher could get a good swing
at them. Everyone tried to raise them higher to lessen the
blow from the strap as it swiped through the air towards our
freezing hands. You had to time it right though, leaving it
to the last millisecond before contact, otherwise you'd get
an extra whack for being a Smart Alec. The pain and the
numbness lasted for hours. I hated Latin, hated maths and
hated French, but didn't mind geography and English. For
art we had Miss Grant, a young, blonde teacher who wore

hippy-type clothes. We played rugby, football and, the odd time, hurling.

We got the school bus to the college up in Carnhill. One morning on the bus another First Year student pulled down the front of his elasticated trousers, showing everyone his dicky, which was hard. He said, 'Look at that, ya boy, ye!', before putting it away again. All the other boys laughed. While I joined in the laughter, I wondered why his dicky was hard.

Brian Deery was in our class. He had dark hair, a bird's beak for a nose and a permanent smile on his face. He invited me and Malachy Bradley down to his house in Ivy Terrace one lunchtime, saying that his ma had a pot of soup ready. Ivy Terrace turned out to be much like Hamilton Street, with the houses painted a variety of clashing colours. His ma was in the scullery at the back of the house. We sat down in the sitting room as she brought the soup, along with some bread for dipping, as usual.

'Can we take the soup upstairs, Ma?' asked Brian.

'Naw, ye'll have soup everywhere. Yis can go up when yis are finished.'

Brian had been telling us about his bedroom and we couldn't wait to see it. It was full of army toys, like Action Man. He even had a huge army tank, which sat on his bedroom floor with an Action Man inside it. Class! Neither Malachy nor I had an Action Man. They were far too dear. We played with the toys for a while before heading back to school.

On the way, I happened to ask Brian something about his da.

'Me da doesn't live wi' us,' he said.

'What d'ye mean?' I asked.

'He lives in his own house.'

'What d'ye mean?'

'They're split up and I live wi' me ma.'

'What? Your ma 'n' da don't live in the same house?'

'Naw. They're split up a brave while now. Me da lives out the Glen.'

Jesus, I thought, *I've never seen the likes of this before!* And from the look on his face, neither had Malachy.

We went back down to Brian's house after school. Brian's ma was still in and I looked at her when we went in the front door to see if I could see anything different about her. I wondered if not living with her husband would change her appearance, but she looked perfectly normal. We went up and played with the Action Man toys again, putting plastic guns and belts on them, and changing their helmets and berets.

After a while we decided we should head down to Foyle Street to get the bus home. We began to sing pop songs as we dandered across Ivy Terrace and on to Abercorn Road, Malachy with his briefcase and me with a new brown-and-white Kung Fu bag over my shoulder. We were singing 'Shang-A-Lang' by the Rollers as we headed down Abercorn and past the tall, three-storey houses towards the even taller red-brick factory, when I noticed that my shoelaces were undone. I stopped and bent down and, as I went to tie them, the way me da taught me when I was eight, a huge monkey wrench fell right in front of me with a loud smack, cracking the concrete footpad. Me and Mal looked up to see two grown men in navy blue overalls looking down at us from the steel scaffolding they were working on. They didn't speak and neither did we. They didn't move, but just looked down at us with stern faces. I didn't know why. I hurriedly tied my lace, grabbed my Kung Fu bag, and we scurried on down the street with the crack of the monkey wrench ringing in my ears. Me and Mal agreed that they must have been loyalists and one of them had dropped the wrench on purpose.

***

In the first few months of 1975 I decided I really hated the college and wasn't going back. Our Patrick had been dobbing since his first year in St Peter's Secondary School in Creggan, and had been caught a couple of times. Our house was like a sanctuary for dobbers, full of the older Boyles, Julie and Bobby, our Karen and Patrick, and the twin Hogan sisters. Me ma was back working in the shirt factory since Glenn, the youngest in the family, started school. I was off sick one day and couldn't believe my eyes – they were in our sitting room, drinking tea, eating gravy rings, smoking and watching 'Roobarb and Custard' cartoons on the TV! I decided to dob too, and instead of going to school, me and Seán Boyle walked around the various building sites that had sprung up around Bloomfield and Brookdale. It was snowing and freezing cold, but we had our lunch money so we bought some tarts in a local shop and ate them in one of the half-built houses that had windows and a roof. We did the same the next day, and then the whole week went by without us going to school.

On the Sunday, Seán told me he'd have to go back to school, so I persuaded our Paul to dob along with me. Paul was still in Primary 7 at Long Tower.

'On'y wan day, Paul,' I said.

'What if me ma finds out?'

'Sure, she's in the factory all day. She'll never know.'

The following day, we headed to the building site. We had a pack of cards to play Snap on the dusty wooden floors of the unfinished houses. The workmen never seemed to be working when we were dobbing. The dobbing days turned into weeks and we still weren't caught. Every day we bought jam tarts in the shop, played cards and dandered around.

One particularly cold and snowy day, we couldn't get into any of the half-built houses to keep dry. They were all boarded up. We had to stand against a gable wall to shelter from the falling snow. Our leaky shoes were soaking wet and our feet and hands were freezing.

'D'ye think we should go home?' asked Paul.

'Naw, someone'll see us and tell me ma. That Dolly Bradley wan has eyes like a hawk!'

'It's effin' freezing!' Paul still didn't curse and neither did I. The snow was still falling as we stood at the miserable gable.

'What d'ye reckon? Will we take the chance?' I asked.

In five minutes we'd crossed the snow-covered green up to our back gate, lifted the spare key from its hiding place behind the concrete fence-post and were inside our empty house. Once in the sitting room we lit the gas fire, took off our shoes and wet socks and huddled around the heat to thaw out. We thought we'd celebrate by making tea and toast, but as we settled back on the white leather sofa, ready to take our first bite of the warm toast, I saw the flash of me ma's latest car, a bright-yellow Cortina XL, pass the steamed-up sitting-room window. It drew up in the drive at the side of the house which we shared with the flats next door.

'Jesus! There's me ma!' I shouted, and both of us jumped up. Sure enough, there she was, getting out of her car and heading across the garden to the front door! Me and Paul cleared out the back door, leaving our warm tea and toast on the floor in front of the gas fire, as well as our steaming socks.

The shock of the freezing snow on our bare feet was fierce, but before we knew it we'd run along by the back fence and hidden behind the garden wall of the flats next door. There we stood for a few minutes in the falling snow, breathing puffs of frost into the air, our hearts racing in panic.

The back door opened.

'Tony and Paul, git in here *now!*' called me ma from the back step.

We said nothing. We just pretended we weren't there as we froze, knees knocking and teeth chattering, attempting to deny our fate.

'Tony and Paul Doherty! C'mon on in before yis git yer death out there!' Her tone had softened. We stood on for a few more moments, still not answering. It took a minute or two for it to dawn on us that there was no good way out of this.

'We'll have to go in,' I said to Paul, whose mop of sandy hair was coated with snowflakes.

'I know,' he said sadly, and we tiptoed back the way we had come. Me ma was at the sink in the scullery.

'How long have yis been dobbin' for?' she asked.

I looked at Paul; he looked towards the floor. I was the eldest.

'A few weeks jist,' I replied.

'A few fuckin' weeks! Holy Jesus this day, what am I goney do wi' yis!'

Me and Paul stood facing her as she turned away towards the sink and put her dark head down and shook it slowly from side to side, confirming that she *really* didn't know what she was going to do with us. We were not to be allowed out to play with our friends and would be sent back to school the next day. Being kept in turned out to be two weeks of mental torture as we watched every wain in the street skidding by on the ice outside our window and making snowmen in their front gardens.

When I went back to the college the next day I discovered I'd forgotten any French and Latin I'd learned, and some of the teachers referred to me as 'The Absent Mr Doherty'. I'd fallen too far behind in almost all the core subjects. The only things I looked forward to in the college were getting a battered sausage and a scoop of chips at dinner time, singing pop songs with Mal on the way home, and smoking. I'd taken up smoking from Benny. You could get a single fag, a Sovereign or a No. 6 for a few pence in any shop. Sovereign were the cheapest, but Benny said they made you fart.

In the spring, when it was warmer, me and Seán Boyle decided to dob again. We were rambling through fields when we came across three donkey foals lying dead at the foot of a steep slope of a small, grassy quarry. One was a brown-and-white piebald, another was chocolate brown all over, and the third was dark grey. They looked like stuffed animals just lying in the sun. We stroked their dead faces and contemplated burying them, then thought the better of it and rambled on.

The whole house, except me ma, got boils all over us, though not on our faces. The doctor had to come out and brought large brown jars of white cream to rub on them. We all gathered round him in the sitting room and he used Patrick to show us how to put it on with cotton wool.

'Now, make sure you don't put it on your face, or it'll sting you,' he said.

We rubbed the freezing cold cream on the fiery red boils and let it dry in before putting our clothes on over it. Karen and me ma put the cream on Colleen and Glenn. It was great because we were allowed to stay off school. The boils went away, though, after a few days, and then it was back to the college.

Me ma was out a lot. I worked out, as Karen and Patrick had, that she just wasn't sharp enough to know what we were up to. She was out nearly every night, even during the week. I still lay in bed at night, refusing to go to sleep until I heard her car pulling up outside. Sometimes John would be with her and sometimes not. One evening, I thought I heard something break outside as me ma's car swung into the drive. The next morning I got up for school and saw the yellow Cortina had been driven through next door's fence, with the front wheels in the garden.

Me, Patrick and Paul all helped out in the house, normally with Karen as leader, and if me ma was working in the factory, we made the dinner in the early evening. There was no choice. It was either do it ourselves or depend on me ma who, between working and being out at night, had passed control to Karen. Hoovering, dusting, shining brasses and making the beds were all shared between us, just like in Hamilton Street. Me ma still made the Sunday dinner, and if John was about, the two of them made it. They made the most gorgeous roast dinner together. Some Sundays we went to the Grianán of Aileach Hotel, just across the border, for our dinner. Benny often came with us. When the weather was good we went to Buncrana in the car.

'Will we take Brandy, Ma?' asked our Paul.

'Naw, she'll smell up me car if she goes into the water.'

'Aw Ma, g'won let us bring her,' we all said. Brandy was sitting in the front garden wagging her tail and looking at us with uncertain eyes as we argued.

'Naw. I'm not bringing her and that's it! She'll be gran' in the street till we come back.'

We all piled into the car and drove off, leaving a sad-faced Brandy sitting in the garden. As we drove off our Paul rolled down the window and shouted 'C'mon, Brandy! C'mon!' and Brandy took off on her four running legs after the car.

'Ach Ma, ye'll have to let her in now!' said Karen in the front seat.

'Naw, Karen. I'm not havin' it the day,' me ma snapped back at her.

She's probably finished wi' John, I thought.

Brandy sprinted after the car as we drove out of the estate and onto the road. 'C'mon, Brandy! C'mon, ya girl ye!' we shouted from the window, as if we were shouting after a racing dog at the Brandywell. Brandy kept coming after us but was a good two hundred yards behind. At one stage we thought she'd turned back, but then she appeared again round a bend when we were at a T-junction. It was make or break for Brandy as we turned onto Buncrana Road, as there was no hope of her catching up on the main road till we reached the Brit checkpoint. As we took off down the main road all our eyes were looking out the side and back windows of the car to see if she was still in sight. There she was! Running with all her might! She was a wee brown speck galloping along at the side of the road.

'Aw, Ma! Ye canny do that to the wee dog!'

'Aw, I suppose so,' me ma sighed as she slowly pulled the car in to the kerb.

'C'mon, Brandy! C'mon, ya pup, ye!' we called to Brandy who, seeing the car had stopped, sprinted even faster. I got out and opened the boot as she approached. She leapt straight in and jumped over the back seat where we rubbed and petted her as she gasped and panted for air. Me and Paul travelled the rest of the journey in the boot along with her and were clattered in dog hairs by the time we smelled the sea at Lisfannon.

On the last Saturday in August, just as I was dreading going back to the college the following Monday, a letter came informing me ma that I'd been expelled. I was over the moon! No more *Ecce* effin' *Romani* or *Celts and* scabby *Normans* for me! Instead of going to the college, I was to go to me granny's on Monday for her to take me to St Joseph's

Secondary School in Creggan. Benny was in the Third Year at St Joe's and I was looking forward to walking up and back with him.

Me and me granny walked down Westway from Central Drive, passing a Brit checkpoint on the way.

'Don't you open yer mouth to them boys, OK?' she said.

'OK, Granny,' I said as I threw dirty looks at the soldiers who were stopping cars on the road. Others lay between hedges pointing their rifles up the street.

At St Joe's we waited outside the office of the Principal, a man called Ted Armstrong. The floors were highly polished and the paintwork on the walls and doors was new and neat. The smell of floor polish competed with the smell of new paint.

'Hello, Sally! How's your John and the rest doing?' said Ted. He didn't look at me as I sat on the chair next to me granny.

'Aye, they're all doin' gran'. Not wan on the bru. John's up working in Belfast. He's a social worker,' said Sally.

'God, isn't that great!' said Ted.

'Our Joseph's still here.'

'Ach, sure I see Joseph every day,' said Ted. 'A right fella he is! How's his asthma?'

'Ach, he's up an' down wi' it, but he jist batters on.'

Mr Armstrong shifted his eyes from me granny to me. I was enjoying the banter but not him looking at me. He had a yellow fringe on his otherwise pure white hair, parted at the side and swept across his head.

'So, young Doherty, you've been up to no good,' he said from his woman-red lips.

I stayed quiet but looked back at him with eyes that I hoped said, 'I don't mean any trouble for you!'

'I don't know if I should take you in, young man. You've squandered a wonderful chance in life, haven't you?'

'I have, sir,' I said, not meaning it.

'What did you do?'

'I dobbed for weeks.'

'You dobbed for weeks?'

'Aye, I hated the college and ...'

'You dobbed for weeks? There'll be no dobbing here!' he said, pulling a huge leather strap out of his drawer.

'No, sir! I'll be here every day.'

'Stand up, Doherty.'

I stood and so did he. He came round his desk, walked towards a cabinet and took out a thick, red-leather Bible. He placed it before me on the desk. He was really close to me. I could smell the stale smoke off him.

'Put your hand on the Bible, young Doherty,' he said in a low voice.

I put my hand awkwardly on the red Bible. I'd never liked drama.

'Say after me: "I swear".'

'I swear.'

'I swear to God that I will attend St Joseph's School every day.'

'I swear to God that I will attend St Joseph's School every day.'

'And that I will be the perfect student at this school.'

'And that I will try my hardest to be the perfect student at this school.'

'Not try, young Doherty, not try!' said Mr Armstrong, his voice raised. I couldn't believe what I'd said!

'And that I will be the perfect student at the school!' he repeated.

'And that I will try my …' I'd said it again! *Jesus, what was I on about!* I screamed inside.

'Tony!' me granny hissed from her chair.

'No, young Doherty, no!' roared Ted from his red face into my red face.

'Sorry, sir, sorry. And that I will be the perfect student at this school! I definitely will, sir,' I said with pleading eyes and a face redder now than Ted's own beetroot chops.

'Very well,' said Ted. 'Go you outside while I have a chat to your grandmother about this.'

I left and sat on a chair outside, looking out the high-panelled windows at the houses on Westway.

I started St Joe's the next morning, getting the bus with wee Benny.

'Your form teacher's in the IRA,' said Benny one morning as we travelled to school. St Joe's didn't have a uniform, so we could wear our parallels and hooped socks. My form teacher, Kevin McCallion, was a tall man with brown, curly hair and glasses. He was from Creggan. He was big into English, forcing poetry and Shakespeare on us twelve-year-olds. I accepted what Benny said, but had great difficulty squaring that a Shakespeare-loving schoolteacher could also be in the IRA.

'He's not the on'y wan,' said Benny, clearly in the know.

Even though Benny was smaller than me, he was older and wiser. It was his smallness that earned him the name Benny, from the 'Top Cats' TV cartoon. We bussed to school each morning and walked back each afternoon, smoking and singing pop songs. We often dallied so as to be at the Collon as the Thornhill girls' college bus came in. Anything Benny wanted to do, I wanted to do as well. In robbing the plum orchards on the Buncrana Road, Benny led and I followed. In stealing pens in the APCK Stationers in Shipquay Street, Benny showed me and I copied. In telling me who he thought was in the IRA, teachers or otherwise, Benny spoke and I took all in. Except when it came to cursing. I'd never uttered a single curse in my life. Benny cursed. Boiler cursed. Our Karen cursed. Everybody effin' cursed! Even our Paul cursed by that time. I related my non-cursing habit to me da. Me not cursing was me being loyal to him, as the main reason I'd never cursed

227

was out of fear of him. I'd resisted Benny's numerous invites to curse until the following conversation took place:

'G'won, curse, Tony,' said Benny.

'Naw!'

'Say fuck!'

'Naw!'

'Say bastard!'

'Naw, Benny!'

'G'won, jist the wan fuck!'

'Naw, I don't wanny!'

'G'won, Tony, jist say fuck!'

'Naw, eff you off, Benny!'

'Eff off, Benny!' he mocked in a girly voice. 'For fuck's sake, Dutchie, jist the wan fuck!'

'Naw, I'm not sayin' it!'

'Here, I'll give ye wan o' these,' he said, taking a pair of two-bob coins from his pocket.

'Naw, Benny, I don't wanny,' I said, eyeing up the silver in his palm.

'Wan fuck and it's yours!' he said, rubbing the two coins between his hands.

'Fuck!' I said. It just came out!

'Jesus!'

'What?'

'Ye said it!'

'Fuck?'

'Aye! Ye cursed!'

'Ah know. Gis me two bob!'

'Naw!' he laughed and let on to run away. We were on the green behind our back fence.

'See you, Benny!' I said and began to walk into the back garden with my head down and about to cry.

'Aw here, Dutchie!' said Benny, running after me and catching me by the arm. I felt him fingering the two bob into my hand.

'You're a wee fucker!' I said, feeling the strange bluntness of the fuck word on my tongue.

'Ye didn't say bastard yit!'

'You're a wee fucking bastard!' I laughed, revelling in the cockiness of my new, long-forbidden words.

Just then, as I stood facing Benny in our back garden, there was a massive explosion. I felt tremors in the ground beneath me and heard all the windows in the whole street rattle and shake.

Oh gentle Jesus! I screamed silently, as Benny fixed his wide eyes and open mouth on the sky just behind my head.

Oh Jesus, what's he lookin' at? I screamed silently again, afraid to look around. I turned my head slowly, to see a huge, white plume, a cloud like a nuclear explosion, rising from the back road several fields away from us.

Thank Jesus! I said to myself, relieved that it was only a bomb and not the earth opening up for me for cursing. We headed down to the shop for a loose Sovereign fag and some sweets. I didn't curse again for a brave while, but the spell had been broken.

***

Benny was renowned as a rioter and knew by whatever means when a riot was due to take place in the Bog. After school one day, me, Benny and Martin 'Monga' McMonagle from his class headed down to Rossville Street to the riot. Monga was from Carnhill, and his big brother, Neil, was in the INLA. Rossville Street was full of teenagers just out of school, many in their college uniforms and black Oxfords, with steel-tipped heels so they click-clacked along the hard footpad when they walked or ran. Oxfords were a shoe to respect, to save up for and cherish when you got a pair. They didn't come with the steel tip on the heel: they were left with the shoemakers in the Collon at the bottom of Racecourse Road to be tipped. I had me ma tortured for months to buy me a pair. When she did eventually, I walked the two miles from our house to the Collon to collect my brand new shoes with tips. They smelled strongly of Evo-Stic and boot polish. I put them on in the shoemakers, as I wanted to be heard and seen, clicking and clacking my way up the Racecourse to Shanty to show them off. Oxfords were worn constantly, till your big toe wore its way through the upper or they got too small.

The soldiers were lined up behind their tall shields at the

junction with William Street and we bombarded them with bricks and bottles. Blue-uniformed girls from St Mary's and green-uniformed girls from St Cecilia's and Thornhill lined the street in clumps, smoking and watching the boys rioting, and the boys watched the girls watching them. One long-haired boy in a full Wrangler suit and clickety Oxfords led us rioters repeatedly down towards the corner to throw our stones and bottles at the Brits.

Benny was full of good advice on rioting: 'Always make sure ye have plenty of room around ye, so ye can run if the snatch squad comes,' he said.

I had strange, mixed feelings of hatred and pity towards the Brits, but I didn't tell anyone that I pitied them. Most were only a few years older than us, covered in spots, the same yellow-headed pimples that were appearing on my chin and jaw blade. I aimed every stone, though, thrown with all the might of my strong right arm, and hoped it would connect with a Brit's body.

Many of the young soldiers had little or no education and would have been regarded as dunces if they'd attended a school like St Joe's. This is one of the reasons I pitied them as much as I hated them.

One evening, I was stopped by a teenage soldier on Racecourse Road in Shanty. I gave him my name and he asked: 'Can you spell Doherty, please?'

'Yes, I can.'

He smiled and said, 'But can you spell it for me?'

'OK. D-O-B-R-O-W-S-K-I.'

He wrote it down in his wee black book and, without batting an eyelid, moved on to Boiler, who gave him an equally Polish-sounding spelling of Boyle, which the soldier wrote down, before walking away with the rest of his patrol into the streetlit alleyways of Shanty.

The riot was now in full swing on Rossville Street.

'Hi you, ya black bastard! Away back to the jungle!' a boy screamed as he threw his stone at a black soldier dodging behind a shield.

'Fuck, Seamus, there's yer ma!' someone called.

'Where?' said Seamus, the leader in second-hand Wranglers and Oxfords, looking around him in panic.

'She's coming down the street. Git behind me! Quick!'

'Aw, fuck!' said Seamus.

'You, boy!' shouted his ma, who was wearing her light-blue factory overalls and an orange headscarf.

'You, boy!' she repeated, grabbing Seamus by his long hair and walking him out of the throng up Rossville Street.

'Aw, Ma, wise up!' he cried as the Brits banged their shields, laughing their heads off. His Oxfords sounded a hollow and pathetic click-clack as his ma walked him up the street past dozens of giggling girls.

'Git up to that fuckin' house, boy!' we heard her hiss into his ear.

I loved the feel of the hard stone in my hand. I gripped it really tight in my throwing hand while holding another in my left. I was a good long thrower with a deadly aim. I didn't care to hide my face the way the older boys did, using hankies tied behind their heads. I didn't care who saw me as I ran the length of Rossville Street, stopping only a few yards from the corner, before throwing my stones with all my might. Seeing my own stone smacking the side of a Sixer or whacking a riot shield full-on gave me a great feeling.

At the end of the riot, me and Benny had to get into the town for the bus. Our hands were boggin' with dirt so we knocked at a house and asked the woman could we wash our hands and she let us into her scullery. We decided to go up past the Rossville Flats towards Butcher Gate. We stood for a moment at me da's green-painted square which someone kept neat and tidy with new paint, before heading up the steps towards the Butcher Gate checkpoint. The Brits checked our hands for dirt from throwing stones and searched us as we stood with our hands up and our legs spread, before letting us into the city centre for the bus home.

'The OC of the Fianna was down at the riot the day. Did ye not see 'im?' said Benny on the bus. Fianna na hÉireann was the junior wing of the IRA.

'Naw, I didn't,' I said, disappointed.

***

The Shantallow IRA started hanging around Brookdale. They wore Wrangler suits with the legs turned up at the bottom and Oxfords. They clicked and clacked quickly up and down the street in groups, talking out of the sides of their mouths. You could hear their Oxfords coming from a country mile away! Our Karen was going out with one of them. He had long, brown hair, parted in the middle like everyone else. They came to our house to drink tea and eat biscuits before heading off again when someone else called for them. I heard them talk about a place called Castlereagh, where boys were badly beaten until they made statements incriminating themselves. *An Phoblacht (The Republic)*, which we got every Friday night, gave accounts of men and women from Ballymurphy and Turf Lodge being tortured and thrown out of windows. It sounded like a very dark and scary place.

We reckoned that a big part of the attraction for the Shanty IRA were the nearly finished houses in which they could keep stuff, probably for days on end. By 1977 new housing estates had sprung up in the fields surrounding Brookdale, and a new chapel had been built on the far side of the green below Brookdale to accommodate the growing population. Me ma's John had moved into a new house nearby with his wife and wains. A schoolfriend of Boiler's, Conor McCloskey, moved into a new estate called Fergleen Park, which you could see from the back of our house. His family was from Ardmore and had been intimidated out by loyalists. Everyone in his family had black hair, except the da, who was grey. Conor had huge hands, spoke with a country accent and talked about his big brother Dermot's collection of music. When Dermot was out, Conor brought some of his records to our house to play on our smart teak 'music centre', which had a record player, radio, tape-deck, built-in speakers and a wee press to hold the records.

Our Patrick had joined a record club and got brand new records in the post for free. Sometimes he didn't even have to order them. They did send letters now and again looking for their money, but Patrick just said, 'Fuck them and all belongin' to them', and threw the letters in the bin. The record press was bunged with The Beatles, Simon & Garfunkel, the Eagles, Fleetwood Mac's 'Rumours', and hits of the 1950s and 1960s.

I called at Conor's house one evening to bring him over to our house to play records. He came out with a bag of LPs under his arm and talked the short distance from his house to mine about Bruce Springsteen's *The Wild, the Innocent & the E Street Shuffle*, David Bowie's *The Rise and Fall of Ziggy Stardust and the Spiders from Mars*, and someone called Boz Scaggs.

He fair knows his stuff, I thought, as we made our way in the back door.

'Our Dermot said that *Ziggy Stardust* is the best album ever made,' said Conor. I hadn't known what an album was, but quickly worked out that it was an LP. We put *Ziggy Stardust* on first. When 'Starman' came on I realised it was the first time I'd heard it in a brave while. 'Starman' was me and me da's secret, so I didn't tell Conor what it meant to me.

Our Patrick came in. I knew he'd joined the Fianna and had begun hanging around with them. He showed us how to tune in to the Brits and cops speaking on long wave on the radio. It was very crackly, but if you listened carefully you could make out some of the messages. It became hard to concentrate as there was a row going on in the street.

'Brian and Janice are at it again,' he said.

We gathered over the back of the sofa to look across the street. Janice was screaming at the top of her voice from inside the flat at Brian, who was standing outside the open door on the footpad. As she continued to scream, he backed further off onto the grass. There was a pause in the screaming and Janice appeared in a flowery frock outside the flat. She tore paper up and threw it in his face, like large confetti, before stomping in again and slamming the front door. Brian walked away, his head down, on another sad and aimless ramble. The paper she'd torn looked like blue fivers. It was Brian's bru! It *was* blue fivers! It was *money* she'd torn up!

Our Paul had been in the front street playing Padsy with Aiden Glenn, bouncing the football off the edge of the opposite kerb. They'd seen the row and stopped playing to take all in. Patrick went to the front door and called Paul over in a whisper. He had to move fast.

'Brian's bru! That mad eejit jist tore up Brian's bru!' he said.

'I know, we saw it as well,' said Paul.

'G'won, sneak over and lift as many of the pieces as ye can.'

'Naw, I'm not goin' near it! She's a lunatic!'

'Tony, will you go over wi' 'im?'

I looked across towards the flat. The curtains were closed in her front window and the door had been slammed shut. It seemed safe enough.

'Aye, c'mon Paul,' I said, and the two of us and Aiden Glenn quickly walked to where the torn-up money was strewn on the grass and footpad: red, white and blue – all fivers. We gathered up all the strips and took them to our scullery table, where Patrick, using Sellotape, pieced them back together like small jigsaws.

Later that night I heard Brian wailing like a banshee as he walked around the back lanes of Brookdale Park with nowhere to go. Me and Benny were in our sitting room when we both decided to take matters into our own young hands. We'd write a letter!

'Dear Janice, this is the 3rd Battalion Provisional IRA in Shanty. You are battering your husband and leaving him yamming in the street every night. We have received complaints from your neighbours and they are all browned off with it. Stop battering your man. If we receive any more complaints about you again, we'll do ye. There will be no more warnings.'

We put the letter in an envelope, wrote 'Janice' on it, and

sneaked round the long way, posting it through the letterbox before tearing back the way we came, in case she caught us.

Over the next few nights we listened to the Brits and cops on long wave on the radio to see if Janice had reported the letter. There was no mention of Janice or the letter, but Brian's beatings stopped.

***

We were woken early one morning; the Brits were raiding the house. I'd heard the two Jeeps squeaking to a halt outside, followed by loud knocking on the door. I was up when me ma came in to tell us all to get dressed and come downstairs. There were around six soldiers in the scullery and sitting room. They'd lined their SLR rifles neatly along the scullery wall and allowed me ma to search them in case they planted something before they started their own search upstairs. Karen and Patrick made tea and toast, which we ate and drank sitting on the white leather sofa as the soldiers took their time rummaging around the house. One stood at the scullery door and one in the hall beside the front door. Some of the neighbours had gathered outside the front garden, standing with their arms folded, looking concerned. The search went on and on. We could hear one of the soldiers climbing up to the attic, beds rolling in and out, and furniture being shifted.

Karen stood up in the sitting room.

'C'mon, Colleen and Glenn, wi' me: I'm goin' to git yis

ready for school,' she said, and led them upstairs past a soldier who stepped out of her way. A few minutes later Colleen and Glenn came down, washed and dressed, and were allowed to leave the house to walk to school. I was hoping the search would go on long enough so that we'd be too late for school. My wish came true, as, when they'd finished searching the house, they began searching the back hall and the alleyway, and poked around the gardens. At around ten o'clock, as they were getting ready to leave, the leader brought me ma out to the scullery to search each soldier to confirm they hadn't stolen anything.

'Mrs Doherty,' the soldier said, 'will you sign this to say that there was no damage to your house?'

'What is it?'

'It's just a chit to say there was no damage.'

'Naw, I'm not signing anything. Yis finished?'

'Yes, ma'am.'

'Well, away yis go and may it be a long time before yis darken my door again!'

When they left, me ma agreed that it was too late for us to go to school, so we spent the day playing cards and Monopoly.

One day shortly after this, there was a mini riot outside St Joe's. Just a few stones and a bottle or two.

'Hi, Kunta Kinte!' someone called across the street to the young black soldier on patrol. He was kneeling at a gable wall with his rifle across his thighs. He was the last man in the patrol. The last man was usually black. The last man was the most likely to get shot in an attack. We were starting to walk home from school, having spent our bus money on fags.

'Hi, Kunta Kinte, away back to the jungle ye came outa!'

As the black soldier looked away into the distance, pretending not to hear, another soldier called, 'Hey, Chalky! He must be talking to you!' and all the other soldiers laughed. We all laughed. The mini riot came to nothing and I began to walk home with Jim Duddy. Jim was a thin, scruffy fella about my height, but with a permanent frown creasing his forehead. He was the smartest boy in our class.

'Paul Harvey's brother's missin', ye know,' said Jim, as we walked through Rosemount, where he lived.

'Aye?'

'He didn't come back from the Training Centre wan day and they're lookin' for 'im. They think he might've thrown 'imself in the Foyle.'

'What d'ye mean, "thrown 'imself in the Foyle"?'

'Fuck, but you're slow!'

'What?'

'They reckon he's drownded 'imself.'

'He drownded 'imself?' I'd never heard of such a thing before. 'What would 'e have done that for?'

'I dunno. Nobody knows.'

'Jesus, man. Why?' I asked as we parted at the Rosemount factory. As I began the long walk home, I wondered why Paul

Harvey's brother, who I didn't know, could put himself into such a cold and grey river.

Our Karen's boyfriend was arrested and charged, and was in prison for a large number of serious IRA activities. Karen told me ma in the scullery that he'd been tortured and was forced to sign statements, but that he was hoping some of the more serious charges would be dropped. It appeared that everyone arrested was forced to sign statements in Castlereagh or Strand Road RUC Barracks which would put them away for long years. Karen went up to the Crumlin Road Gaol to visit him and came home crying each time. Nearly all his Shanty IRA friends had been imprisoned as well.

9

THE AGE OF CHANGE

While the Fianna was a secret organisation, it was in many respects a fairly public one too, as among our age group it was open season for speculating as to who might be in it. This public secrecy was a great attraction. All the talk at school and elsewhere was about who was in the Fianna and who was in the Urps. All the talk in Shanty was about the Fianna, who we thought was in it and the possibility of us being allowed to join. My first cousin, Danny Doherty, was rumoured to be OC of the Fianna in Derry.

Eventually, my own opportunity came when I was fifteen. We were dobbing school up in McDevitt's, a ruin of a large old house set in grounds down by the river beyond Culmore Road. Robbie, who for certain was in the Fianna in Shanty, was dobbing the same day. Six of us sat around smoking under the ancient oak trees.

'I'm looking to join the Fianna,' I said to Robbie when I had the chance, out of earshot of the others. We stood amid the high grasses near the arch of a tall doorway.

'How d'ye know I'm in it?' he asked, smiling.

'I jist know,' I said, smiling too.

'Your Patrick was in the Fianna wi' me. I never liked 'im,' he said, crooking his hand downwards to signify that Patrick was too effeminate for his liking. I ignored it.

'Why d'ye want to join?'

'I jist want to.'

'You know that you'll probably end up in jail, on the run or in an early grave?'

'I do,' I said, but I thought he was being a bit dramatic.

The British Army and the RUC had tortured and imprisoned dozens of boys not much older than me, and they were now on the Blanket Protest in the H-Blocks of Long Kesh prison. They had to protest because the British were trying to make out that the IRA were criminals. Our Karen told me that her friends, the twin Hogans, hadn't seen their brother in over a year and they said they didn't know if he was alive or dead. Stories about torture in police barracks and in Long Kesh prison were in the *Republican News* each week.

Long Live The Provisionals! was written in tall, white letters on the flats above the Shanty Shops. All the talk up at Devlin's shop, where we hung around at night with the Carnhill girls in their long skirts and champagne tights, was about the IRA in South Armagh and what weapons they had. On the way home at night, me, Boiler and Conor would munch a deep-fried steak and kidney pie or a single red fish each and talk about Ireland, what kind of person could kill another with a gun up close, and what we would do to withstand torture if we were ever lifted.

At some stage each night, the Brits and the RUC would drive by in their Jeeps. Sometimes we stoned them. One such night, after pelting them, we scarpered into the square behind Devlin's, only to run smack into a waiting Brit patrol on the other side. We'd fallen into their trap! The officer lined the three of us against a wall, searched us, took our names, then took off his black leather gloves and slapped us about the face with them! The Brits all laughed, then let us go, and we walked home feeling silly for getting caught and humiliated at being slapped with the gloves.

I'd stopped saying my prayers at the foot of the bed each night. Paul had stopped too. I joined the Shantallow Library instead and took out several of Walter Macken's historical novels: *The Scorching Wind*, *The Silent People* and *Brown Lord of the Mountain*. Macken's books brought to life the drab history I'd been taught, first at the college and then at St Joe's, about the Famine, the Tan War and the Civil War that followed. I read in bed at night before saying a short prayer and thinking about me da. Me da was usually the last thing in my head at night. It was 1978, but I still missed him and felt hatred at the fact that he'd been taken from me, me ma and the rest of his family. I didn't really hate ordinary soldiers in the street, though I had no love for them, and if my endeavours at joining the Fianna were successful, and I eventually progressed into the IRA, I often wondered if I could kill one of them the way me da had been killed.

On other fronts we were moving steadily in the direction of girls and drink. One summer evening I was out with Monga. We'd talked about drinking a few times and decided to take our first alcoholic drink as soon as we could. Monga's big brother, Neil, bought us three tins of Smithwick's each, and we stood with Neil behind Carnhill Library and drank them. The drink tasted unpleasant, much like the disgusting dregs of beer bottles we sometimes sipped in the mornings after house parties. I nearly boked while forcing the third tin down. Neil guffawed, calling out, 'Git it down ye, ya boy ye!' as the beer came down my nostrils.

The effect of the bitter brown beer was pleasant afterwards, though, as me and Monga headed to the Carnhill disco nearby. We had a newfound confidence that let us speak to and have a laugh with girls, and take them out for slow dances. I must've been staggering a bit, as Mrs Barr, the Youth Leader, said to me, 'I'm keeping an eye on you and your antics, young Doherty!' In my mildly drunken state, I wondered how she knew my name.

The Carnhill disco on a Saturday night became a regular destination and we nearly always had a few tins of beer round the back before heading in. The Undertones played at the disco one night. Monga and wee Benny loved the Undertones. Benny had become a punk-rocker, leaping up and down with other punks and non-punks like myself to 'Teenage Kicks', The Boomtown Rats and The Stranglers.

One day, as we came back from school through the Guildhall Square, wee Benny spied Feargal Sharkey of The Undertones. 'Hi! Fisheye Sharkey!' he called out, jooking out from behind Shipquay Gate. Sharkey made a bolt for us across the square in his big red Dr Martens boots, but we ran up Shipquay Street and hid behind rows of hanging jeans in Speer's Wrangler shop.

As well as hanging round the shops and going to discos regularly, girls were beginning to present themselves as serious subjects of interest. I'd gone out with a few, including Kathy White, but her entire family emigrated to Australia to get their teenagers away from the Troubles. Then I went out with a dark-haired girl called Deborah from Belmont, just across the road from the top end of Carnhill. We stood and kissed for hours, with a few smoke breaks, in whatever darkened, out-of-the-way place we could find near her home. I loved kissing and rarely had the nerve to slip the hand, but sometimes I couldn't help myself. Not that it ever got me very far!

Later, I went out with a girl called Maire, whose ma owned a hairdressing salon at the bottom of Racecourse Road. They were well off. I first noticed her when she and her friends got off their school bus at the Shanty Shops, where we usually hung around for a few hours after school to watch the talent.

Maire had long legs – all the way up to her backside, as me ma would say, short, brown, styled hair and lovely pale blue eyes. I watched her one day as she dandered away from the shops with her pals and remembered seeing her before at a disco.

Our other interest at the Shanty Shops was Brenda Cooley, who took us into her house in Shantallow Crescent for tea, tarts and records. Shantallow Crescent is where, years before, I'd tried to sell the heavy bags of sticks before getting left behind and eventually lost. At Brenda's we learned to jive and double-jive in the sitting room, pushing the furniture out of the way to make space. One day, her da, Danny, came home early from the jeweller's shop he owned. He'd been evacuated because of a bomb scare. He proceeded to give me, Eddie O'Donnell and Boiler a lecture about staying away from the IRA, that it would only lead to heartbreak for our parents. Brenda sat rooted to her chair, grim-faced, staring at the carpet until her da left again.

'I'm really broke to the bone,' said Brenda, raising her eyes to the heavens.

'He's on'y doin' what any da would do,' said Eddie. '*My* da has me tortured about it.'

'I know, but that's *your* da,' replied Brenda, covering her face with her hands. 'I'm really affronted!'

We'd started going to the Shanty Community Centre for their disco on a Sunday night, in a sports hall doubling up as a dance-hall. The films *Grease* and *Saturday Night Fever* were all the rage. Brenda and a blonde, curly-haired fella called George Ryan, or 'Gorgeous George' as we nicknamed him, practised 'Summer Nights', as performed by John Travolta and Olivia Newton-John, in the sitting room, before transferring their slick dance routine to the floor of the Community Centre. Me, Boiler, Monga and Conor scranned whatever money we could to buy a carry-out of McEwan's lager from the Shanty off-licence, though we had to wait until a sympathetic older boy came along to buy it for us. Along with Skin McCauley and Eddie O'Donnell, we drank our tins of cheap beer in out-of-the-way alcoves around the huge, red-brick Carnhill High School, which was planked in a field between Carnhill, Shanty and the newly-named Galliagh, to which Brookdale, Bloomfield, Fern Park, Fergleen and other small estates belonged.

***

It was arranged that I'd be sworn in to the Fianna in a house in Creggan. I held a folded Irish tricolour in my hand and repeated an oath in the company of the Fianna Brigade Staff. The OC came down to a meeting with us in Shanty one evening. After 'falling in' in the bedroom of a house, he asked, 'Is this all we have?' We were six or seven Fianna boys sitting around a double bed. When I nodded back he said, 'God save Ireland!' It was hard to say whether he was joking or not.

Our meetings were usually held in the bedroom of a supporter's house. We 'fell in' at the beginning of each meeting and 'fell out' at its conclusion. This meant that all present stood erect and facing in the same direction, with the most senior person in the room giving orders in Irish to stand to attention, stand at ease and fall in. This meant the meeting was in session, that it was official business. It was difficult sometimes, if there were too many of us in the room, to negotiate the carpet, standard lamps and other bedroom furniture.

The Fianna acted mainly as a feeder into the IRA. We were schooled in small groups by Terence, an IRA veteran from the 1950s. He was a small, grey-haired man who sucked on a pipe, lit or unlit, as he patiently talked us through Irish history over the course of many evenings in a house in Carnhill. Another man, Jackie, who had black hair and black-tipped fingernails like me da, talked to us about our responsibility as junior IRA men. He told us not to drink or make fools of ourselves, either through taking drink or while sober, and to become young men that others would respect. Keeping out of fights was another rule. He warned us that joining the IRA would likely result in death, imprisonment or going on the run, and that, in all cases, our families would suffer. He gave us lectures on anti-interrogation techniques and how to outsmart our captors in the event of being arrested. One of the things he told us to do under interrogation was to imagine ourselves in a dark room with nothing but a flickering candle in it. We thought that was a bit mad and laughed about it as we dandered up to Shanty afterwards. It sounded a bit too religious for us as by that stage we only went to Mass reluctantly, when put under pressure.

The advice about not drinking was ignored by one and all. Each Friday night we went to the Marian Hall at the top of Shanty, and the Community Centre on a Sunday night. Having spent our money on McEwan's lager or Colt 45, we often tapped for odds in small groups outside to gather the money to get into the disco. While tapping one Sunday night I saw Maire and her friends approaching us outside the Community Centre.

'Have ye any odds on ye?' I asked her.

'Aye, why?' she asked with a generous smile.

'G'won, gis them to git in.'

'Here,' she handed me 20p.

'Sound! Can I git a wee slow dance later?'

'Aye, dead on,' she said, and I couldn't tell if she was saying aye or not, as 'dead on' could also mean 'Do you think I'm an eejit?'

All the fellas walked round and round the hall anti-clockwise in small groups with their hands in the pockets of their half-mast trousers or jeans, eyeing up the talent and waiting for the slow-set to come on. The girls danced in small groups around their handbags, or sat at tables sipping Coke or cordial and pretending not to watch the fellas on their circular travels.

Dopey Joe, the DJ, played music for all tastes. Shanty had more than its fair share of rockers with long hair and denims, who were mad into Status Quo, The Horslips and Deep Purple. When their songs came on, the rockers sprang to their feet and played air guitar as they dandered, bandy-legged, up to the front of the stage. Sometimes me, Boiler and Conor joined in for the craic, but the rockers were *really* into it, shaking their long hair all over the place. The air guitar changed swiftly to solo air drum roll and then back to air guitar as they shook their dandruff about under the flashing disco lights. Dopey Joe also played punk rock for Wee Benny and a group of Shanty punks, mostly fellas with a few girls, who stuck safety pins in their ears and spiked and coloured their hair. They pogoed up and down and shook one another by their leather coats clattered in studs and badges of punk bands. Again, we joined in, jumping up and down and pulling each other by the furry hoods of our Snorkel jackets, which everyone wore and rarely took off.

Once the slow-set started, the floor would clear. Fellas going steady with girls were usually the first to make a move to take them out for a dance. Once the floor was populated with slow-dancing couples it gave the rest of us the chance to break from the pack and head in someone's direction to ask them out. It was mortification to get bombed out, as you had to make your way back to the pack with your redner. The beer made things a bit easier, but not completely.

I thought I'd seen Maire look in my direction a few times earlier on as I dandered round the hall. She was now sitting with her friends in a row of seats against the wall. I caught her eye through the disco-lit darkness and shuffling couples, and she caught mine. This was my chance. Without warning I slunk off, pretending to head to the toilet, then veered off in her direction. She saw me coming.

'Ye fancy a dance?' I asked with a hand out. Her friends all turned away, pretending it was none of their business.

She took my hand and said, 'Aye, dead on,' and we walked out to the floor. For a slow dance you simply put your arms on the girl's waist, she placed her hands on your shoulders and you shuffled around in the one spot until the song was over and, if you liked her, you kept a hold of her till the next song came on.

'You're Maire, aren't ye?'

'Aye, and you're Tony. You went wi' my friend, Deborah.'

I quickly calculated that Deborah mustn't have said anything bad about me, otherwise Maire would have bombed me out. I remembered Boiler telling me that the girls liked the Neil Diamond song 'Red, Red Wine' and that, at a certain point in the song, if you put your hands further round the waist and pulled her in, they would let you. Sure enough, 'Red, Red Wine' came on and, about halfway through it, I put my hands right around Maire's waist and pulled her in and she let me. A sure sign of her interest.

'Can I walk you down home after?' I asked.

'Aye, dead on,' she said.

***

Fights at dances and discos were commonplace. One evening outside the Carnhill disco there was a huge and seemingly unstoppable melee as Shanty boys fought with the 'hoods' from Pennyburn. Conor McCloskey had somehow become embroiled in it when a local IRA man appeared out of no-where with a pistol in his hand and waded into the crowd.

'Aw, Jesus, don't shoot me, mister! Please don't shoot me!' shrieked Conor's unmistakable country voice. The IRA man had him by the scruff of his Snorkel and was dragging him onto the road to do, it appeared, just that!

We all survived to slag him as we dandered together down the Sticky Pad towards home.

'Aw, Mammy, don't shoot me, don't shoot me!' we shrieked in laughter into the dark night.

Marmalade, a band from Scotland, were playing in their pink suits on the stage of the Marian Hall one evening when two local republicans appeared and took the mike from the lead singer. The guitars and drums came to a clanging end, stopping jivers jiving and boppers bopping below on the floor. One of them read out a statement from a piece of sodden paper:

> The Republican Movement in Shantallow hereby gives warn-
> ing to any young person who sees these dances and discos as
> a place to practice their boxing, wrestling or Kung Fu skills.
> Somebody'll be killed if it doesn't stop. Yous know who yous
> are and so do we! This is your last warning!

When he finished, he beckoned the terrified lead singer back
to restart his pop song where he'd left off.

***

Eddie O'Donnell lived in Ardnamoyle Park with his da,
also Eddie, his ma Sally, and his sisters and brother. Their
house was only a few doors away from me Aunt Celine and
her family. We became great friends as we said goodbye
to 1978. At the Christmas disco in the Marian Hall every
fella kissed nearly every girl in the hall. We broke from our
normal staggering and swaggering anti-clockwise dander,
and roamed freely in packs until every girl had been tracked
down and kissed. These were great, big and deep film-star
kisses, not wee pecks on the cheek.

Eddie had a simple style about him. He wore lambswool
jumpers, checked shirts, parallels down to just above the ankle
and tipped Oxfords. He had dark, coppery hair and a cute,
freckled face. When he walked, his feet splayed outwards,
earning him the name 'Eddie Duck' and then 'Eddie Dirk'.
The girls loved his cuteness.

No bars or off-licences opened in the north on Sundays. One Sunday evening someone had the brainwave to walk out to the Rock Bar at the end of the Rock road to get a drink. It was around two miles away along a hedged country road, which, at the border with Donegal, was blocked off by huge concrete 'dragon's teeth'. You could just about squeeze through the gaps. It was daylight when we started off, but was getting dark when we reached the Rock Bar. We were all only sixteen and seventeen, and unsure if they'd serve us. We sauntered in to the sound of country and western music – played by a wee man on an electric organ and another on a snare drum and cymbal. The country pub was filled with older couples out for a Sunday night tipple.

Bobby Boyle, Boiler's older brother, went up to the bar while the rest of us hung back expecting to get thrown out. When Bobby came down with a tray full of Harp and Smithwick's we retreated to a corner, so as not to be noticed. We drank the beer and ate nuts and crisps until it was time to head along to the Shanty Community Centre. It was very dark. Not like night-time in Derry, with streetlights. This back road really was pitch black. You literally couldn't see your hand in front of your face. We were half-cut but determined to make it back in time to get into the disco. Guided by I don't know what, we took to the dark road and sang rebel songs to keep us company.

'If wan stops for a slash, we all stop, OK?' said Bob, the

voice of experience. We stopped and slashed loudly into the ditches, then kept walking towards the orange haze of Shanty far off on the horizon. Every now and then someone would step in cow-dung to the sound of 'For Jesus sake! I'm leggered in shite!', or someone would hit a pothole and fall to the ground with a squeal and then a laugh. We were dandering on through the blackness when, all of a sudden, we heard a yelp a few yards behind us.

'Jesus Christ!' There was a crunch of leaves and twigs, followed by a splash.

'Who is it?' someone shouted.

'It's me, Eddie!'

'Where the fuck are ye?'

'Ah dunno! I'm in fuckin' sheugh water!'

We followed the voice in the black ditch until we found him and hauled him out by the arms. He was soaked right through and had to go home while we headed for the last half-hour of the disco.

Over the summer months, me and Eddie were rarely out of each other's sight. I really enjoyed his company and I was sure he enjoyed mine. We had the whole summer to ourselves. We spent our days playing football and helping his da with the garden or me ma with hers. One evening we had made an arrangement to meet at seven but didn't agree where. I walked to the right side of Carnhill Secondary School towards Shanty, where Eddie lived, and had a feeling that he'd be walking down to my house on the other side.

'Eddie!' I called at the top of my voice, cupping my mouth with my hands. 'Eddie!'

'Dutchie!'

'Eddie!'

'Dutchie!'

We met at the bottom of the school, near the main road in Galliagh, and laughed at the thought of us calling to each other over the tall school buildings.

One Sunday evening after the disco in the Community Centre, Eddie got stabbed in the chest by a punk rocker. While fights and melees happened frequently, they were usually harmless enough. The worst you would expect to receive would be a black eye. No one ever used knives in fights. Until that night. An ambulance came and took Eddie to hospital. He got out the next day and, from his bed, showed us the black-stitched cut just below his chest. He was kept at home for a few days but was out again before we knew it.

On the evening of 9 August the anniversary of internment without trial was marked by bonfires in many nationalist areas. The Shanty bonfire was to be held, as usual, in the donkey field behind the Community Centre. Me, Eddie, the brothers Paddy and Trigger Brown from Carnhill, and a group of girls went up to the Plantain, a wooded area away up behind the Marian Hall, carrying hatchets and saws to chop down trees and take off branches for the bonfire. As it was a warm summer's day, the girls sat on tree stumps or lay on the grass smoking. Eddie scaled a huge tree like a monkey and was soon chopping with all his might at a thick branch that he was sitting on. He hugged the tree with his left hand and chopped to his right.

'Ye want this butt, Eddie?' I called up to him. He stopped chopping. I could see his Oxfords from below, tipped and yellow-soled.

'Aye, scoot it up.'

I flicked the butt up to him; it landed on his shirt and he grabbed it and sucked on it, blowing smoke as he sat on the branch fifteen feet above the ground. Suddenly, we heard a sharp crack which appeared to come from inside the tree trunk. I was a bit concerned.

'Eddie, I think you should come down; that didn't sound the best.'

'Nah, it'll be grand.'

'Ye sure, Dirk?'

'Aye, give me head peace,' he laughed.

I walked away from the tree and began bantering with the girls. Suddenly, there was another loud crack, as sharp as a rifle shot. As I turned around, I heard Eddie shout 'Jesus Christ!' and saw the blur of his arms, legs and red lambswool jumper heading downwards.

When we reached where he was, not fifteen yards from where we'd been sitting, Eddie was lying under the thick branch he'd been perched on, which had simply snapped from the main tree-trunk. His eyes were wide open. In panic, me, Trigger and Paddy and the girls wrestled with the colossal weight but it wouldn't budge.

'Are ye OK, Eddie?' called Trigger into Eddie's face. His eyes stared back but he didn't answer.

'Jesus!' shrieked Trigger. 'After three, lift the tree! Let's go! Wan, two, three!'

Our collective strength lifted the timber up and dropped it on the barbed-wire fence beside Eddie. The weight of the thick bough sagged the barbed-wire fence almost down to the grass. Eddie didn't move. I was rooted to the spot. Trigger and Paddy lifted Eddie and when they did, we could see that he'd been impaled on a flat-topped fence-post which had entered him just below his armpit. His eyes were still open and he let a deep sigh out of him when they lifted him.

'Run to fuck and git an ambulance!' shouted Trigger.

We could see the chimney of a house behind a red-brick wall a field away. Me and Paddy took off across the field, scaled the high wall and rushed past an Alsatian dog in the yard that, luckily for us, cowered in a corner as we went in the back door of the house. A woman appeared us as we entered the scullery.

'Missus,' puffed Paddy, 'can we phone an amblience?'

The woman smiled nervously at the mention of 'amblience' and looked at us with some suspicion.

'Sorry, missus,' I said, seeing her fear. 'Our friend, Eddie O'Donnell, fell from a tree. He's in a bad way.' Even as I said this I was certain he'd live. There was no chance my best friend would die! The woman rang 999 and we took off again over the wall back to where Eddie was lying beside the fence. He hadn't moved.

'I better go and git his da,' I said, taking off in a flight of panic down past the Marian Hall towards Eddie's back square and straight in the back door. Eddie's ma, Sally, was in the scullery and Eddie's da, hearing the back door hit the wall, came in from the sitting room.

'Eddie fell out of a tree,' I panted and, seeing the shock on Sally's face, I lied, 'but he's all right.' He was far from all right and I knew it. Eddie changed out of his house-slippers into his shoes without saying a word.

'Where is 'e?' he asked as we rushed out the back door and up through the square.

'Up the Plantain.'

'How is 'e?' he was looking at me as we ran. I couldn't look at him.

'Not good, Eddie,' I said, keeping my eyes on the ground.

As we approached the Marian Hall the ambulance had arrived and its back doors were open. We ran past it to the side of the hall and saw two ambulance men grappling with a wheelchair down a slope. There was a body in it, wrapped from head to foot in a long, white blanket. Trigger, Paddy and the group of girls were following behind, all crying. My best friend, Eddie 'Dirk' O'Donnell, was dead.

His sisters arrived one by one from their work, still wearing their blue factory overalls. As they approached, they could see the crowds that had gathered round their front door and they knew that something had happened. They were greeted with the news that their brother was dead. As the last person to speak to him before he fell to his death I was their sole link between Eddie's life and his sudden and brutal passing. I also felt strangely responsible, as my words to him were the last he heard before the bough broke. My words were in his final sequence on this earth.

I was inconsolable. Sometime later I found myself walking down towards home in the blue-sky heat of that summer's day. I needed me ma. For the first time in several years, I needed her. John gradually living more in our house than his own, and all that flowed from their connection, had changed our relationship. She was still me ma, but her priorities had changed. At that moment, though, I needed her. But when I went in through the door in floods of tears she wasn't there. I headed out right away, accompanied by our Brandy, towards me Aunt Mary and Uncle Jimmy's house in Moss Park, where I sat on their sofa and told them that I'd lost my best friend a few hours ago. I told them in the way I wanted to tell me ma. Jimmy gave me a cup of tea, which I drank with shaking hands while Brandy sat upright in the corner of the room watching me with sad brown eyes. When me ma and John came in shortly after, I felt resentment towards her that she hadn't been there for me when I really needed her. I could tell by her eyes that she knew how I felt.

Me, Trigger and Paddy Brown went back up to the Plantain the night of Eddie's funeral. We wanted to go up at night so we waited for the dark to arrive. When we reached the spot where he'd been killed, we stood in silence as the wind blew the tops of the tall trees together. They looked like a group of Mass-goers in conversation outside chapel, each making their contribution before moving back to the edge of the circled throng. The stars shone bright in the black sky beyond the swaying, chattering trees.

***

Exactly two weeks later, I woke to find a big, dark-uniformed RUC man standing at the foot of my bed. He didn't say anything, but I had the distinct feeling I was going to be arrested. The house was full of soldiers searching the bedrooms and all around the house. When they were leaving, the big cop said to me ma, 'Which one is Anthony Christopher?'

'Why do ye want to know?'

'Because he's coming with us.'

'It's OK, Ma. I'm Anthony. Tony.'

'I'm arresting you under the Prevention of Terrorism Act,' the cop began.

'He's not goin' anywhere till he's somethin' in his belly!' called John from the scullery.

'He's going now, with us. Transport is outside waiting.'

'He's goin' nowhere without his toast 'n' tay,' said John, at the scullery door.

One of the soldiers looked at me and said, 'It's OK, have your tea and toast. Any for us?' he joked.

'Ye can fuck off! Yer gettin' no tay here!' John was a docker; dockers didn't take jokes from soldiers.

After the tea and toast, I was put into an army Jeep and driven up the town towards Strand Road RUC Barracks. The back doors of the Jeep were left open and the cool August air wafted right through the vehicle. The Jeeps had stopped at the lights at the Collon and a car pulled up behind us. The male driver waved at me and I gave him the thumbs up. It was a nice, reassuring encounter that reminded me that I wasn't alone. I needn't have worried. When the RUC detectives began questioning me, they let me Aunt Celine into the interrogation room as I was under eighteen.

I sat across the desk from two slick-looking detectives. One was black-haired and the other blond. They questioned me about an event I'd had no part in, which was further reassuring. My problem, however, wasn't the two cops.

'We've brought your Aunt Celine in because you're too young for us to question on your own. You understand, young Doherty?' said Blondie.

I said nothing, just looked silently into his eyes.

'You not talking to us, young Doherty?' said Blondie.

'You're well trained in the Fianna, young Doherty, aren't you?' said Blackie. 'What do think of this boy, your nephew, Mrs McCourt, not co-operating with our enquiries?'

Celine started by poking her finger into my arm as she sat beside me in the hard chair. 'You, boy!' She had a wild, high-pitched voice. 'These gentlemen are here to keep ye outa bother! Ye weren't brought up to be ignorant like that!'

Holy Jesus! What under God is she at now? I roared inside my head. On the outside I was calm.

'Come on, young Doherty; you're in the Fianna, aren't you? Your so-called comrades have told us everything. You may as well admit your part!' said Blondie.

Nothing from me.

Celine was poking at me with her sharp nail. 'I'm tellin' you this day, your father, may God have mercy on 'im, is turnin' in his grave knowin' that his son's got 'imself mixed up wi' a bunch of gangsters!'

Git you outa my hair for Christ's sake, ye oul witch! I screamed in my head.

'And you boys hijacked a bus and put a booby-trap on it to kill poor innocent soldiers!' Blackie pitched in.

'Jesus and his Blissid Mother! You're running around Shantalla hijackin'?' she screamed, slapping her hand on my knee.

'Take it easy, Mrs McCourt,' said Blondie, getting up and putting a hand of concern on her shoulder.

'Take it easy! Take it easy! This is such a disgrace to our family!' she cried with her head in her hands.

Jesus! It's me against the three of them. I'm fucked here! I roared again silently, so that only I could hear the panic in my head.

'I'm not in anything and I didn't hijack any bus,' I said. The first statement was a lie, the second the truth.

'Oh, you're speaking to us now, are you?' said Blondie.

'Oh, you're speakin' to them now, are you?' repeated Celine.

I said nothing more. I had to escape from her somehow! I thought I'd try conjuring up the flickering candle in the dark room. There it was, the bright, flickering light in the dark. I locked my open eyes on it, watched the flame moving, bobbing and drifting under its own weightlessness, and thought what a fiercely beautiful candle it was. The soft, white wax dripped down its rounded sides, gathering in a terraced mound on the white saucer below. It was so bright, but yet it didn't penetrate the darkness around it. It was a bright, dancing, flickering light, beautiful and entrancing. It drew my eyes and held me with its magic. Suddenly, the flame was blown to a wisp of white smoke.

'Wh–, wh–, what?' I hadn't heard a word they'd said for I didn't know how long.

'You haven't heard a single word we said,' roared Blackie across the table at me.

'Not a word! Ye'd think he was reared in a cesspit of ignorance!' screamed Celine.

Then I felt her foot. She placed it over mine on the floor behind the desk, pressing it for a second to the floor. I looked at her foot and then at her. Blackie and Blondie were staring at me across the desk, wondering what had happened.

'Now you, Tony Doherty! You speak to these grand fellas and tell them all ye know!' shouted Celine, as convincingly as before.

'That's right, Tony. C'mon, tell us what you've done! Get it off your chest before you destroy your whole life!' said Blackie.

Piss you away off, ya half-wit! I laughed into myself.

Me and Skin McCauley got out the following morning and met at the Shanty shops the next afternoon.

'Hi, Skin, we defeated the full might of the British Empire!' I laughed and shook his hand before we headed over to Brenda's for tea and a well-earned tart.

10

RISING UP

Jackie sat with his thick fingers entwined, rubbing his work-roughened hands on the white Formica, drop-leaf scullery table in Wee Owen's grey-brick house in Shantallow. It wasn't the first time I'd met him. He'd warned us then, 'If yis ever see me in the street, don't speak to me or I'll put me toe up yer arses! OK?' It wasn't the first time we'd used Wee Owen's house either. We were now lined up around his sparse scullery, standing against the back door, the sink-unit and the scullery presses. The window and the Venetian blinds were closed, which kept out the noise of wains gallivanting in the back square, and cast a sepia sullenness over the gathering. When we fell in, our heels echoed loudly on the oilcloth floor. Six of us stood looking down at him as he angled his stern, swarthy face up at us. The first few bars of *Coronation Street* filtered through the thin adjoining door, the music blending with the legacy of the cabbage and bacon that Wee Owen and his wife and wains had eaten for their dinner.

'I'm here to warn yis off, boys,' he said. 'To do yis a favour.'
No one spoke.

'There's very serious consequences to your decision the night, isn't there?' he said, as he picked the dirt from under his black-tipped fingernails with a key. We were now on the cusp of progressing into the IRA. We nodded in agreement.

'What are they?' he asked, looking round the ranks of seventeen-year-old soon to be ex-Fianna boys.

No one spoke.

He paused. There was an argument on the TV in the next room.

'It's death, it's jail or it's a life on the run. That's what the consequences are, boys.'

I could tell he'd said this before.

Still no one spoke.

His eyes swung to the left, and settled on the first boy in the line. Like school.

'What's your name, son?'

The boy answered.

'Why do you want to join the Irish Republican Army?'

'To get the Brits out of my country.'

'What about you?' he asked the second boy. 'Why do you want to join the Irish Republican Army?'

'To get the British out of Ireland.'

Jackie smiled. He got the same answer from the third boy. Then he came to me.

'What's your name?'

'Tony Doherty.'

'Why are ye joining the Irish Republican Army?'

I hesitated, intending to follow the others. Then it just came out: 'To get revenge for me da's murder.'

Fuck! What did I say that for? I screamed inside at myself.

He paused, all the while looking through me.

'Are you Paddy Doherty's son?'

I smiled at the familiar way he said me da's name. 'Aye, I am.'

His eyes travelled onwards to the next boy, then stopped, and came back, fixing his gaze sternly on me. 'That's not a good enough reason for joining the Irish Republican Army.'

My heart sank. I'd been waiting for this moment for months and now I'd messed it up! In resigned silence I stood observing him as he moved back to the next boy in the recruiting line.

Later, I walked with two of the others across the Shantallow pitches.

'What the fuck did ye say that for?' asked one in disbelief.

'I dunno. It jist came out.'

'You're a right dick.'

'I know. I could kick meself.'

'Ye know, I'm not joinin' for any different reason than you.'

'What d'ye mean?'

'Me da told me all about Bloody Sunday and internment and all them men being tortured by the Brits. He was nearly shot 'imself that day.'

'God, but the Brits are bastards, aren't they?' said another.

'And so are the fuckin' cops. What about all the boys from around here that they lifted and tortured in the Strand Road and Castlereagh? Seamus and Tony Brown, Sa Gallagher, Paddy O'Carroll, Willie Hogan, Pete McCallion and all. They're all on the Blanket.'

'And Thomas Starrs and Davy McKinney from Hamilton Street, where I used to live, are inside as well,' I said, 'and so's me cousin, Danny Doherty.'

After some time walking, I said in disgust, 'Why didn't I jist say the same as yous boys said?'

'Well, ye'll know the nixt time, won't ye, Dutchie boy?'

'I certainly will. D'ye think I'll get another chance?'

'Aye, sure he said we're all to come back nixt week. We're meetin' in the house in Carnhill.'

So it was with a blend of justifiable vengeance and moral authority settling in my head that I veered home towards Brookdale Park, having been refused entry into the IRA. By the next time we met with Jackie I had my reasoning thoroughly revised.

***

My journey into 'The Army' as we called it, began just after Easter 1980, when many of the older Fianna reached the age to move up into the IRA. The Fianna had prepared well for the Easter march. We practised marching in halls in a number of places in Derry alongside the Cáilíní, which was the female equivalent of the Fianna. The pressure was on, as the Cáilíní paraded very neatly and in step, whereas the same couldn't be said about us. On Easter Sunday we'd arranged to meet at a house in the Bog to collect our black uniforms and get dressed. It was a scorching day and I could hear the whirr of a British Army chopper in the distance. When we were given the uniforms there was a bit of a scramble for the best ones, and the OC had to negotiate to sort out the best fit for everyone. When we all put on our new, black polo-neck jumpers we discovered that the Fianna badges had all been sewn on upside down.

The *Green Book* is the list of rules and regulations I had to learn to become a new member of the IRA. When I was in St Joe's Secondary School I'd heard a rumour from Benny (one of hundreds) that Kevin McCallion, my form teacher, met new recruits at night in his classroom. I didn't really believe it, though, as I still couldn't square up the connection between his apparent obsession with Shakespeare's *Macbeth* and fighting the Brits out of Ireland! Events, however, made it more than plausible, as I went on to receive my own schooling in the *Green Book* from another teacher, Mr McGregor, in his classroom in another Derry school.

Not being a pupil, I didn't know my way around his school or its grounds. As I approached it via a darkened pathway I could see a light in a window a few floors up. It stood out starkly against the rest of the building, which was in total darkness. I'd heard stories about the ghosts of monks walking the floors of this school at night trying to kidnap anyone who crossed their path. There was no one around as I went in through the squeaky double doors and headed towards the stairwell, which was also in darkness. When I reached the corridor on the correct level it too was in darkness, except for the light shining through a door panel at the end.

I knocked and went in. Mr McGregor came out from behind his desk to shake my hand. He didn't tell me his name. He was dressed in a black polo-neck jumper, a shiny black leather coat and black trousers. He had black hair, a black moustache and long, black sideburns. He had a copy of the *Green Book* and told me to read the first few pages. He then chatted for a while about what I'd read, asking me if I understood it OK and had I any questions? This pattern was repeated for five or six weeks. On the final evening, he sat me down on a chair opposite his.

'Could you hold out under intensive questioning for five to seven days in Castlereagh?'

'I think so,' I said, but my confidence had recently been dented a bit because a former Fianna leader had signed his life away in Castlereagh.

'You have to know so, Tony!' he glared at me.

'I know I can do it!' said I, smartening myself up.

'Grand. But do you know that giving information to the Brits or RUC is a crime punishable by death?'

'I do.'

'So why have we had so many informers?'

'I don't know.'

'Weak people and money don't mix very well. That's why!'

'I see. I couldn't give a damn about dough.'

'Grand. You're to get sworn in this time next week at this address,' he said, placing a strip of jotter paper into my hand. It was an address in the Bog.

'Did you read it?'

'Aye.'

'Good, give me it back.' He stood up and put out his hand. 'All the very best of luck, young Doherty. You're goin' to need it!' he smiled.

'I know,' I said.

The following week I went to the address in the Bog and waited in a long hallway with another fella I didn't know. There was a framed picture of the 1916 Proclamation on one wall and a red-bulb-lit Sacred Heart the other. A door opened and Jackie nodded me in. There were two other men in the room: Mr McGregor and a man called Éamonn. The two of them stood behind a table draped in the Irish tricolour.

'Place your left hand on the flag and raise your right hand,' said Éamonn.

I did as I was told.

'Say after me …'

After I took the oath, the three of them shook my hand.

I left the house to dander through the dark streets of the Bogside, past the high-walled Gasyard, taking my first steps as a sworn-in member of the Irish Republican Army.

Instead of being placed in the 3rd Battalion in Shanty, I was made a member of a new unit up the town. Any night I had a meeting I had to walk the few miles from our house and back, passing Maire's house on Racecourse Road. As I neared her house on the far side of the road I always put my hood up so anyone looking out the window wouldn't recognise me. I never talked to Maire about being in the IRA because I knew she didn't like it. It was something I just had to do.

***

I looked at the passengers on the Lough Swilly bus as we bumped along the narrow, hedge-bordered roads of Donegal. I was en route to my first IRA training camp. As I searched for faces of boys my age who might be travelling down for the same reason, I concluded that there were at least five possible candidates. The arrangement was that I was to go to a café on the square and wait. When I got off the bus, two of the five possibles walked in the same direction as me, eventually forming a three-person queue at the café counter, where I ordered a cup of tea and a bun. I sat down on a grey Formica bench at a grey Formica table, sipped my tea, nibbled my bun and waited, looking out of the large window onto the square. There were tractors and trailers, mud-stained Datsuns and

Hiace vans, all competing for space to park, while mammies and grannies guided their steps and stairs offspring into shoe shops and clothes shops. Flat-capped farmers stood in groups deep in earnest talk, their pinky-red jowls breathing fag and pipe-smoke into the small-town air.

The other two boys sat separately on their grey benches, sipping their stewed tea from white mugs, and knowing, but pretending not to know, why each of us was there. Shortly afterwards, another Derry man came in through the door. Dermot was older than us. He came to me first and swung himself onto the grey bench on the far side of my table.

'Are you Tony?'

'I am.'

'It's three o'clock now. At a quarter past exactly, you and the other two boys head down to the end of the square,' he said, pointing to the right. 'Walk along the road and keep walking and we'll pick you up. OK?'

'Aye, no bother. A quarter past?'

'Aye, a quarter past.'

He got up, spoke briefly to the other two and left in the direction his hand had just shown us. Now that we knew officially what we'd suspected anyway, the three of us slid together around one table, slurped our tea, chatted awkwardly and waited for the time to pass.

At 3.15 p.m. exactly, the three of us got up, said 'Churrio' to the woman behind the counter and walked to the end of the square. We turned onto a country road and walked three abreast in the heat of the early summer Saturday. After about a half mile, a car passed us and pulled in at the side of the road. The driver, who I knew as Snowy, rolled the window down and waved us into the back seat. Dermot was the front-seat passenger.

'Hope that back seat isn't too bumpy for yis boys,' laughed Snowy as he drove along.

'It's grand, so it is.'

'Stick yer hand down the back,' said Snowy into his rear mirror, 'so ye see what I'm on about.'

I slid my hand down the back of the seat and felt hard wood and metal. It was a rifle!

'That's the gear for the day; the best 'o vintage for yous boys!' he smiled as he sped along the country road. We laughed politely back, wondering what he was on about, until he pulled the car off the road onto a track behind hedges and stopped.

'That's us boys; out yis git!' said Dermot.

The three of us slid out of the back seat and Dermot reached in, pulling the back seat up to reveal three rifles, which he lifted out one by one, standing them upright against the car.

'Here yis are, boys,' he said. 'Lift wan o' them each. Don't worry, they're not loaded!'

We grabbed a rifle each. I hadn't held a rifle since 1969, when the first English soldiers were stationed in a sangar at the foot of our street. It was a substantial weight. Its smooth, aged bulk felt good in my hands. It felt like something that could do damage. We walked with our rifles across rugged, unfarmed land for a short time until we met another man, Philly. He'd been sitting under a tree, waiting for us. He shook each of us by the hand before leading us further along until we reached a ravine. Dermot gathered us in a circle.

'This is us,' said Philly. 'Me an' Dermot are yer trainers for the day. Listen very carefully to every word I tell yis. Someday it might even save yer lives! We've three rifles and an automatic pistol; where's the pistol?'

Snowy reached his right hand under the rear flap of his blazer and produced the dark pistol, pointing its muzzle towards the ground.

'First things first,' said Philly, in a serious and commanding tone. 'Never point a weapon at anyone unless you intend to use it. And when I say never, I mean *never*! OK?'

'OK,' we all agreed. This was not an occasion for messing about.

Pointing to us in turn, he said, 'Tony, you have a German Mauser; you have a British Lee-Enfield .303; and you have a semi-automatic Remington Woodmaster. They are all powerful weapons, all very accurate and, if used in the right circumstances, can kill a target from a range of nearly a mile.

'Tony's rifle,' he said taking it from my hands, and standing back a few yards so we could all see, 'is a bolt-action. It's clip-fed, meaning you can put a full clip of rounds inside it, so you don't have to load it every time you fire.' He pulled the metal bolt back, showed us there was nothing inside, then slid the bolt forward, aimed it to the sky and pulled the trigger. It went off with a disappointing 'click'. He passed the rifle back to me.

'Right, Tony, grip with your left hand and pull the bolt – this wee knob – back hard with your right.'

I pressed the rifle butt against my lower chest, gripped the bolt, slid it back, pointed it into the air and fired, exactly as I was shown.

'Dermot, will you and Snowy take Tony across to the range with the Mauser? I'll stay with these two.'

'Aye, OK. Let's go, Tony. Have you the rounds for the Mauser?' asked Dermot. 'Did you bring the sheets, Snowy?'

'Aye, I've the sheets here.' He began unfurling them from inside his blazer.

'OK, Tony, we only have five rounds for the Mauser. I'm goney show ye how to load and fire it.'

We walked about fifty yards away from the group. Snowy disappeared into a small valley before appearing again fifty yards ahead, where he fixed a large white paper sheet to the grass on the far side. Dermot pulled the five bullet rounds out of his coat pocket, pulled back the bolt on the Mauser and pushed it sharply forward.

'You watchin'? That's it ready to fire, but you're not goney fire it yit. Can ye take the round out?' he asked, handing it back to me. I took the Mauser again, slid the bolt back as I had before and the brass bullet flew out of the rifle onto the grass.

'I'm goney teach ye how to snipe, and to learn to snipe you have to be aware of your sights, your breathin' and your trigger. The Mauser has a rear V sight and a forward bead,' he said, fingering the raised band of metal just above the butt with a small V cut into it. Then pointing to the tiny, raised metal bead at the end of the muzzle, he said, 'Ye line the rear V sight with the forward bead; that's what gives ye an accurate shot. Lie down and try it.'

I lay down and pointed it across towards the white sheet. Snowy, who was still standing nearby, took off like a startled hare, shouting, 'Houl on, fuck ye!'

'I didn't tell ye to aim it at the sheet!' cried Dermot. 'I told ye earlier, never aim a gun at anyone unless you're goney use it!'

'Right, OK, I forgot,' I said, from my redner on the ground.

'Now, finger the trigger. Ye see it has a wee bit of give in it?'

'Aye.' It felt loose up to a point and then stopped.

'Right, aim now at the sheet,' he said, 'but only do as I tell ye. Aim. Have ye got the front bead lined up with the rear V?'

'Aye.'

'Press the butt up tight, but not too tight, against yer

shoulder. Check yer sights. Line up the rear V with the front bead. Take a breath. Hold it in and slowly let half of it out, squeezing the slack on the trigger. Check yer aim and let the rest of your breath out slowly. As you do, squeeze the trigger.'

Click!

'OK, that was gran'. Now we're goney load the five rounds into 'er. Up ye git on yer hunkers.'

I held the Mauser upright with the butt on the grass, and slid the bolt back as Dermot handed me the first round, which I clicked into the empty chamber, then another and another until the five rounds were clicked into place. I slid the bolt over and lay down again. Dermot got right down beside me on my left-hand side as I eyed up the white sheet across the glen.

He repeated his list of instructions, and, at the end, re-minded me, 'Let the rest of your breath out slowly and, as you do, squeeze the trigger.'

Bang! The shot rang in my ears and it felt as if the force of the blast sent me backwards along the grass! Snowy slid over to the white sheet, then turned round and crossed his arms to signify a miss.

'Ye closed yer eyes, Tony,' said Dermot with a reassuring smile. 'Ye'll not hit anything if ye shut yer eyes when firin' a weapon, son. OK? Now, eject your round.'

'OK.' *I'll not effin' close them this time*, I thought, as I snapped the bolt back, springing the empty shell, smoking, onto the grass.

'Right, away ye go again: butt to the shoulder.'

I went through the same methodical procedure until I let my breath go and squeezed the trigger.

Bang! Again, the loudness hollowed out my eardrums! There was no need for Snowy to check the sheet this time, as the shot had blown it up and out from the grass.

'Great shot, Tony. Great shot!' smiled Dermot, as Snowy ran to fix the white sheet up again. I ejected the empty round without being asked and lay eyeing up the white target across the glen.

***

I felt the pleasantly dull soreness in my right shoulder for days afterwards. 'Me mammy knows you're in the IRA, ye know,' said Maire. She'd been crying again. Her eyes were red.

'How does she?' I asked.

'Somebody told her in the shop.'

'What? They were talking about me as they got a colour in?'

'It's no joke, ye know, Tony.'

'I know. What did she say? Your ma, I mean.' I thought her ma had been a bit distant when she answered the door earlier. We were in their back room listening to records.

'That's all.' She fell silent. I looked out of the window. When I looked round at her again, there were tears flowing out of the corners of her eyes.

'What's wrong wi' ye, Maire?'

'You know what's wrong; you don't have to ask,' she said coldly, wiping her eyes.

Silence followed. There were many silences between us. They used to be nice silences but now, more often than not, they were tense and unpleasant. I knew what they were about, but always pretended not to.

'I love him, but I'll never have him,' she said, not looking at me.

'What are ye on about?'

'I spoke to me da about you. About us. He knows you're in the IRA too.'

'What did he say?'

'"You love him, but you'll never have him", that's what he said.'

'But you *do* have me. I'm here, aren't I?'

'You're only here 'cos you have no meetings to go to, or whatever you do in the IRA. I don't know,' she sighed, slowly shaking her head.

'God's sake, Maire. Gimme a break.'

'No! I can never have you the way I want to! Ye may as well have another girlfriend!' she cried.

'I don't want another girlfriend. I love you, Maire.'

'D'ye know that, on the nights you're away up the town, I know what time you're goney pass our house on your way home?'

I looked at her, astonished. I never knew. I thought I was incognito, rushing past her house with the hood up!

'Ye pass by with your hood up on the other side of the road. I wait at the bedroom window, dying to call to you. But I don't. It's like your goin' wi' another girl!' she cried into her hands. 'I'm fed up at seventeen crying myself to sleep as you're out there doing I don't know what in the dark!'

'I'm sorry, Maire,' I said gently, putting my hand on the side of her face.

'But you're never goney change, are you, Tony? That's what me daddy said: "It's too deep in him, Maire; he can't change now."'

'Sure, what would your da know about me?'

'Me daddy knows more than you think, Tony. His own daddy and uncles were steeped in the IRA in the 1950s.'

Silence followed. ELO's 'Horace Wimp' fought with the tension between us. The tension won.

'This isn't goin' to work out, Tony. I love you with all my heart, but you canny love me back the same way and you canny change now.'

***

It was a bumpy ride. The Hiace van groaned up and raced down, braked, twisted and sped along for miles and miles on the road to God knows where. We didn't know where we were, or where we were going. The windows at the back were blacked out so we had no view of the countryside to occupy us. Friday was for travelling, Saturday for training and Sunday for heading home.

These camps were serious. At the first weekend camp, Tommy Carlin had laughed at the camp leader because he made us lie in a field after he'd heard the sound of a tractor several fields away. When we got back to Derry, Jackie had chewed the bake off Tommy for showing disrespect to someone in charge.

This time I was with Martin and Patsy. Martin was my height and age, while Patsy was also the same age but carrying some beef. We had great craic coming down in the van, playing cards and guessing where we might be.

The van turned sharply and stopped. We sat in silence, bursting for a pee, as the driver and his front-seat passenger got out. We heard accents that were not northern. After a few minutes, the back door of the van flew up, letting in the fresh country air and the fading light of a Connacht summer evening. The two camp leaders introduced themselves as Bernard and Peadar. Our digs were an old farm cottage inhabited by an ancient character who reminded me of me great-uncle Paddy Stewart. There was no electricity and the toilet was out in a small courtyard. They fed us a beef stew with very little beef, and afterwards, in a small stone outhouse, we were shown the mechanical workings of the .303, the AR15, the Remington Woodmaster and a .22 rifle with a telescopic sight. We were shown how to press the nodes to strip the rifles down and how to reassemble them. We also learned how to load the magazines into the AR15 and the .22, and how to eject them.

Instead of a rear V sight, the AR15 had a tiny circle, the 'rear aperture sight', through which you centred the front bead. None of us liked the rear aperture sight. Peadar and Bernard knew their business as they patiently and gently put us through our paces, reminding us of the damage that such weapons can do and warning us again not to point them at anyone unless we intended to fire.

Later we were told to get some rest in sleeping bags on the hard sand-and-cement floor of the sitting room. Whatever was in the beef stew played desperately on Patsy's bowels and he blasted his way through the night, having me and Martin in fits of giggling and nose-holding into the early hours.

Each of us, including the camp leaders, took turns keeping watch. Outside, I paced around the hedgerows under a silvery moon, armed with an empty Lee-Enfield .303 rifle. There wasn't a sound, not even a breath of wind, except for the odd rustle of hedgehogs, rats or field mice in the thick undergrowth of the hawthorn hedges. Every now and then I saw bright silvery flashes in the far distance, the lights of vehicles miles away. Their headlamps were like swords of light piercing the blanket-folds of pitch-black darkness spread out below me as I stood guard high above them. I wondered about the lives of the drivers. Were they farmers' sons coming back from a dance, or were they gardaí searching high and low for subversive threats to the nation, like me?

You don't really feel the cold until you come back into the warmth. I was glad when my ninety-minute stint on guard was up and I could wake farty Patsy for the beginning of his shift. I handed him the .303 as he staggered, sleepy-eyed, out through the door.

'Git out, big Patsy, ye smelly hoor!' laughed Martin as the door banged shut.

The following morning we dressed in combat gear and rubber boots and set off holding a rifle each, with knapsacks on our backs. Bernard was in charge and, to prove it, he wore a pair of field glasses round his neck and halted us with a raised hand every now and then to scan the landscape for signs of the Irish army or the gardaí. At one stage he flagged us all down under a hedge because he saw movement on a high cliff overlooking us. He studied and scanned the cliff, twiddling and fiddling with the sights of his field glasses, for what seemed an inordinately long time, until he gave Peadar a go on the glasses to get a second opinion. We could see nothing.

Peadar looked for a minute at the suspect spy. 'It's a mountain goat, Bernie, ye fookin' half-wit!'

Bernard was mortified and took the field glasses back off him, nearly pulling his neck off with the strap. 'Be Christ, 'tis a mountain goat all right, so!'

'Look at the size of the horns on the hoor!' laughed Peadar.

Peadar shook his head in feigned disgust and we resumed our trek. Eventually, we reached the campsite, which looked as if it could have been an old quarry, not unlike the small glen of the first camp. There was a long mound in the middle running lengthways, which, from a height, looked like a large, overgrown grave. When we got down to it, Peadar and Bernard pulled branches away to reveal an upright car tyre, and after more branches were cleared, another car tyre on the other side of the mound. When you looked through you could see that the inside of the long mound was made from around sixty tyres tied together and camouflaged with sods of grass.

'This is for rifle fire. The tyres muffle the sound so it doesn't escape into the countryside,' said Bernard.

'Yeah, like the fookin' mountain goat, so!' laughed Peadar. Bernard laughed too; they were good-humoured, the pair of them.

'OK, I know yis have all fired rifles before, isn't that right?' asked Bernard. We all nodded.

'Today, we have an AR15, a .22 automatic rifle with a silencer and a Remington Woodmaster. We also have a Webley .38 revolver and a 9mm Browning automatic pistol. Now, what is the first rule of handling a weapon, loaded or unloaded?'

'Never point a weapon at anyone unless you intend to use it,' I answered, before either of the other two could.

'Got that, everybody?'

'Yip.'

'The three rifles are gas-operated and magazine-fed, meaning they eject the spent shell and load a live one automatically. Yes?' he said as he rubbed at a midge on his forehead.

'Yip,' we answered, rubbing our faces and necks in response.

Having shown us how to load the magazines with live rounds, I chose the AR15, or Armalite, and headed with Peadar over to the firing range. I took up position, leaning into the tyres.

'I don't like the sight on this, Peadar,' I said.

'Oh, the rear aperture sight?' he said. 'No one does at the start, but you'll get used to it. It's hard to keep the front bead centred, isn't it? OK? Remember your breathing and the trigger-squeezing.'

'OK,' I said, as I took aim through the tyres at a large cardboard sheet placed about eighty yards distant, and fired. I didn't see the weapon ejecting the shell, it happened that fast. I could hear the others behind me firing their weapons. I fired again and again until I'd finished my fifteen shots. Peadar ran to get the sheet of cardboard. When he brought it back it had around seven tiny bullet holes in it. Peadar got out a marker and put a T against each hole.

Then it was my turn for the .22 rifle with the silencer. The midgies were becoming a wee bit annoying, biting into my neck and face. I loaded the toy-like magazine, the shells of which were brass but, unlike the AR15 and most other rounds I'd seen so far, the bullet-heads were a shiny grey. Bernard pointed up to a hole in the quarry face about a hundred yards away and told me to fire. I aimed through the small telescopic sight, making sure that the cross-hairs were centred, and fired at the hole. There was no sound and hardly any recoil on my shoulder.

'Good shooting, Tony,' said Bernard, looking through his field glasses at my handiwork.

I emptied the magazine as he watched, and when I was finished, I stood with the rifle on my hip and looked around me. As well as Martin and Patsy loading and shooting, it appeared that the midgies were getting good target practice too, as everyone was rubbing their faces and hands.

'Christ, them midgies is gettin' bad,' said Peadar. 'Ye think they're a plant by the British or by the Free Staters?'

'Here, I've heard they hate cordite,' said Bernard, taking the .22 from me and loading in a full magazine. 'I'll blast a dozen or so into the air; that'll send them on their way!'

Having fired off his rounds into the blue sky things took a turn for the worse. Our midgies appeared to be the cordite-loving type as they converged in their millions, crawling into our noses, into our ears, through our hair and, when we tried to speak through the furious clouds around us, into our very mouths.

'We'll have to abandon camp, so,' said Peadar to Bernard, while blinking, rubbing and slapping furiously.

'We will, so,' agreed Bernard, snorting midgies out, a nostril at a time. 'Take all the magazines out, make sure there's nothing in the breach and get ready to follow me immediately!'

Martin, who was the only one with a hood on his combat coat, had it up around his head and face so all you could see was a dark gap for the eyes. He was running around rubbing his head through the hood, almost in hysterics. We took off without delay up the side of the sandy quarry, but when we reached the top, our heads were still surrounded by the tiny enemy forces biting lumps out of us.

Peadar reached into his backpack and brought out a yellow tube of ointment, instructing us to hold out our hands as we walked hurriedly away from the firing range. We each got a squirt of bright yellow stuff on our hands, which we rubbed onto our poor, smarting faces.

'That should do the job, so,' said Peadar, but I realised immediately, not only was this type of Connacht midgey big into cordite, they had a certain penchant for bright yellow ointment as well!

We took off at a steady trot across a field, oblivious to the dangers of the Free State army or suspect mountain goats as we tried to escape the furious, hungry clouds nipping at our sticky yellow faces. We kept going till we reached a stream, where we dunked our heads in the water, holding them under in the hope that the midgies would wise up and go back to where they belonged. After several minutes of dunking in the cold stream, it appeared safe to take stock, get our bearings and begin the long trek back to the old man's cottage. As we trekked on with our rifles and backpacks, our swelling faces still yellow and studded all over with tiny black, dead and dying midgies, I thought to myself, *What a hoorin' way to free Ireland!*

11

THE DEAD BESIDE US

It was set for a Wednesday afternoon in February 1981. We were to firebomb a furniture shop at the bottom of Clarendon Street. The owner had collaborated with the state forces, our unit leader, Johnny, told us, and it couldn't be tolerated.

The small, two-door car pulled in at the top of Clarendon Street. I had the two devices in black plastic bags between my feet. When the car stopped, I lifted them out with my thick-gloved hands. 'Never put your dabs on anything' was another rule that was drilled into us. They were heavy enough; two full plastic containers of petrol, with a large industrial detonator squeezed between them, wrapped in plumbers' black tape to keep it intact during the journey.

Clarendon Street is a steep, elegant avenue, lined on both sides with four-storey Georgian houses. As I began my solo walk down towards the furniture shop, passing the ornate, black-painted railings and the broad, panelled front doors, a woman backed off against a car with a look of horror on her face. I wondered momentarily what she thought she'd seen until I spotted something else: an undercover car with two

Branchmen in it driving slowly up the steep hill towards the traffic-lights. They weren't more than ten yards away from me. I was sure, though, that they hadn't noticed me, as it was getting dark, I was carrying the firebombs low and there was a line of parked cars between them and me. *Strange though*, I thought, as I kept walking with the weighty devices taxing the strength in my arms.

As I came to the junction with Queen Street, I noticed a cluster of RUC and Brit Jeeps parked with their lights on and a crowd of people gathered round something on the ground as if there'd been an accident. They were no more than seventy yards from me. *Strange*, I thought, as I kept going at a steady pace, *this is a bit too close for comfort. If one of the soldiers or RUC men turns round they'll see me and call on me to halt.* When you have such a cargo between your hands, unlike the heavy bags of sticks that I couldn't sell nine years before, your choices are limited: keep going until you reach your destination; ditch them somewhere, behind a wall or up an alley, and make a beeline out of there; or take them back where they came from. Our car had left as planned, so there was no way back. Anyway, I was close enough, so I kept going in the direction of the furniture shop, my ton-weight cargo stretching the sinews of my arms.

I went in the main doorway, taking the narrow flight of steep stairs up to the furniture shop on the first floor. All must have gone as planned because when I stepped in, the shopkeeper and a customer had been taken into a back room and were being held facing a wall so they couldn't identify anyone in the event of a court case. I placed the firebombs on a large mahogany table and tore the black plastic from around them, revealing the petrol-filled containers and the two small wooden boxes holding the timer and battery. I tried to prime one but my thick goalkeeper's gloves made it very difficult. One of the other two volunteers in the shop saw my difficulty and came over. He removed the stubby dowel rods to prime them and said, 'That's them now; twenty-five minutes. Here, away you go!' He placed the dowel stubs into my hand. It was my job to bring them back the following day to prove that I'd detonated the firebombs properly.

I stuck the dowels in my coat pocket and headed downstairs again to leave. As I got halfway down the stairs, I heard loud sirens piercing the hum of traffic in the street outside. I hesitated for a few seconds before deciding it was best to keep going, so I left the shop to cross the street. As I did so, a number of RUC cars raced round the corner from Strand Road RUC Barracks. I stood on the white line in the middle of the road as the first one passed by within inches of me. I was so close I recognised the passenger as Maurice Johnson, a local bigwig in the RUC. I remained rooted to the white line for what seemed like an eternity until the cavalcade of vehicles had all passed by. They were heading in the direction of Queen Street, where I'd seen the crowd a few minutes earlier. I walked up Strand Road to Foyle Street to get the bus home, dumping the dowels down a grating on the way. There was too much activity going on and I didn't want to get caught with them on me. It felt weird getting a bus away from an IRA operation. As I wondered whether I was the first IRA man ever to do so, I realised that the route this bus took was back down Strand Road! Sure enough, as we passed the junction of Strand Road and Clarendon Street, all the workers had been evacuated from nearby shops and were standing in groups thirty to forty yards on each side of the furniture shop, looking towards the open door I'd exited ten minutes earlier. The Brits hadn't got round to blocking Strand Road off, so the bus just kept going in the direction of Shantallow and home.

One week later, I was woken by the sound of the boots of a burly, uniformed RUC man tapping at the end of my bed. I jumped up, startled and confused. *Fuck!* I thought. *This is it now.*

'Anthony Christopher?'

'Aye.'

'Good, we want to speak with you, boy!'

'Aye, big deal,' I said, but inside I was too jumpy and nervous and I knew it.

Soldiers searched the house, then gathered in the front street. They were getting ready to leave when the RUC man put his hand on my shoulder and said, 'Anthony Christopher Doherty, I'm arresting you under the Prevention of Terrorism

Act in connection with terrorist offences carried out in the Londonderry area.'

'It's yous that are the terrorists! Not him!' hissed me ma into the big RUC man's face.

Even though my mind was racing and my jitters hadn't abated, I felt I needed to be calm and defiant in front of the rest of the family. They were all there in the sitting room, except Patrick, who'd gone to live in London.

'It's OK, Ma. I'll see yis in a few days.' Even as I said this, I couldn't help the feeling of dread inside.

The February darkness was giving way to a low, lead-coloured sky as we walked out of our house. The big RUC man kept his hand on my shoulder until I was placed in a red armoured RUC Ford Cortina outside the house, handcuffed to the inside of the door, and away up the road we went.

I hope it's to the Strand Road we're goin', I thought as the car sped through the empty streets towards the city centre. It stopped outside Strand Road RUC Barracks, just round the corner from Clarendon Street. There were two other armoured cars there as well, with their lights on and their engines running. I guessed one of the passengers must be Tommy Carlin; I'd got to know him very well since joining the IRA. The police radio crackled a message and, ours first, the three cars headed on up the road and across the Craigavon Bridge; we were heading to Castlereagh Interrogation Centre.

'The only person that can break you is yourself,' we'd often been told, during the secretive 'lectures' in houses in Carnhill, Shantallow and in the school with the Green Book. 'They'll try every trick in the book: we'll lift your ma and bring her in; your mucker's told us everything, so you may as well own up to your part; you're too good a fella to be involved in this silly nonsense.'

The two-hour journey to Castlereagh gave plenty of time for a dark cloud of doubt and trepidation to settle on my mind. That was before we arrived in the courtyard and the motor was switched off. The dark-grey sky blanketed the dull-red brickwork of Castlereagh's three-storey buildings. Looking up, I wondered were those the windows that boys had been thrown from not long ago. I was put in a cell with nothing in it but a steel-framed, hospital-like bed with a chocolate-brown plastic-covered mattress and matching pillow. Two heating pipes ran along the length of the wall below the bed, baking the stale air even on this bitter February day.

Knowing what is about to happen is bad enough, but not knowing is worse. Not knowing meant that each sound was a signal they were coming for me. Every jangle of a key near my cell door heralded an imaginary squad of grisly interrogators, ready to hang me from the nearest hook; every squeaky-booted walk was someone coming to my cell door; on the wind of every muffled voice in the corridor I heard the Belfast-accented words *Anthony Docerty*, pronounced with a hard c.

I debated what I should do when they did come for me.

Get ready to fight? Greet them with a smile and the 'Yous have got the wrong man' approach? Lie on the ground, refuse to move and make them carry me upstairs to beat me? Get laid into them with my wee fists? When the cop had taken my photo at reception and noted my height, eye-colour and weight, he'd looked at me and asked, more of himself than me, 'Build?' before mouthing the word *thin* as he wrote it down. I was raging.

I lay on the bed. I stood up. I paced up and down the wee cell. I read the graffiti scraped into the heating pipe:

'Geordie, Newlodge, 7 days – Don't let them break you!'

'Sam, Twinbrook, five days – fucked!'

'Brendan, Nowhere, 7 days – say fuck all!'

The longer I waited, the more agitated I became. No one had told me that waiting would be such a killer! I lay on my chest on the bed and felt my heart thumping so hard I swore it was going to lift me off it. On the road up to Castlereagh, the cops, who were only a few years older than me, talked about their girlfriends, playing football and eating in fancy restaurants. They even talked about a soldier getting a lift in one of the other cars to a hockey match in Antrim! Girlfriend? *Jesus, Maire, I'm very sorry about all this!* I thought about Maire's ma finding out about me being in the IRA and her distancing me afterwards when I called to her house. I understood but it hadn't put me off Maire or the IRA. They were an unhappy combination.

After what seemed like ages, the keys rattled in my door. I jumped to my feet, ready to meet whoever or whatever came in. The door opened to reveal two suited interrogators, one with dark hair and a bushy moustache. The other was brown-haired and ruddy-faced, like he was a drinker.

'Anthony Doherty?'

I didn't respond.

'Are you Anthony Doherty?'

I just looked back at them. They both laughed and the dark-haired one said, 'Jesus, this boy's a gag! Are you Anthony Doherty?'

Eventually I nodded. They beckoned me out of the cell and walked me through brightly lit corridors, past series after series of doors – open and closed, from which I could hear the odd scream and the tumble of furniture.

Oh, gentle Jesus, I thought, as the two suits, one on each side of me, guided me into a room, empty but for a single desk and three chairs.

'Stand you there,' said Darkie, pointing to the corner. He approached me and I flinched as he moved the chair on my side of the desk away. He came back at me and made a sudden move with his hands. I flinched again, worse this time, as he turned away and took off his jacket. He was playing me. I was a 'hooked fish'. I looked at a camera fixed high up on the wall. He saw me looking and shouted, 'That's a camera.' I turned my head to look at another camera on the opposite wall, and again he shouted, 'And that's a camera,' right into my face, then turned and hung his jacket over one of them. 'And that's for your human rights!' he said, pointing to his coat, and both of them laughed and shook their heads. He slid the chair on my side back into position with his foot and said, 'Sit yourself down, young fella.'

Not another word was spoken for the next God knows how many minutes. They sat, Darkie and Brownie, across the table making notes while looking up at me every few minutes. I could hear shouting and screaming nearby, doors slamming and the heavy crump of bodies hitting floors.

Darkie sat back on his chair with his hands behind his black head. He had deep brown eyes and a Burt Reynolds moustache.

'Bloody Sunday was a terrible, terrible day for this province. You know, I was a constable in Londonderry that afternoon. I saw what those soldiers did and I hope they rot in hell some day! They left us policemen to deal with their mess. We had to maintain law and order after they fucked off back to England. Someone has to do this job, but they made it very hard for us.' He paused. 'I was at Queen's University in the 1960s. All the wee Civil Righters wanted to do was ride each other in sleeping bags. Did you know that, Tony? They were at it like rabbits,' he laughed, closed his eyes and shook his head in feigned disgust.

I just sat and looked at him, knowing that this was his way of getting me to identify with him.

Brownie, who'd been sitting looking at me and doodling with his pen, laughed and said, 'They did not, did they?'

'They fuckin' did!' guffawed Darkie. 'Like fuckin' rabbits. But that's not why we're here, is it, Anthony? Or is it "Tony"?'

I said nothing.

'Which is it?' asked Darkie, smiling broadly under his moustache.

I said nothing.

'We'll call you Tony, shall we?' asked Darkie. And then, feigning surprise, 'Hold on, what did the boy up the corridor call him?' he asked Brownie.

'Ducksie? Or was it Dutchie?'

I said nothing.

'Dutchie! That's it! Dutchie! We have a boy squealin' like a stuck pig, you know that? He called you Dutchie.'

I still said nothing but I resented these people addressing me by my nickname.

'You see, Dutchie, we know everything. How d'you think we know about you? It wasn't my own wee mammy that told us. No, it's one of your own. You want us to show him to you?'

'Will we take him a wee walk?' asked Brownie.

'No, we'll let it go for a while,' said Darkie.

'I think we should walk him to show him who's singing like a canary,' said Brownie.

'Maybe later, yes?' asked Darkie.

'OK, later,' agreed Brownie.

During this discussion, Brownie sat fiddling with his pencil, rubbing his stubble and picking at his ears. Sometimes he fixed me with his eyes, while at other times he seemed distracted. Darkie sat with his hands on the desk, fingers entwined, or rested them behind his head. He hardly took his eyes off me, though, except to address Brownie directly.

'It's up to you, Dutchie,' said Darkie. 'What are you gonna do here? You gonna tell us your part in the bombing of Clarendon Street?'

My eyes widened and my heart raced at the mention of the bombing. *They know the heap*, I thought, and wondered how they'd found out. Still I said nothing.

'The bombing of the furniture shop in Clarendon Street, Dutchie,' continued Darkie. 'That's all we want from you, Dutchie, nothing else!'

That fucker loves saying Dutchie, I thought.

'Tell us what you did, Doherty, or I'll beat the fuckin' head off you!' shouted Brownie, ready to do damage. I thought he was about to come across the table at me.

'Now, there's no need for that behaviour!' said Darkie in a raised voice, putting a hand out to calm him.

'We're doin' all the fuckin' talkin' here! A good boot in his skinny wee balls'll make him talk!' shouted Brownie, punching the table.

Fuck, I don't like the look of this, I thought. *He'll be hard to calm down.*

'Why don't you go and get yourself a wee cup of coffee,' said Darkie, with his hand on Brownie's arm. 'I know you've been under a bit of pressure recently.'

Brownie sat down. He rubbed his face with his hands, breathing heavily in agitation. He looked like an unhappy man. Suddenly, he sprang up again, pulled the door open and walked out, slamming the door behind him. His departure left a hollow silence in the room. Darkie sat staring into my eyes. I looked away.

'Are you ashamed to look at me, Tony?'

Still I said nothing.

'You know you've fucked up, don't you? It's not the end of the world. We can sort this out together. I'm here to help you.'

Silence followed each sentence, punctuated only by the echoing sounds of tumult and violence coming from the cells surrounding us.

'I'm your only friend in here,' said Darkie after a few minutes of heavy silence. 'Finlay's in very bad form these days. His best friend was shot dead by the IRA. He'll come back, though, and hopefully he'll have calmed down, but he might try to bash your head against that wall behind you. If he does, I'll try and stop him, but I can't keep an eye on him all day. I have to go home to my wife and children. Finlay's divorced from his wife – he doesn't give a flying fuck any more.'

I still remained silent. I was thinking, though, about Finlay coming back. *He looks like he really doesn't give a fuck all right.*

Darkie has the measure of him, though. As long as Darkie stays in charge.

'You carried the bomb down Clarendon Street, didn't you, Dutchie? And you couldn't prime it and one of the others had to do it for you. Isn't that right? You must've felt like a right tit, not being able to do a simple job like that.'

Jesus, somebody has told them the lot! I thought.

He paused. 'Now, is it Tony or Dutchie you want me to call you? Finlay won't give a fuck what your name is when he gets back, you know.'

I still said nothing, but I didn't like the idea of Finlay coming back and swinging for me.

'Aw, come on, Tony! You can hear all the other Finlays in the cells around us, can't you? All the messed up policemen whose nerves are fucked? So is it Tony or Dutchie?'

'Tony,' I said, and found myself exhaling relief at the sound of my voice.

'Tony. That wasn't too hard now, was it?'

'Naw.'

'Are you hungry, Tony?'

'Sort of,' I said.

'It's nearly lunchtime; you'll be going back down to your cell soon.' He leaned forward on the desk. His smiling face was about a foot from mine.

'Have I laid a finger on you?'

I said nothing.

'Have I?'

'Naw.'

'Can we be civilised to one another?'

'I suppose so.'

'Good.'

***

The jailer came round with a fry on a plastic plate and tea in a plastic cup. The fried egg looked and tasted like it was made of soft rubber. I sat with one leg on the bed and the plate on the brown mattress, eating what I could. Afterwards, as I lay on the bed thinking about the morning, my mind was racing and my heart pounding in my chest. I wasn't in control and I knew it. My mind and body felt like they were pulling apart. I wondered what was worse, the waiting or the questioning? I sprang to my feet at every noise in the corridor. I heard other cell doors opening and closing, names being mentioned, and gangs of tramping feet along the corridor. I lay down and tried to close my eyes to sleep, but my heavy heartbeat scared me. In the end, I sat up or paced the cell.

This time it was Darkie who came to the cell door. There was no sign of Finlay. We walked in silence up wooden stairs and along the corridors until we came to the same cell as before. Finlay stood facing the corner with his back to us. I could feel my racing heart sink at the sight of him. It was a strange feeling of losing control. I didn't like it and it wouldn't leave me.

'You better tell me that this boy talked after I left,' he said into the corner.

'He did. He said a few wee things, didn't you, Tony?'

'A few wee things? A few wee things?' He swung round. 'My best mate was shot to death by these fuckers, and you're telling me that this skinny wee fucker said *a few wee things*? I'll fucking see about this!' He tried to push past Darkie to get at me.

'Finlay, don't do this! Stop yourself!' said Darkie, with a grip on Finlay's shoulders. 'Calm down, or you'll have the sergeant up with us again!'

Finlay sat down on the chair opposite me and leaned forward, putting his head in his hands. Darkie looked at me and shifted his eyes as if to say 'He's mad, ye know.' I sat looking at the top of Finlay's head and reckoned that he'd try and kill me before the day was out. I also reckoned that I'd admit my part in the bombing, as long as Darkie kept Finlay away from me.

Darkie asked me if I was ready to talk. I felt it better to say nothing than say a little so as not to aggravate Finlay any more. He asked me again and again while Finlay just rolled his head in his hands on the table, puffing and panting now and again. Towards the end of the session, Darkie asked me did I want more time to think about it and I nodded back in affirmation.

'Will we see you later on then?' asked Darkie. I nodded

again. Both of them walked me back down to the cell in complete silence. They had their fish biting on the hook.

I lay in the cell listening to the noises in the corridor. Keys jangling, bolts sliding and doors banging. The noises were a distraction from the loss of control I was feeling inside, and from the realisation that I was probably not going to make it out of Castlereagh unscathed and a free man. They appeared to know everything about the bombing. The thought of another five or six days of this level of interrogation, of continuing to brazen it out against their accusation, true as it was, and the likelihood of a sustained hammering at Finlay's hands bore down heavily on me. I had less and less control over what might happen and was scared almost to death. It was a vicious circle of self-defeat from which I had no way out.

In the evening I was brought back up, knowing I was going to tell them about my part in the bombing. I sat down opposite Darkie and Finlay.

'Well, Tony, are you going to admit your part in the bombing in Clarendon Street?' asked Darkie. He smiled broadly when I confirmed that I was going to tell them my part and my part only. I made a full statement about the bombing, even down to dumping the dowels down the grating on Strand Road. They wrote down every detail on sheets of dark-lined paper before reading it out to me and allowing me to read it for myself. I signed 'Tony Doherty' at the bottom of each sheet.

'You'll not regret this, Tony,' said Darkie. 'You'll do a few years, and when you come out you'll be able to put your life back together.'

The following morning, I was met in my cell by two new suits and taken upstairs again to the interrogation room. They were wasting their time. I'd already decided they were getting nothing more from me. I wasn't that surprised that Darkie and Finlay had tricked me; that's what interrogators do. I was surprised, though, and to an extent disappointed, that these new suits thought they could get me to give them more information. Like an informer. Their strategies were similar to those tried by Darkie and Finlay, but by Thursday evening they knew their own game was up and sat back, called me a stupid whore for signing a statement and generally made a laugh of me. I thought they were a slimy bunch of fat hoors with foul tongues. Even the way they talked annoyed me, with their Ballymena accents and not pronouncing their Ts. They talked about their wages, cars and houses, and what it was like at the 'Coun'ry Club on Sunday nigh'.' I hardly said a word the whole of Thursday and Friday. I accepted my fate – I'd sunk myself by my own words and would be in jail before the end of the week. By Friday, knowing what I'd learned about their techniques, I was regretting not holding out until the first full day was over. I'd heard it said before that if you got over the first full day, you could do five or even seven days, no bother. I knew Tommy was in too as I'd seen his name written down somewhere when I was having my fingerprints taken. I hoped he hadn't signed a statement like me.

On Saturday morning I was taken back to Derry to the Strand Road Barracks to be charged. The cells in the Strand Road were medieval compared to the modern luxury of Castlereagh, with hard wooden beds. As I was placed in a cell and the door closed, I heard the name 'Carlin' in the short corridor outside. I knew then that Tommy must have signed as well. After a while they brought me back out to be formally charged. Tommy was standing in the corridor already, as was the big cop who'd arrested me. He had the yellow charge sheet in his hand and a broad grin on his well-fattened face:

Anthony Christopher Doherty, of 15 Brookdale Park, Londonderry, you are charged under the Prevention of Terrorism Act 1976 with causing an explosion with intent to endanger life and cause damage to property at Clarendon Street, Londonderry, on 18th February 1981; you are further charged with possession of a firearm, namely a .32 automatic pistol, with intent to endanger life, on 18th February 1981; you are further charged with being a member of a proscribed organisation, namely the Provisional IRA, between June 1980 and February 25th 1981.

He then read out a similar charge to Tommy, to which he replied, 'Nothing to say.'

Shortly afterwards, we were transported to Bishop Street

courthouse in a large, dark-blue police van that resembled a mobile cell-block. The sheet-metal cubicles inside were tiny, the metal freezing to touch. When we reached the courthouse there was a huge cheer, which got louder as we alighted from the van, each of us handcuffed to an RUC man. Familiar faces greeted us, cheering as we walked the short distance into the building. I was delighted to see and hear how people felt about us after several days of verbal abuse from interrogators and confinement in Castlereagh.

The purpose of the court hearing was for the judge to decide whether to let us out on bail or to remand us in prison. Me ma, John and our Paul were in the public area, along with Tommy's ma and his sisters and brother Frankie. I'd never been inside a courtroom before and found the formality very strange. It was also strange to be so close to our families and yet, for the first time in our lives, not be able to be with them or to be among them.

We were remanded to Crumlin Road Gaol. As we were taken out of the courtroom we had to pass through the public area, still handcuffed to our RUC guards, who wanted to drag us through as quickly as possible. We didn't like being dragged, so we pulled our hands back, slowing the procession down, while the RUC men used all their strength to keep us moving at a smart pace. On seeing this, Paddy Brown, who'd come to the courthouse along with our Paul, decided to launch himself at my RUC man, who was at least a foot taller than he was. Paddy missed with a right hook, and went skidding in his rubber boots along the floor, coming to an abrupt halt at the black-booted feet of a group of equally tall RUC men. A brief scuffle ensued in the crowded public area and our little procession slowed almost to a halt as the RUC men wrestled with Paddy.

'Get those prisoners into the cells right now!' someone in charge called out. I felt an extra pair of hands pull strongly on the handcuffs and we were dragged, puffing and panting, into a holding cell. The door was slammed behind us as the scuffling and shouting continued outside.

'Did you sign?' I asked Tommy, already knowing the answer.

'Aye, for Jesus' sake. You?'

'Aye, on the first night.'

'Me too.'

There was a commotion outside. The door opened and Paddy Brown was flung into the room along with us. His Snorkel jacket was mucky and torn, its white lining gaping through in several places. He got up immediately, laughing. The three of us laughed.

'I'm not lettin' them hoors off wi' that!' He banged on the door with his fists. 'Open this door, ya black bastards, and give me in me boots yis stole on me!'

'Fuck's sake, Paddy! Yer goney git us kilt!' laughed Tommy.

The cell door opened and Paddy's mucky boots were flung into the cell, hitting him on his lower legs.

Me, Tommy and Paddy returned to the Strand Road Barracks in the same vehicle. Paddy was later charged with assault. Tommy and I were put in a cell together, and me ma, John and Tommy's elderly ma were allowed in for a visit. Tommy's father had been an IRA man who was killed in 1970 in an explosion that also killed two of his comrades and two young children. I watched as his mother sat weeping at the thought that her youngest child now faced a long prison sentence. I could see that Tommy was upset too. An RUC man stood at the cell door watching us as we said our goodbyes to our widowed mothers.

***

The cream-painted cell with a shiny, red-painted floor had two single beds, a single chair, two small lockers with a Bible in each, and two plastic piss-pots with lids. There was a heavily barred window on the back wall. We were in the basement of Crumlin Road Gaol. The cell door opened. A screw and a stripe-shirted orderly stood there.

'Yer teas!' snapped the pudgy, round-waisted screw as the orderly shuffled through the doorway with a metal tray in each hand. When the orderly left the cell, the screw slammed the door. The noise echoed around the myriad of metal bars and stone surfaces of the basement.

'He must be out a fortune on doors, that boy!' I laughed. The flap on the outside of the door lifted, revealing a pair of searching eyes, before banging down hard again. The screw had heard us laughing.

'Orange bastard,' said Tommy, not so loud.

Me and Tommy sat on the edge of our single beds with the trays balancing on our laps. It was a Saturday night fry. The rounded, plate-sized dip in the metal tray held sausage, rolled up bacon, a fried egg and a slice of fried soda; all floating in an enticing pool of hot lard. There was a large plastic mug full of fine-looking tea, though, set in another rounded hollow on the silver tray.

Bacon is a food I always associate with my childhood. The crispier the better! But this rounded, decrepit, curled-up piece of pig-flesh on my tray was drowning in lard, so I picked it up with a hankie to dry it off, before placing it back down on the edge of the tray to cut it with the plastic knife and fork. I cut through the first slice and then the knife wouldn't go any further. I was slicing across something hard. I prised open the bacon with my fingers and pulled out an inch-long sliver of shiny glass. I placed it with a clink on the side of the metal tray.

'Jesus, Tommy, look at this,' I said. 'It's real glass!'

Tommy lifted the sliver between his fingers to see if it actually was real glass. Both of us stared at it for a while, trying to comprehend. We never thought about complaining.

Prison is a quiet place after teatime. I lay back on my pillow and chatted on and off to Tommy, lying parallel to me on his own bed. Tommy was reflective and sad about leaving his old mother, at times going quiet when I wanted to talk. We talked about Paddy Brown skidding across the shiny floor of the courthouse in his mucky oul boots!

'Where was he going in them rubber boots anyway?' I mused, and both of us laughed. 'The big cop must've been three times the length of 'im!'

'It was great to see so many up at the courthouse, wasn't it?' said Tommy, and we went over who was there and who they were married to or had connections with.

'What was the glass in the bacon about, do ye think, Tommy?'

'I don't know, Dutch; it could've been either of us who took the wrong tray.'

'D'ye think it was meant to kill one of us, or what?' I asked him, not really expecting him to know.

'It would kill ye all right if ye were simple enough to swally it!' said Tommy, setting both of us laughing again.

'I know; a bit obvious, wasn't it!'

'I reckon it was that fucker of an orderly,' said Tommy. 'Did ye not see the scowl on his bake?'

'Probably was him all right,' I agreed. 'Then again, that big fat screw hates you wi' a passion!'

'What did I ever do on 'im, d'ye think?' laughed Tommy.

'God only knows.'

We lay staring at the arched ceiling, chatting between bouts of silent reflection.

'That oul good cop/bad cop routine is as old as the hills and we fell for it,' said Tommy.

'I know. You wouldn't think it was one of the first things we were taught in the Fianna.'

'Worked a treat on us, so it did,' said Tommy.

'Sure did. Hook, line and sinker, as they say.'

'I'm really pissed off wi' meself, ye know,' said Tommy. I could see the disappointment in his face.

'For signing?'

'Aye.'

'Me too.'

'We'll not be seein' Derry for a right few years, ye know?'

'I know. What d'ye reckon, how long?'

'Dunno, Dutch. We could get ten years.'

Ten years in jail! I'd never thought of my life in years before. It was a new and terrifying prospect. Now, as I lay in the echoing basement of Belfast's crumbling prison, the silence broken only by an occasional jangle of keys slapping off a screw's thigh, I measured my life in years for the first time. I was eighteen years, one month and twenty-eight days old. It was exactly nine years and twenty-nine days since me da had been killed by a British soldier. I wondered if his executioner was living or dead, and if he'd killed again since then.

Me da and Tommy's da had been killed within eighteen months of each other and now we, their teenage sons, lay in prison within inches of each other. It felt for a moment that the dead were beside us. I wondered if Tommy had a special song or something to remember his da by. I had 'Starman'. I'd never told anyone about it. I didn't want people to think I was a weirdo or something. I loved having a song to remember me da by. I knew by instinct that it wasn't over between me and me da. I knew our paths would cross or converge again on the road to God knows where. *A world of difference between then and now. And tomorrow*, I thought, as I drifted off to sleep.

***

New prisoners weren't admitted to the prison wings at weekends. So, on Monday 1 March 1981, I was separated from Tommy as we came through the prison circle, the main intersection between the four wings of Crumlin Road Gaol. Tommy was taken to A Wing. Escorted by two tall screws whose shiny black boots squeaked on the highly polished floors, I found myself facing down the broad, black, shiny floor of C Wing.

'A.C. Doherty 606' shouted the tall, moustachioed screw, his words, describing me anew, echoing and calling back to him from hard stone through ascending stairwells of cast-iron and black-painted steel. 'Mr Kyle; C Wing, one on!'

Mr Kyle appeared from a room halfway up the corridor, made his way towards us and led me along C Wing towards my new home in Cell 5.

It would be many a day before I would walk on Derry's streets again.

GLOSSARY

BA	British Army
bake	mouth
block	log of wood
blone	a promiscuous woman; a Derry word for a whore, or a woman or girl who is free with sex
bluttered	drunk
boggin'	filthy
boked	vomited
bru	Bureau, weekly payment from the Unemployment Bureau
Bush (a glass of)	Bushmills Irish whiskey
cheevy	a chase
chew the bake off	chastise severely
clattered	covered in mess
dabs	fingerprints
dandering	walking/meandering
dobbing	truancy, avoiding school
doobs	breasts
ecker	exercise – school work
Ferret	small, tank-like army vehicle
footpad	footpath
fried soda	fried soda bread
Geembeddy God	'Oh, dear God …'
gerning	whingeing/crying

give me head peace	stop bothering me
gravy rings	ring doughnuts
grumped	huffed
gulpin	ignoramus
haymaker	a wild thump or swipe
heads and thraws	lying in a crowded bed head to toe
hoor/hoorin'	curses: whore/whoring
INLA	Irish National Liberation Army
IRA	Irish Republican Army
IRSP	Irish Republican Socialist Party
jook	a quick look
keeping dick	keeping watch
Kunta Kinte	a character in the novel *Roots*
leggered	covered in mess
longy	a football game with only one player in each team – kicking the ball the length of the pitch towards the goal
messages	errands; shopping
my tail was up	I'd grown in confidence; had the upper hand
OC	Officer Commanding
odds	spare change
oul	old
piece	sandwich
Pig	a large, four-wheeled army vehicle
pish-the-bed	dandelion plant
poke van	ice-cream van
press	cupboard
quare half	a good-looking woman or girl
red fish	battered smoked fish

red/redding up	clean/cleaning up
redner	a red face/embarrassment
rifts	burps
RUC	Royal Ulster Constabulary
scoot	flick with your fingers to someone else
scranned	scavenged
sheugh	a ditch
Sixer	a large, six-wheeled army vehicle
skitter	a small rascal or rogue
slabber	dribble
slabbers tripping someone	salivating, a phrase used to describe someone very hungry
slag	tease
Snorkel	a style of parka jacket with an elongated hood
spla feet	big feet
stall a boat	stop; stay here, or stay where you are
steever	a good kick, usually in the backside
steps of stairs	a family of children with only around a year and a few inches of difference in height between them
Stokes	a common surname for Derry Travellers, often used as a collective noun
stoolying	giving information
taking the hand	making a fool of someone
taking his oil	accepting his defeat gracefully
tap (for odds)	ask for small change
tap her up	ask her for a date

the bars/see the bars	see what's new/what's happened
the craic	fun/enjoyment
the day	today
the marra	tomorrow
the night	tonight
themins	'them ones'; those people
thon	that one – used derogatorily
thran	stubborn
tig	a children's chase game, also known as tag
urps	colloquial pronunciation of IRSP, the political wing of the INLA
wan	one
wains	children
wance	once
wile	from wild, meaning terrible, or very
wipe his eye	to make a move on someone he fancies
yamming	crying
yes	hello (in Derry)